RUNNING THE RIVERS OF NORTH AMERICA

RUNNING THE RIVERS OF NORTH AMERICA

by Peter Wood

Barre Publishing
Barre, Massachusetts

Distributed by Crown Publishers, Inc.

Published simultaneously in Canada by General
Publishing Company Limited
First edition
Printed in the United States of America

Designed by Mary Gale Moyes
Maps by Robert Porter
Illustrations by Clay Ghiosay
Cover photograph by Barton Silverman

Library of Congress Cataloging in Publication Data
Wood, Peter, 1930–
Running the rivers of North America.

1. Canoes and canoeing—United States. 2. Canoes
and canoeing—Canada. 3. Rafting (Sports)—United
States. 4. Rafting (Sports)—Canada. I. Title.
GV776.A2W66   1978   917.3′04′926   77–26833
ISBN 0–517–53313–8
ISBN 0–517–53314–6 pbk.

TABLE OF CONTENTS

Part II: The Rivers

PREFACE

Considerate hosts, given a moment, will brief a new arrival to the party about those he is shortly to meet. Such is the intent of these preliminary words. The formal introduction is much longer. It comprises, in fact, the entire body of the book.

Those already familiar with the guests inside will not find much here that is new, though it never hurts to brush up if one has allowed acquaintance to lapse. Those who have never taken an extended canoe trip, learned to balance a kayak, or floated a raft through white water should discover a great deal to please them. Even those who are not dedicated outdoor people, do not care to carry their food and shelter on their backs, up hill and down dale, should find river running the ideal entry into a calmer and cleaner world. It is hoped that once the full introductions are made, friendships will follow, casual or passionate, as the case may be, and that the future will then take care of itself.

So far as the assemblage inside is concerned, the number of honored guests are four: running water and the three major modes of transport on it—raft, canoe, and kayak. How to plan a trip and camp beside a stream are also present. For the rest, they are the rivers themselves—some sixty of them selected with an eye toward geographical balance as well as the superior character of each. There is a notable gap in the guest list. Alaska is missing. Mounting a boat trip to Alaska is such a specialized enterprise that it falls well beyond the scope intended here. Alaska is not for the beginner. Better try running some rivers in the lower forty-eight before you tackle the Big One. To be sure, Alaska is a grand place for river running. In fact, to find true wilderness rivers one must go there. If you like what you find inside, you will want to do so one day.

Meanwhile, dear reader, allow me to present a representative gathering of the rivers of the United States and Canada. You will, I am certain, find them fascinating and rewarding company, while the many diversions you can enjoy together are bound to lead to long and lasting friendships.

GLOSSARY OF RIVER TERMS

BOIL: A mound of water created by an upwelling of the current.

BRACE STROKE: A paddling technique used to stabilize the boat. In a brace, which can be high or low or in the middle depending on the position of the hands on the paddle, the paddle blade is pulled toward the boat against the water.

BREAKOUT: An abrupt turn resulting from a boat's entry, bow first, into an eddy. Breakouts occur when the movement of the bow is arrested while the stern is still subject to the currents of the stream.

CARRY: *See* PORTAGE.

CFS: Cubic feet per second. A measure of the volume of water flowing per second past a particular point on the river.

CHUTE: A constricted channel through which the flow of water is faster and usually deeper than in the surrounding river.

"COLORADO SANDWICH": One of the dangers of rafting on powerful rivers. The passenger is trapped in the middle as his raft is bent backward on itself by an oncoming wave. As a safety measure, it is usually best to keep more weight in the bow.

COMBING: The cockpit lip of a kayak or other boat.

CURLER: A steep and high wave that curls or falls back onto itself.

DORY: A rowboat with a pointed bow. River dories are usually built with watertight compartments for personal gear and equipment that enable them to remain afloat if capsized. Dories, which are heavier than rafts, may be constructed of wood, aluminum, or fiber glass.

DRAW STROKE: A paddling motion intended to pull the boat sideways, toward the paddle side. Used for small, light boats or rafts.

DROP: A sudden, sharp descent in the river.

EDDY: A countercurrent, any discontinuity of flow, where the water either stops or turns upstream.

EDDY FENCE: The boundary between two contrary currents. Crossing an eddy fence can be dangerous.

FEATHER: A part of the recovery stroke, this movement, in which the paddle is pivoted 90° about its long axis, offers minimal resistance to the air.

FERRY: To move a boat sideways across a current. Ferrying involves rowing or paddling upstream at an angle sufficient to counter the force of the current.

FREEBOARD: The distance between the waterline and the top of the boat or buoyancy tube. The more freeboard you have, the dryer your boat will be, although boats with a lot of freeboard are likely to be heavier and are more subject to wind than others.

GUNWALE (or GUNNEL): The upper edge on the side of an open boat.

HEADWATERS: The source of a stream.

HOLE: An opening in the river with strongly defined boundaries. These reversals in current created by backward tumbling water can be both exciting and dangerous for the river runner.

HULL: That part of a boat that provides buoyancy.

HYPOTHERMIA: A condition in which the body gets so cold that it can no longer warm itself. A threat whenever the water temperature drops much below 60°F, hypothermia is perhaps the greatest danger, next to drowning, that boaters face.

JOHNBOAT: An inexpensive planked scow formerly used for runs on the streams of the South and often abandoned when a run was through. The johnboat has largely been replaced by the canoe.

KEEL: A longitudinal projection extending along the center of the bottom of some boats. When present—on lake canoes, for instance—the keel can help the paddler keep a straight line and guard a boat from being blown over by the wind. Keels are either minimal or entirely absent on white-water canoes.

KEEPER: A hole with enough power to trap a boat or swimmer for an extended period.

LINING: The use of two ropes 50 to 100 feet long, one controlling the bow and the other the stern, to maneuver a boat from the river bank or edge of the stream. Lining, which relies on the force of the current, is helpful in guiding boats through difficult passages or against strong currents. Also called tracking.

LOAD: The earthy debris carried along by streams. Vigorous young streams usually carry loads with large particles but relatively modest total quantity. Most mature streams lack the energy to carry anything except a small amount of fine debris.

PAINTER: A line, usually around 20 feet long, attached to the bow or stern of a boat and generally used for lining, rescue, and to secure the boat when not in use.

POLING: A method of controlling a boat both up and downriver with a pole. Poling is most often used to propel a boat upstream through the swift currents of shallow rapids.

PONTOON: Extra-large inflatable rafts, from 22 feet to 37 feet, used mainly by commercial outfitters to carry many people on big rivers such as the Colorado.

PORTAGE (or CARRY): A method of getting around obstacles in the river or from one body of water to another by carrying the canoe on one's back. Portage also describes that portion of a river trip during which the canoe is carried along the banks of the river.

PUT-IN: The starting point of a river trip, where a river can be entered.

RAPIDS: A stretch of river with fast-moving and turbulent water. The water surface is broken by obstacles and generally erupts into waves.

REVERSAL: A meeting of currents caused by a current swinging upward and revolving back on itself. Reversals can be treacherous. This term includes holes, keepers, stoppers, souse holes, and other current formations.

RIFFLE: A shallow rapid producing very small waves.

ROCKER: A curved keel line in the hull of some boats. A rockered boat is slightly banana shaped and pivots like a top. These boats are easy to turn and useful for the quick maneuvering rapids demand.

SHIP: To take water over the side of a boat.

SLEEPER: A large rock creating a mound of smooth water that erupts into a boil on the far side. Boats may bounce over sleepers and come to grief in the froth at the bottom.

SOUSE HOLE: Narrow to moderate in width, this hole is found below underwater obstructions, such as boulders.

SPRAY SKIRT: These skirts, made of neoprene rubber and elastic hems, fit over the cockpit lip of a kayak and around the paddler's waist. The spray skirt provides a watertight seal between the passenger and the boat.

STOPPER: A hole or reversal powerful enough to arrest the forward progress of a boat.

TAKE-OUT: The end point of a river trip, at which it is possible to leave the river.

TAPER: The degree of narrowness of the stern and bow of a canoe. A boat with a narrow V-shaped bow will knife through waves rather than ride over them, but this boat is less stable than the slower flat-bottomed canoe.

THWARTS: Cross supports running from gunwale to gunwale in canoes. Thwarts supply tensile strength and make possible the construction of boats of greater volume and more seaworthy shape.

TIE-DOWNS: The metal rings fitted to the tubes of a white-water raft for lashing down cargo. Tie-downs, which can serve as good handholds for passengers, should be plentiful and sturdy.

TONGUE: Fast water in a smooth V-formation usually found at the head of rapids.

TRACKING: *See* LINING.

TROUGH: A depression between waves.

TUMBLEHOME: A term describing the inward slant of a boat's gunwales. Boats with tumblehome have a slightly pear-shaped appearance in cross section. When the gunnel is tilted in, the paddler doesn't need to reach so far outboard for his strokes. However, as this shape doesn't slap down waves as well as vertical or outward-slanting sides, most modern canoes are without tumblehome.

WHITE WATER: Water that has encountered an obstacle and its surface is broken. White water can be characterized by a smooth surge and a small breaking wave and back eddies curling in from the side.

Part 1
AN INTRODUCTION TO RIVER RUNNING

WHITE WATER

THIS is a book about river running—how to do it and where to do it. But, most importantly, it is about why to do it. The simple one-word answer is *fun*. For some people this translates as thrills (plenty of those); for others as tranquility, or challenge, or just plain sport. River running is all these and more. But whatever you are looking for, indoors or out, it is axiomatic that the quality of the experience is increased with understanding. The place to start, then, is not with the craft and techniques of river running—subjects of subsequent chapters—but with the stuff itself, water in motion as perceived by someone fresh to the sport.

WATER IN MOTION

Consider, then, the babbling brook. It may be too small to boat on, but it provides a nearly perfect model of how running water behaves in a rough and twisting channel. The first glance reveals little more than a random confusion of conflicting motions, flowing generally downstream, to be sure—gravity sees to that—but in a cadence that is hopelessly undecipherable. In a word: babbling.

Actually, that jumble of waves, depressions, slicks, shoots, riffles, currents, and countercurrents (we will learn to call them *eddies*) *is* comprehensible once you know what to look for. It follows predictable patterns imposed by the shape of the stream bed and the configuration of the obstructions in it. And these principles are largely independent of stream size, which is convenient for us since we are looking at a brook but

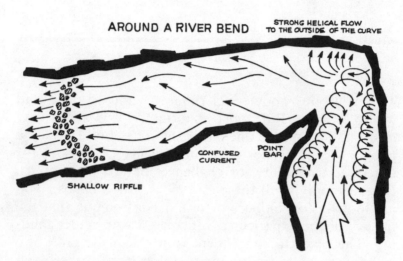

Where a river bends sharply, the current flows farthest along the outside bank. As the river comes out of the turn, the current is confused but regains positive direction by the time it passes the shallow riffle a little ways downstream.

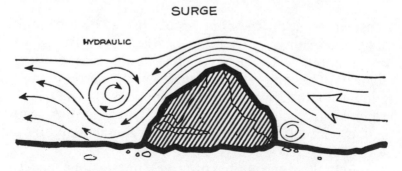

A surge is created when a river flows over a submerged obstruction, usually a boulder, deep enough to cause the water merely to hump up.

imagining a mountain river. A kettle-sized rock lying barely submerged in a freshet will produce the same smooth surge of water over its top, with perhaps a small breaking wave just below its downstream side and with back eddies curling in like pincers from the side, as will a house-sized boulder in a fast river. A twig or leaf carried over the small rock by the current will accelerate on the crest, tumble down into the trough below the rock, and be tossed back by the wave that curls upstream. For a moment or two it might struggle there until the balance of forces acting on it shifts to one side, propelling it back into the mainstream. Later the same bit of flotsam might shoot across the boundary between the main current and a back eddy. It lies motionless near the bank, then moves eerily upstream. The very same motion might befall a kayak or raft as it shoots over the submerged boulder or darts into a back eddy.

Though a babbling brook can teach us a lot about the behavior of white, or turbulent, water, nothing can replace actual experience. For that, you must put yourself on a large white-water river, preferably in the hands of an experienced boatman, and see what happens —as we did last year on the Snake River with a group of friends.

EXPERIENCING WHITE WATER

The Snake is a white-water river, a young giant that bulls its way out of the heart of the Rocky Mountains toward the Pacific. Rising in Yellowstone National Park in Wyoming, the Snake draws early strength from snow-melt off the craggy heights of the Grand Tetons. It crosses the full width of Idaho in a lazy loop before turning north to form the boundary between that state and Oregon. The Upper Snake, in Grand Teton National Park, attracts thousands of river runners each year. But it is the Lower Snake, particularly the mile-deep canyon that separates the Wallowa Mountains of Oregon from the Seven Devils of Idaho, that concerns us here.

Only a decade ago the Snake in an exceptional spring run-off flushed through the entire thirty-two-mile length of this tremendous gorge at up to 85,000 cubic feet per second (or cfs, the river runner's measure of stream flow). Squeezed between rock walls, blocked but by no means stopped by house-sized boulders, the torrent gave the gorge its name, Hell's Canyon. Today, the giant has been gentled. Three large dams restrain it, and in the process have drowned what many thought to be, after the Grand Canyon of the Colorado, the most magnificent wild-river canyon in America. Mercifully, an eighty-mile section below the third dam remains to remind us of what once was—though that, too, is threatened by the proposal of yet one more dam across the Snake.

Our first look at the river is disappointing. From Joseph, Oregon, we have descended by truck and micro-bus through forests of pine, spruce, and Douglas fir into the V-shaped valley of the Snake. We cross the river at Ox Bow Dam—more bridge than dam, as the water on either side stands roughly at the same level. Now, as we follow a gravel road down the right bank, the river lies beside us placid and wide as three empty football fields and doing little more than reflecting the blue of the afternoon sky. The former riverbed was movingly portrayed by photographer Eliot Porter in his *Wildness is the Preservation of the World* shortly before the sluice gates were closed. Now it lies hidden under more than two hundred feet of water. Where the water laps at the steep hillside of gray rock and parched grasses, it is hard to discern any current.

At Hell's Canyon Dam the lakelike tranquility ends, as if cut with a knife. At the base of a three-hundred-foot-high concrete wall a froth of water bursts from the outflow of the generating plant. More dramatic, still, is a great plume of water that gushes from one of three gates at the top of the dam. Unseasonable summer rains have filled the reservoir, and Hell's Canyon Dam is dumping its excess.

The boatmen in our truck crow at the sight. The river will be fuller than usual, perhaps running at 30,000 cfs, they think. Wild Sheep and Granite, the two major rapids that lie ahead, will be special challenges this run. As if eager to fulfill the boatmen's prophecies, the river charges away from the dam like a wild thing, frothing and dancing out of sight around a distant bend. But here the Snake becomes its old self again, lean and sinewy enough for someone with a good arm to hurl a rock across. The banks are rough talus slopes descending to a margin of water-worn boulders and bedrock. As we cross the top of the dam, the roar of river and rock rises to meet us. It is a sound that will echo in our ears for the next six days.

In a pelting thundershower, we launch and load the boats we trailered with us. They belong to an outfit called Grand Canyon Dories which runs commercial trips on the Colorado and a number of other western rivers, including the Snake. As a white-water craft the dory is still in the development stage. Our three boats represent three variations of flat-bottomed, double-ended fishing boats—the type that Spencer Tracy rowed on the Grand Banks in the movie *Captains Courageous.* River dories, designed for passengers rather than fish, are larger (eighteen feet) and wider abeam. They also have watertight compartments for personal gear and equipment and to keep them afloat should they turn over. Like the houses of the Three Little Pigs, each of the Grand Canyon boats was built of a different material: wood, aluminum, and fiber glass.

Clarence Reese, thirty, muscled like the Idaho State champion wrestler he once was and wearing his sun-bleached hair à la Prince Valiant, gathers his thirteen charges together for a lecture on river safety.

To escape the sudden downpour we crowd into the microbus. "It is not likely," Clarence tells us, "but boats do flip—turn over, that is. That's why every one of you has a life jacket. You don't have to wear it all the time [not true on nationally administered rivers, where to be caught in a boat without a life jacket on, even when the boat is beached, is to risk a fine].

"But when your boatman puts his on, you had better do the same, no matter how strong a swimmer you are. You can't swim in a river rapid anyway. Should a boat go over, above all, don't panic. You may come up under the boat. You'll know that's happened if you open your eyes and it's dark [nervous laughter]. Reach up, feel for the rail, and move yourself to the side. Once out, stay on the upriver side of the boat. The worst danger you face is to be pinned between the boat and a rock. Stay with the boat. You may have to help the boatman right it."

A DAY ON THE RIVER

At 3 P.M. we push off. The sun is out again, but so low that it reaches into the canyon only in spots. We will get wet, we have been told, so most of us are wearing a minimum of clothing and our fat orange kapok life jackets, with collars designed to keep an unconscious person's head above water.

Forest Woods, Peter Bull, and I are seated in the bow of the *Stanislaus*, the aluminum boat named for the Stanislaus River in California. David Phillips and his blonde wife, Lore, occupy the stern seat. Between us sits our boatman, twenty-four-year-old Jim Barton, bearded, wearing strong glasses, and gripping a pair of oars. Jim does not face aft, as is customary in most rowboats; in river dories the oarsman faces forward, toward the upswept bow. He can push the boat in that direction with a forward thrust of his arms, but when he pulls, really putting his back into it, the stroke propels the boat backward. For this the stern is also pointed. The arrangement means that the boatman can face the dangers—call them challenges, for we are all here to enjoy ourselves, are we not?—head on and pull away from them when need be. Rafts are rowed according to the same principle. The essential difference between rafts and dories is that the heavier dory, with its pointed bow, smashes through waves while rafts ride up and over the top of them. Sometimes this means that the dory gets swamped and may capsize. Rafts do not lose stability when they swamp, but sometimes they ride so high on a wave they are tipped over backward or, in some cases, bent double, making, in the vernacular of the river, a neoprene sandwich. There are advantages and disadvantages to each craft. Beauty, however, has never been an attribute of rafts. Dorymen, a proud bunch, are condescending to raft jockeys, although to handle either craft requires a thorough understanding of white-water hydraulics.

This will be the thirteenth trip Jim has made down the Snake; however, it is his first time in the aluminum *Stanislaus*. Now he spins the boat around twice in the current to get the feel of it. Spaced about fifty yards apart, the three boats sweep down through a few easy stretches of choppy water, clear of protruding boulders. The water is moving swiftly. A horseman would have to hold a steady trot to keep up. Where the canyon widens, sunlight suddenly pours in. Its warmth is welcome. Bow pointed downstream, Jim holds the *Stanislaus* at a forty-five-degree angle to the current. He meets the larger waves by swinging the bow into them, the way one turns into the wake left by a speedboat. But there is little that is regular or predictable about these waves, and sometimes one sloshes over the bow, or rolls in amidships, dousing us. Then we take plastic buckets and bail. The water is warmer than the air. The long loop the Snake makes through southern Idaho kills the original glacial chill, and in the reservoir the water has been soaking up the sun all summer. In the mountains around Joseph it snowed the night before we set out, but here the river almost invites swimming.

Jim, seated in the middle of the *Stanislaus*, with his feet hooked under a stout wooden dowel for leverage, is letting the river do the work, rowing just enough to keep us in the current while swinging the bow this way and that to meet the oncoming waves—standing waves, really. It is we, borne on the current, that are oncoming.

On rivers the size of the Snake, most large rapids are the product of steep side streams that carry down with them the boulders and debris that obstruct the flow, creating drops, shoots, and fearsome holes. After about an hour on the river, we pass the mouth of Wild Sheep Creek and pull into an eddy. Ahead, the river seems to disappear, dropping from sight into a boil of turbulent water. Wild Sheep Rapids, Jim tells us. Our campsite, assigned by the U.S. Forest Service, lies beyond it around a bend. We beach the boats and climb the bank to have a look. Clarence tells us he has been accused by other parties of stopping to look these rapids over only to build the drama of the upcoming run. The truth is, every new water condition changes the shape of a rapid and the strategy for running it. Serious rapids, like Wild Sheep, biggest on the river, must be scouted, no matter how familiar a boatman is with the river.

So we survey Wild Sheep. Perched at a strategic spot on the big rocks above the river, we see it all. No question, this does build drama. Three tongues of smooth water bend over the drop, hard to measure in real terms because the froth below the falls will not hold still. Six feet, perhaps? Not a very big drop, to be sure, but when one figures that 30,000 cubic feet of water, weighing 960 tons, is pouring over it every second, one begins to get a better handle on the enormous forces loose on a river like the Snake. The tongue of water farthest from us is aimed straight for a large rock buffeted by waves reflecting off a rock face on the Idaho shore. The middle tongue, the main stream, bends toward the perpendicular, scouring a deep hole in the river into which a great wave is constantly breaking. A boat or raft plunging into that hole would swamp

SUCK HOLE

*A suckhole, also called a keeper or a sousehole, is
caused by an obstruction so large and steep that it causes a
wave to break upstream. The water piles up over it and
then drops steeply, cutting into the water below and creating a hole and a reflex current that can trap a boat for days.*

immediately and be thrown backward by the wave. The
same would happen to a swimmer. The hole is what
rivermen call a *keeper*, perhaps the single most dangerous phenomenon on big water. Keepers have been
known to hold boats, rafts, and/or swimmers inter-
minably. They cause the most drownings. Boatmen
steer clear of holes like this one, which are too big to
punch through.

    The tongue nearest us appears to be the way to go.
It points downriver between a mound of smooth water
and a protruding boulder. The mound is the work of a
large rock, clearly visible through the half-foot of water
that pours over it on all sides, creating a nasty boil on
the far side. This is a *sleeper*. The danger of sleepers is
that one may run into them. Boats will normally bounce
over them but then come to grief in the froth at the
bottom. A large raft, on the other hand, may actually
hang up on a sleeper, bending around it like a fur
piece on a matron's neck, and be pinned there. Sometimes the force of the current is so great that the raft
cannot be pried loose, even by pulling with a rope from
shore. In that case there is nothing to do but abandon

SLEEPER

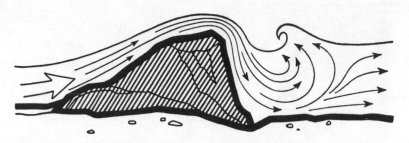

A surge becomes a sleeper when the depth of the water flowing over the obstruction is insufficient to float a boat over it. A jumble of currents awaits the boater on the other side.

ship and wait, sometimes for weeks, until the water level on the river changes.

"Our course," Clarence explains, "will be to shoot down this closest tongue of water between the sleeper and the rock that protrudes beyond it, skirt the big hole in the middle of the river, and meet the waves at the bottom of the drop head on." The first wave, really a breaking ridge of water reaching out from shore, will be the hardest. It is highest where the channel is deepest. We will want to miss that part if we can.

The tongue of smooth water and the breaking wave below it are basic elements of any rapid worth the name. The V-shaped tongue points downstream. When in doubt, and if you have not scouted ahead, the V indicates the way to go—providing it is pointing downstream. Vs pointing upstream represent a turbulence streaming backward from a protruding or nearly protruding rock. Beware Vs pointing upstream! The downstream V, on the other hand, usually signals the deepest water, while the waves curling in on either side of it spell trouble. What one must be mindful of is that the V does not lead to some other obstruction, as does the one farthest from us now, or that it does not drop so steeply that the water pouring down it piles up at the bottom, creating a dangerous hole and breaking wave.

FALLS

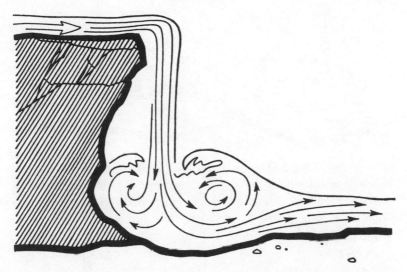

*Two suckholes are created at the base of a waterfall,
one in front of and one behind the downpouring water.
With a two to three foot drop, the suckholes may not
be too dangerous; but with drops over six feet they could
prove fatal.*

Clarence takes his boat through first while the rest
of us watch and take pictures from the riverbank. For
a moment he hangs in limbo, sideways at the top of the
V—then he slides down it, past the big hole, and is flung
into a frightful jumble of waves. Pulling right now to
miss the worst of the standing waves, bobbing up and
down, he is safely through. Straining like a Trojan, he
pulls left, driving his boat into an upstream eddy, which
brings him back up to a point just below the first big
drop. From there he and his passengers can watch us
run the rapid and render assistance if needed.

The eddy, or countercurrent, is another basic element of stream flow. Technically, an eddy is any discontinuity of flow. Eddies come in an infinite variety.
Those that are useful flow upriver, usually along either
bank, but also behind obstructions such as protruding
boulders. When a river narrows, is obstructed, or the

BREAKING HOLE

A breaking hole results when a great deal of water flows over a boulder or ledge without enough of a drop to make a suckhole. Instead, a stationary crest forms at the bottom. This standing wave can easily flip a small boat or raft.

gradient increases, water accelerates. It gains momentum, and at the end of the obstruction or drop, it is moving faster than the configuration of the river at that point calls for. To compensate, water flows upstream to replace it. That is an eddy. An eddy fence is the boundary between two contrary currents. Crossing it can be as dangerous as entering a buffer zone between any two opposing forces.

Now it is our turn to run Wild Sheep. Jim stands in the middle of the boat to get a better look over the edge where the river disappears. His passengers scrutinize his face for signs of nervousness, any twist of the mouth or cast to the eye. Unfamiliar with this kind of water, we have no other way to judge the degree of danger we are facing. Jim shows no sign. We are reassured. And just in time, for we, too, are in the grip of the current—no turning back, no chance to pull for a friendly eddy. We slide quickly down between our Scylla and Charybdis, the sleeper and the opposite rock. I am surprised how long Jim holds the *Stanislaus* sideways. We sweep past the big hole. At the bottom Jim swings the boat to meet the wave. It towers over us. It crashes down on us. The *Stanislaus* swamps. But Jim seems to know what he is doing. Certainly, we will push through. Then we turn over, rolling from starboard to port. I am sitting on the port side, and the boat comes down on me like a lid. By God, it is dark. In a confusion of foam, boat, and bodies, I start to work my way out and am struck on the back of the head. The blow is nothing compared to the confusion I feel. Then I am free, clinging to the overturned boat. But I am on the downriver side. Lore, wide-eyed, is next to me. We work our way around the boat. The life jacket holds me unaccustomedly high in the water. It is hard to swim. But now I have a chance to look around. All hands are accounted for, as we sweep and bob along in the rushing water. It feels warm and rather pleasant. So this is what it is like to turn over in a big rapid.

Jim is fumbling with the painter, the rope attached to the *Stanislaus*'s bow. Uncoiling it, he leads it around the oarlock on the downriver side and throws it over the back of the boat, as if roping a huge turtle. He comes back to our side again and uses the rope to climb up on the overturned boat. I look past him down the river and understand his haste. Another stretch of nasty water lies ahead, with breaking waves and a few protruding rocks. I also notice that Jim still has his glasses on. They have no attachment around the back of his head. Clever fellow. Leaning his weight against the rope hitched to the downstream oarlock, Jim now tries to turn the boat over. Several of us clamber aboard to add our weight to the rope. Slowly the far gunnel rises. We grab it and the boat flops right side up again. Jim is in like a monkey and helps pull the rest of us aboard, not an easy feat as our bulbous life jackets protrude and catch on the gunnel. Only one is left in the water— Peter Bull. But the next rapid is nearly on us. Jim has only one oar, the spare that had been lashed to the thwarts. Better than nothing to get through the rapids with, but hardly adequate. Clarence's boat, having followed our travail, now bears down on us. A man in the bow holds out their spare oar. At the last second he gives it a heave. Not far enough. It goes into the river, but the momentum carries it to us. Jim slaps it into the oarlock and swings the boat around just as we enter rough water. Peter Bull is still hanging on astern. Two of us bail. The others sit shivering with excitement and cold. As soon as we have passed the new rapid we haul Peter back on board and pull for shore. Granite Creek, our campsite, lies just ahead. Our first day on the Snake has disappointed no one.

A LAND OF RIVERS

As I write I am sitting at home on a small island a dozen miles off the southern coast of New England—not, as it turns out, a bad place to consider rivers. For the past half hour a south wind has been pumping fog over the moors, blotting out the summer sun. A river in the making is blowing past my door, gathering the strength and weight that will transform amorphous mist one day, like some larval insect, into a bright ribbon of rushing water.

THE LIFE CYCLE OF A RIVER

This low-lying cloud—for fog is nothing more—upon reaching land will gather warmth, rise, and dissipate in the form of invisible water vapor. High up the vapors will mingle with other currents of moist air, also drawn from the sea by the radiant power of the sun. In time, and at the whim of the winds, these microscopic water particles, separated now from the salts they held in solution while they were part of the ocean, will move inland, and when conditions direct, condense again into clouds. Finally, on high ground, this fresh water will fall as rain.

Dripping from the pointed tips of oak and rhododendron leaves, splashing into puddles, the water gathers in tiny rills and rivulets. Tugged at by such subtle forces as capillary action and its own surface tension, but impelled mostly by gravity, the water, long diffuse, is regrouping again. From a million sources, from rock crevices, bank-seeps, and meadow bogs, from springs and freshets, it gathers momentum. It fills gullies, gullies empty into brooks, the threads draw together, and a stream is born.

Conceived of sun and sea, nurtured in the womb of the sky, all rivers begin as rain. There is no other source. Water flows down to the sea, or into some landlocked basin like Great Salt Lake—contrary to the popular saying, all rivers do not flow down to the sea. Wherever it flows, it eventually evaporates. It is carried back to the heights once more, falls as rain, and runs down again. Around and around and around.

Most running water follows seasonal rhythms, dictated by climate and topography. New England's streams, for instance, are full in the spring and early summer, when rains and snowmelt are at their peak and before the considerable thirst of forest and field has begun to soak up ground water. It has been calculated that a mature white oak in full summer leaf transpires in the course of photosynthesis some five hundred gallons of water every twenty-four hours, water that would otherwise find its way into some stream bed. In steep mountainous areas, streams empty quickly. Some that provide thrilling white-water runs for kayakers and practiced canoeists from April through June become boulder-strewn gullies punctuated by occasional open pools in summer. Except when it freezes or floods, New England's largest river, the Connecticut, remains passable all year. It did so even before its thirteen dams were built to regulate the flow. The lower reaches of the Connecticut, like those of most large rivers, run over a shallow gradient, no more than a foot or two per mile, its waters deep and strong, fine for canoeing but too slow for all but the most lethargic rafter, and no challenge at all for a kayaker.

The relation between cause and effect, deluge and flood, is not always so obvious. For millennia Egyptians in the fertile valley of the Nile accepted as divine Providence the river's annual overflowing of its banks, which laid down rich sediments and watered their crops. The flood came when not a drop of rain could be expected to fall in that desert land. Not until the nineteenth century was the annual bounty understood to originate in equatorial downpours occurring weeks earlier and thousands of miles to the south in Kenya and Ethiopia.

On the other hand, and sadly, many of America's grandest rivers have been stripped of all mystery and surprise. They are entirely controlled by man. The once mighty Rio Grande in the arid Southwest has its waters drained away for irrigation and is reduced to a mere trickle where it marks the border between El Paso, Texas, and the Mexican city of Juarez. Were it not for the influx from the Rio Conchos, flowing north out of Mexico, the glorious Rio Grande Canyon at Big Bend National Park would be dry. And what will happen when the Mexicans more fully exploit the Conchos?

Left alone, streams, in the manner of most natural phenomena, experience discernible life cycles, from birth to death. The aging factor is the power of water to dissolve and abrade. Water is not only the single most important element in support of life on earth, it is the most potent geological tool. Water comes the closest of any natural substance to being a universal solvent. Even without the additional abrasive energy it achieves in tumbling down a mountainside, it breaks apart the hardest rock, molecule by molecule. In climates where freezing and melting occur, the process is accelerated manyfold. No sooner does one continental plate of the earth's surface jostle another to make a mountain than running water goes to work to flatten it again. Geologists have calculated that the sediments carried to the oceans by the rivers of North America are sufficient to lower the land mass by one foot every nine thousand years. That is a theoretical average. In fact, the mountains are coming down much faster than that. Most of the material cut out of them is deposited during times of flood in the lowlands long before it reaches the sea. It took the Colorado River millions of years to carve the mile-deep stream bed of the Grand Canyon, exposing layers of rocks all the way down to the primal continent of a billion years ago. Most of that material now comprises the flood plain at the head of the Sea of Cortés.

TELLING A RIVER'S AGE

In running downhill, whether guttering a country road or washing down the face of Mount McKinley, water soon carves its own channel. It then becomes, by definition, a stream. We call our largest streams rivers. The name we use for smaller streams are legion—rill, brook, freshet, creek. However, there is little difference in behavior between big and little streams. Gradient, not size, determines the character of a stream. A stream is said to be young when it is a torrent dashing down an irregular slope, tumbling over falls and rapids. At this stage the banks are usually steep and the water-worn valley abrupt with V-shaped sides. The earthy debris carried along by streams is called their load. Young streams carry loads generally characterized by large particle size but relatively modest total quantity. Such ebullient streams have an excess of energy. Some of that excess is spent down-cutting the stream bed, adding to the load. The rest is spent in creating the turbulence. Down-cutting progressively lowers the gradient, and as it does, the force of the stream diminishes. In time— immense by human standards, but relatively short in geological terms—the stream will be flowing with just enough energy to support its load. At this point it is said to have reached maturity. The gradient now will be smooth, the valley wide and gentle sloping. In those conditions the stream begins to meander, to swing in sinuous arcs from one side of the valley to the other, cutting ever wider loops through material it has deposited earlier. As the loops grow lazier, the actual length of the stream increases, while the gradient grows shallower and shallower. Following this longer course, the stream flows more slowly than before and deposits more of its load. Streams in this state are approaching old age, a time of sluggishness, with the river snaking back and forth across a wide, open flood plain. It has little energy left to transport anything except a small amount of fine debris. Such a river is the Mississippi, whose extensive delta and shifting channels proclaim its venerability. The Hudson, on the other hand, which still flows vigorously into the Atlantic, is just approaching maturity.

Whatever their geological age, river systems are like trees: a trunk that supports many great limbs may be old and gnarled, while the tips of the branches are indistinguishable from those of young saplings. It is the youthful rivers, and the still-vigorous branches of the older rivers, that will command most of our attention in this book. For it is on streams with a youthful excess of energy that river running is most fun.

RATING A RIVER

The volume of water passing a given point in a river is one measure of its energy. But this does not describe its real difficulty for a rafter or canoeist. As white-water sports have grown in popularity, it has become increasingly important to have some sort of universal rating system so that a particular stream or rapid can be described to someone who has never seen it.

Two systems prevail. The first, and less common, is a one-to-ten scale. One equals virtually flat water and ten signifies the "limit of runnability." Any water more difficult than that gets a U rating, for unrunnable.

In wider use across the country and in Europe is a

classification system using Roman numerals I to VI. One in each scale signifies easy water, whereas VI on the Roman numeral scale is the equivalent of U on the decimal scale. Since the Roman numeral scale has a wider acceptance, it is used in this book.

The Rating System

I. Very easy. Slight gradient, channels wide and clear. Riffles and small waves.

II. Easy water. Regular waves not over two feet high. Rapids of moderate difficulty are easily avoided.

III. Moderately difficult water. Waves up to three feet. Rocks and eddies. Scouting advisable on first runs by any but seasoned experts.

IV. Rapids long and violent. Waves to five feet. Dangers include rock drops and souse holes. Should be run by experts only.

V. Violent rapids without letup. Many dangers to craft and life. Must be scouted. Waves over five feet. Large volume of water. Powerful hydraulics that can swallow craft. Falls and holes able to trap boats and swimmers.

VI. Unrunnable or at the absolute limit of runnability. Every imaginable danger. For daredevil experts only. Scouting imperative.

Not only does the fast water add zest, in the same way that steep mountains make skiing more exciting, but it is at the headwaters of large rivers and in their constricting rock canyons that you find them in something approaching their natural state. For these are the last parts of rivers likely to be developed. Competitive kayaking and canoeing—running slalom courses on rapids against time—puts little premium on the ambiance along the riverbank. Indeed, in the Munich Olympics, in 1972, the kayaking competition was carried on in a man-made concrete sluice. But those events aside, it is fair to say that the fun of river running increases in direct proportion to the wildness of the river.

NORTH AMERICAN RIVER SYSTEMS

Having said that, one must admit that few perfectly wild rivers are left within the lower forty-eight states. One has to travel to Canada or Alaska to find whole rivers without the strong imprint of man upon them. Still, there is no section of the continent that is without challenging white water—at least for part of the year—and with many calm and scenic stretches of river still in a semiwild state. A quick inventory east to west begins with the Appalachian range, an old one, dating back to the Mesozoic age, 230 million years ago. This 1500-mile-long range gives rise to the rivers of the entire Atlantic seaboard. They are, by and large, mature streams. Their low stretches flow gently, usually through broad, well-populated valleys. To find fast water and a semblance of wilderness, one must reach well inland toward the stream heads.

West of the Appalachians, across the heart of the continent all the way to the Rocky Mountains and the Continental Divide, the country is dominated by the incredible Mississippi River system. The great trunk that empties into the Gulf of Mexico at New Orleans draws its substance from such disparate sources as the Ohio and the Missouri, whose headwaters rise nearly two thousand miles apart. Here again the most attractive stretches of fast water are found well upstream.

Not so around the Great Lakes and in eastern Canada. The lakes are the youngest geological feature of any consequence on the continent. They appeared in their present form only about 10 million years ago, in the late Pleistocene epoch. Their tributary streams still run with youthful vigor right into the lakes themselves. It is country where canoe travel was born and where it experienced its grandest moment during the era of the voyageurs and the fur trade. Canoeing remains a prime sport around the Great Lakes.

The Rocky Mountains, too, are geologically young. The coastal ranges, the Sierra Nevada and the Cascades, younger still. It is there in the West that the robust river giants flow. Rivers like the Rogue, the Snake, the Green, are in the full blush of adolescence—strong, unpredictable, bubbling with life.

RIVERS AS THOROUGHFARES

It was roughly in the order described above that the New World revealed itself to Western man. And rivers were his thoroughfares. They determined the early settlement of the continent—the English on the James at the mouth of Chesapeake Bay, the French on the St. Lawrence, the Dutch on the Hudson. For centuries rivers provided the paths of least resistance to the interior. The first deep probe of North America came in 1534, when the French explorer Cartier sailed up the St. Lawrence. Just twelve years earlier Magellan had found his way around the bottom of South America and had crossed the Pacific. Europeans who understood the significance of that first circumnavigation of the globe knew they had to go much farther than Columbus had predicted to reach the Orient. Still, each explorer, finding a new Great Lake, proclaimed the Western Ocean to lie just beyond.

The dream of a viable Northwest Passage would not die for three centuries. And if men never did actually sail boats over the Continental Divide in pursuit of beaver pelts, they came within a few short portages of doing so. The waterway provided by the St. Lawrence, the Great Lakes, and the sodden lake and river country of central Canada led the voyageurs toward the end of the eighteenth century, the heyday of the fur trade, to the very ramparts of the northern Rockies.

Were the voyageurs in their long canoes the first true river runners? One is tempted to say so. True, they had learned from the aborigines the craft of canoe building and the art of paddling. And Indians had been skillfully traversing the rivers and lakes of the north woods for centuries before the whites arrived. But one detects in the voyageurs, in their stylized dress (gaudy sashes, stocking caps), in their joyous songs—*"En roulant ma boule," "Youpe, youpe sur la rivière"*— and in their fierce pride, for the first time in the history of the New World a certain sporting attitude toward rivers.

Yet their *canoe de maître* was no toy. It measured thirty-five feet, weighed some six hundred pounds and, though built of bark, could carry a cargo of three tons. Those figures were reason enough for men to take the risks of running rapids in bark boats. The alternative was to carry canoe and cargo on their backs. Four men routinely shouldered the craft, while the furs, packed in ninety-pound *"pièces,"* were toted by the remaining six or eight paddlers, two *pièces* at a time per man. Staggering work, but, in fact, most of the rapids that are duck soup for a good paddler today were portaged by the voyageurs. A spill meant more than a dunking. It could cost many thousands of dollars. Sometimes it cost more, as one contemporary account describes:

> They preferred running the Dalles [a rapid on the Columbia River]. They had not gone far, when to avoid the ridge of waves, which they ought to have kept, they took the apparent smooth water, were drawn into a whirlpool which wheeled them around into its Vortex; the Canoe with the Men clinging to it, went down and foremost and they all were drowned; at the foot of the Dalles search was made for their bodies, but only one Man was found, his body much mangled by the Rocks.

Disaster bred knowledge. The voyageurs learned when to avoid certain types of "smooth water." Without knowing the words, they grasped the principles of riverine hydraulics, how to take advantage of back eddies, to shun souse holes and standing waves. With knowledge came the pride and satisfaction of doing a job with style and doing it better than the next man. And that, certainly, is where all sport begins.

There is no telling where it might all have ended if beaver hats had not gone out of style. The focus of attention shifted, then, farther south, to the great westward-tending Missouri River, the "Big Muddy" as it was known to a generation of rivermen who pitted their muscle against its monstrous flow. With their many tributaries, the Mississippi and Missouri river systems became highways and byways of the Louisiana Purchase. This was water on a grand scale. The keelboats, large enough to carry a small brass cannon in the bow "to teach the savages respect," gradually replaced the canoe as the major cargo vessel of the West—as it, in turn, bowed to the steamboat and later to the iron horse.

In the farthest corner of the American West the extensive Columbia river system was explored. And in '49, when gold was found at Sutter's Mill on the American River in California, hardly a waterway in the West went unprobed for long. Settlers followed like air into a vacuum. Twenty years after the gold rush, the national map contained only one sizeable blank, an area of spectacular erosion lying in the southwest desert, now the northern section of the State of Arizona. It is significant that the man who would illuminate that void, John Wesley Powell, chose to do so by boating down two wild and largely unknown rivers, the Green and the Upper Colorado.

The year was 1869, and the region to be explored, the mile-deep fastness of the Grand Canyon of the Colorado. Major Powell was a one-armed veteran of the Civil War, a self-taught geologist, and an enterprising promoter who had raised the funds himself for this mission. Moreover, he had persuaded nine stout men to accompany him—without pay. Their craft were four double-ended dories (one can still run the Colorado today in modified versions of these boats). When they set out on May 24 from Green River Station, Wyoming, the rail stop closest to the Colorado river system, it was in the face of reports that the river vanished underground, that it plunged over falls higher than Niagara, and that it was inhabited by bands of deadly savages. The odyssey lasted three months. (Today, with one of several commercial outfitters, one can dash through the canyon on inflated rafts in just five days—and expect hearty camp meals ashore each night.) One man left the Powell expedition even before it reached the main canyon. Three others chose to walk out on foot only one day before the last challenging rapid was past. Tragically, these three were killed by Indians somewhere on the rim of the canyon, the only casualties Powell would suffer in either that or a subsequent expedition two years later. The survivors emerged gaunt, clothes in tatters, cowhide boots soggy and misshapen, and near starvation. Two boats had been splintered on the rocks. Their entire stores consisted of a sack of moldy flour, some blankets, some coffee, and a few tools and instruments. But they also had Powell's extraordinary journal. Any of a hundred excerpts from that log of the first run down the Colorado tells more about the future sport of river running than any contemporary account of white-water adventure ever could. Here is one:

June 9—Very slowly we make our way, often climbing on the rocks at the edge of the water for a few hundred yards to examine the channel before running it. During the afternoon we come to a place where it is necessary to make a portage. I land the little boat and the others are signaled to come up.

I walk along the bank to examine the ground, leaving one of my men with a flag to guide the other boats to the landing place. A minute after,

I hear a shout, and, looking around, see one of the boats shooting down the center of the fall. It is the No Name. I feel that its going over is inevitable, and run to save the third boat. A minute more, and she turns the point and heads for shore. Then I turn down the stream again and scramble along to look for the boat that has gone over. The first fall is not great, only 10 or 12 feet, and we often run such; but below, the river tumbles down again for 40 or 50 feet, in a narrow, angry channel filled with dangerous rocks that break the waves into whirlpools and beat them into white foam.

I pass around a great crag just in time to see the boat strike a rock and, rebounding from the shock, careen and fill its open compartment with water. Two of the men lose their oars; the boat swings around and is carried down at a rapid rate, broadside on, for a few yards, when, striking amidship on another rock with great force, she is broken in two and the men are thrown into the river. But the larger part of the boat floats buoyantly, and they seize it, and down the river they drift, past rocks for a few hundred yards, to a second rapid filled with huge boulders, where the boat strikes again and is dashed to pieces, and the men and fragments are soon carried beyond my sight.

Running along, I turn a bend and see a man's head above the water, washed about in a whirlpool below a great rock. It is Frank Goodman, clinging to a rock with a grip upon which life depends. Coming opposite, I see Captain Howland trying to go to his aid from an island onto which he has been washed. Soon he comes near enough to reach Frank with a pole, which he extends toward him. The latter lets go the rock, grasps the pole, and is then pulled ashore. Seneca Howland, the captain's brother, is washed farther down the island and is caught by some rocks, and though somewhat bruised, also manages to get ashore.

And now the three men are on an island, with a swift, dangerous river on either side and a fall below. The Emma Dean is brought down, and Jack Sumner, starting above as far as possible, pushes out. Right skillfully he plies the oars, and a few strokes set him on the island at the proper point. Then they pull the boat upstream as far as they are able, until they stand in water up to their necks. One sits on a rock and holds the boat until the others are ready to pull, then gives the boat a push, clings to it with his hands, and climbs in as they pull for mainland, which they reach in safety. We are as glad to shake hands with them as though they had been on a voyage around the world and wrecked on a distant coast.

DESTRUCTION OF THE WILDERNESS

It is now more than a hundred years since Powell's incredible adventure. The century has been even more cruelly destructive of America's rivers than the two that preceded it. For all their awe at the bounty of the New World, white settlers saw the wilderness not only as boundless but as something to be conquered and tamed. Policies and practices that evolved during the eighteenth and nineteenth centuries have been carried to terrible excess in the twentieth. The wooden dam that held back the mill pond in Thoreau's day has grown to proportions that dwarf the pyramids. Every fifteen years the demand for power in this country doubles. Hydroelectric power, which at first glance appears to be pollution free and inexhaustible—the perfect source—turns out to have serious drawbacks. The expenditure of energy in the first place to build a dam on the scale of Grand Cooly, across the Columbia, is astronomical. Because of the build-up of silt behind it, the useful life of a dam like Grand Cooly is limited.

Other rivers have been channeled for transportation, or bled for irrigation, or burdened with such a noxious load of sewage and industrial waste as to become unbearable to smell or look at. Most nineteenth-century mill towns, in fact, have turned their backs on their once-proud riverfronts. Pollution has relegated most streams running through populated areas to the status of back alleys, dumping places for old automobiles, garbage, and trash. The surface of Cuyahoga River in Ohio was so thickly covered with oil and chemical wastes that it caught fire in 1969. The Millers, a once-famous Massachusetts trout stream, now carries effluvium away from a chemical plant. Not only are the fish gone, but no vegetation grows along the bank. Extreme cases of pollution, to be sure, but the fact remains that one has to travel into northern Canada or Alaska today to find potable water in any sizeable North American stream.

PROTECTING OUR RIVERS

Who cares? The sad answer is that until recently there were very few people in this country who did care, and for the most part they wielded little clout. Some small streams found protection under the patronage of wealthy sportsmen who reserved them for fishing. Some parts of rivers like the Yellowstone and the Colorado, flowing through national or state parks, were partially maintained in their wild state. But obviously that was not enough. It is axiomatic that wherever a river is disturbed—dammed, polluted, or syphoned off—everything downstream and upstream suffers.

The idea of providing federal protection for an entire river, or, where it is already too late to do so, part of a river—in the same spirit that endangered species of wildlife are protected—is a relatively new concept. It comes in the absolute nick of time. There are today far fewer wild rivers left in the forty-eight united states than there are whooping cranes or condors.

What it took to awaken federal concern was a sizeable and vocal body of citizenry who cared about wild, free-flowing rivers. That constituency began to take shape with the growing popularity of river running—in canoes, kayaks, and rafts. Canoeing had long held a small, highly dedicated following, particularly in northern New England, upper New York state, Canada, and around the Great Lakes. Recreational canoeing, primarily as means of travel through wilderness areas, dates well back into the nineteenth century. But it was a pastime indulged in mainly by the leisure class —well-to-do sportsmen and New York, Boston, and Chicago families able to keep rustic "camps" in the North Woods. If it became necessary to protect a stream, they found that the simplest way was to buy it and the surrounding country, at prices often working out to no more than a few dollars an acre. The numbers of these dilettante Thoreaus were infinitesimal compared to the hundreds of thousands who ply our streams each summer today.

With all the horrors committed over the past three centuries to American rivers without so much as a "by-your-leave," it is instructive to note that the first comprehensive step the federal government has taken to protect what is left was prompted largely by the overuse of rivers for recreation. A joint 1963 study by the Department of the Interior and the Department of Agriculture led Congress five years later to pass the Wild and Scenic Rivers Act. In recommending that law, the secretaries of the Interior and Agriculture departments declared jointly: "We have harnessed many of our rivers, dedicating some to navigation, others to power, water supply, and disposal of wastes. [Rarely has "rape" been couched in such sanitary terms.] But we have not yet made adequate provision to keep at least a small stock of our rivers as we first knew them: wild and free-flowing. In a Nation as bountifully endowed with rivers as ours, it is time to do so."

Rivers to be protected must be "free-flowing streams which possess outstanding remarkable scenic, recreational, geological, fish, wildlife, historic, cultural and other similar values." Those that qualify will fall into one of three classes: *wild rivers,* those that are both inaccessible enough and free enough of interference by man to rate as true vestiges of primitive America; *scenic rivers,* those that are accessible in places; and *recreational rivers,* those which are readily accessible by road but otherwise meet the requirements.

When the act was promulgated, on October 2, 1968, eight rivers made up the nucleus. Future rivers would be added pending study. The original eight were the St. Croix, in Wisconsin and Minnesota; the Wolf, in Wisconsin; the Rogue, in Oregon; the Middle Fork of the Feather, in California; the middle Salmon and the middle Clearwater, both in Idaho; the Rio Grande, in New Mexico; and the Eleven Point, in Missouri.

Nearly a decade later only eight more rivers have joined the list, the latest as of this writing being the New, in North Carolina. By the summer of 1976, twenty-seven other rivers were under consideration. Three rivers under study—the Maumee, in Ohio and Indiana, and the Allegheny and Clarion, in Pennsylvania—had been rejected because of existing development.

When dealing with the federal bureaucracy one must learn to curb impatience. Given the centuries of neglect, the Wild and Scenic Rivers Act is at least a beginning—and a promise that for those new to the sport of river running there will, at some future time, still be rivers to run.

RAFTING

IT is hard to prove but even harder to dispute that man's first river trips were made on rafts—simple wooden platforms. In the early days of river running the primary sporting craft were pontoons and inflatable military surplus rafts made of rubber. Certainly there is no more straightforward approach to a river, and, in the minds of many, none better. Paddling a canoe or kayak demands conscious effort all the time, even in the calmest water; the appeal of rafting is different, more basic.

To be sure, the modern inflatable raft, though simple in principle, is built of sophisticated materials available through modern technology. Moreover, running a raft through a big rapid requires a high degree of navigational skill and a thorough understanding of riverine hydraulics. Yet, left to its own devices, a raft would probably get down most of our rivers pretty much by itself. Rafts are agreeably accommodating. Flexible, they mold themselves to angry waves, do not tip easily, bounce off rocks, and carry large loads relative to their own weight. Rafts allow time to devote to the river. Time to lie back and watch the countryside slide by, trace the towering gyre of a hawk, dangle your feet in cool currents, fish, read, contemplate the infinite, listen to the river.

There are moments, however, on big, strong rivers with heavy hydraulics, when rafting calls up the adrenalin and more than satisfies the appetites of the most avid thrill seekers. Rafts easily handle water too rough for open canoes. And big rafts, the thirty-footers, can even venture into holes and over falls that would eat up a kayak or a decked canoe. Thus neophyte passengers who have never been on a river before can taste the delicious terror of truly big water. All in all, with some congenial companions along for the trip, rafting provides a whale of a good time right from the start.

The most careful way to begin your adventures in rafting is to join a commercial float trip that uses small-to medium-sized rafts. This way you can learn firsthand what to look for—and look out for—when choosing your own craft. You will also learn whether you enjoy the sport enough to lay out the price (two hundred to six hundred dollars, depending on size and quality) of a reasonably serviceable craft. These trips are generally great fun and provide a cram course in river running. As vacations go, they are a good buy—costing in the neighborhood of two hundred dollars for five days on the water. The outfitter supplies the meals, you bring (or rent from him) your own camping gear.

If going out into the wilderness in guided groups runs against your grain, a second way to test the water before plunging in is to rent a raft. These services are not widespread, but on some of the popular rivers described in this book you will find rentals available.

If you are certain rafting is for you, you may not wish to waste a penny but instead put all your money into the best raft you can buy. Where to buy a raft? Sporting goods stores and camping stores, if they have no rafts in stock, will order one for you or provide you with the information to order your own. Write for specifics, then order by mail. One of the advantages of inflatable rafts is their packability.

CHOOSING A RAFT

Size:

How big? Two factors rule: the number of passengers and the size of the river. Although rafts have come a long way since the war-surplus type that inspired the sport in the first place, certain conventions die hard. Chief among these is the rated capacity of rafts. A so-called six-man raft, for instance, might well suffice to save the lives of six fliers downed in the ocean, but it would be seriously overloaded on any stream rated higher than Class II—and that is without camping gear along. Three people and their gear would fill the boat. Two would be comfortable. A general rule of thumb is to take the manufacturer's rated capacity of an inflatable raft and divide it in half for river running, or even by one third if you intend to carry a lot of camping equipment. The maneuverability of a raft depends on its riding light on the water. It is possible to load a raft with an incredible weight—to fill it with water, for example. It will not sink, but it will become sluggish, unmanageable, and, in big water, downright dangerous.

When sizing a raft to a particular river, you should know the width of the narrowest passes between rocks. Otherwise you can't get through. Elementary, you say? Well, back in 1964 a group of Americans, most of them experienced river runners, set out on the previously unrun Urique River in the Sierra Madre mountains of northwestern Mexico. The Urique cuts a fabulous gorge called the Barranca de Cobre, or Copper Canyon, which in parts is deeper than the Grand Canyon. The unmapped river had never been run before, and the leaders made a thorough aerial survey before setting out in seventeen-foot neoprene rafts that were eight feet wide. Somehow in studying the Barranca from the air, they had missed the huge rock jams that blocked the river in many places, requiring them repeatedly to portage their four-hundred-pound boats. The Americans

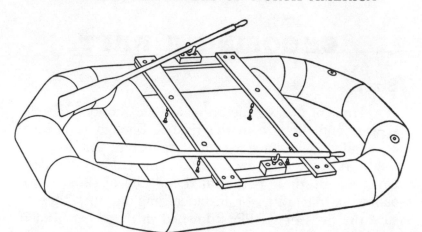

A typical inflatable raft rigged with a frame.

never did make it through the canyon, but ran out of food and were finally rescued by the native Tarahumara Indians.

When figuring boat width, remember the oars. In a really tight squeeze you can, of course, ship the oars. But generally figure that a raft needs at least triple its width for a safe passage. Still another consideration when choosing the size raft you need is the degree of difficulty of the rapids. Everything else being equal, the bigger the boat, the bigger the water it can handle.

Material:

The material your boat is made of is important. Whatever compound is used to make a tube airtight, it needs reinforcement to hold its shape. We speak, remembering the war, of rubber life rafts. Cotton drill was the original backing for rubber. But this natural fiber was found to rot when it got damp, while rubber deteriorated quickly in the sun. Almost no rafts are made of rubber any more. The best modern replacement is a synthetic rubber called neoprene backed with nylon fabric, or nylon sandwiched between two layers of Hypalon, a neoprene-like substance manufactured by Du Pont.

Some inflatable craft, particularly the kayak-shaped Tahiti boats that are popular on rivers today, are made of vinyl urethane—strong enough without a fabric backing to withstand considerable punishment, and lighter in weight than the laminate compound. Like any fabric, vinyl urethane can be punctured, but the trouble with it is that it cannot easily be mended on the river the way neoprene can. Contact cement and patches do not stick securely. Vinyl urethane requires high heat and special tools, and for that reason is outlawed on many federally controlled rivers unless it is used in conjunction with a sturdier inflatable craft.

Neoprene/nylon comes in several weights, measured in ounces per square yard. The bigger the raft, the heavier the material should be. A fifteen-foot raft should use no lighter than twenty-four-ounce neophene/nylon, whereas a giant thirty-footer may well be made of forty-eight-ounce weight. The floors should probably be of still heavier fabric in both cases, as they take the most wear.

Tube Size:

Another variable among rafts is the size of the tube. Seventeen inches in diameter, half the girth of an average man, is generally considered a minimum for venturing on true white water. One of the best manufacturers of inflatable rafts is Avon, a British firm. Although they primarily design dinghies for yachts, a few years ago they began making a line of boats specifically for rivers because they recognized the growing interest in river running. They gave them seventeen- and eighteen-inch tubes (and also made a rowing frame to fit). The only drawback now is price. The sixteen-footer currently costs in excess of a thousand dollars. But an Avon should last a decade or two, if properly cared for.

Flotation Chambers:

Be sure to ask how many flotation chambers a raft has. It may be tedious to inflate each one, but the more you have, the safer the boat. Puncture a two-chambered boat and you are practically out of business. With four or six chambers, your raft can be expected to hold its shape long enough for you to get to shore and slap on a patch.

Rocker:

After size and material, the most common variable among rafts is the amount of rocker, the upward bend of the bow and stern. A rocker helps the craft climb over waves and slaps down spray. It also makes any craft easier to turn. Some rafts are rockered fore and aft, some not at all. It is simpler—and cheaper—to build a raft without a rocker. If you are going to be rafting on white water, you are going to get wet, rocker or no rocker. So the choice comes down to a matter of maneuverability. If the rivers you contemplate running are full of rocks and surprises, you may want to spend the money for a rockered boat. Otherwise, do not bother.

Tie-Downs:

Another thing to look for in a white-water raft is the number and ruggedness of the tie-downs—the metal rings fitted to the tubes. You cannot have too many. The more securely you are able to lash down your cargo, the better off you are. Tie-downs also make good handholds for passengers. Sitting on the gunwale, or upper edge, of a neoprene raft in white water is about as secure a place to park yourself as on the back of a bucking bronco—that's the fun of it. But it helps to have something to hold on to.

EQUIPMENT

Oars:

All right, you have the raft. Now what about the tools to control it? Oars and a rowing frame to stabilize the oarlocks are the most efficient propulsion device. The principle is the same as rowing a dory or other small boat. The oarsman sits in the middle of the craft and pulls a pair of oars that are secured in their oarlocks at a distance approximately one-third down their length. Oars should measure about one-half the boat length, slightly longer if you feel strong. Ash and maple, the same woods used for baseball bats and shovel handles, are the best because they are strong in relation to their weight. Marine supply stores generally sell oars in a variety of lengths. When you first get your oars, it is a good idea to cap each blade with a six-inch strip of sheet copper bent over the tip and tacked down. You are bound to hit rocks with the ends of your oars, and sometimes you will use them to push off. The caps will keep the oars from splintering.

Rowing Frame:

Basic small inflatables often come with reinforced loops on the gunwale, or gunnel, to serve as oarlocks. Anyone who has tried to row such a craft knows the meaning of the word *frustration*. The pivot point is too yielding, and a hearty pull may even collapse the raft. This is where the rowing frame comes in. It provides a solid base for the oarsman and the oarlocks so that the full force of a stroke is transmitted to the water. Now, if the water would only hold still also, instead of flowing around the blade or buffeting it about in turbulence, you would have a nearly 100-percent efficient machine. As it is, a light raft with a good set of oars and rowing frame can be moved forward or aft or spun about with surprising ease for so clumsy looking a craft.

Very few raft manufacturers equip their boats with frames, however. Usually you will have to make your own. A simple frame for a twelve-foot raft can be built from two-by-sixes. Talk to your local sporting goods store about where to get plans.

On large rafts, frames are often built of one-half-inch galvanized iron pipe bent to fit over the tubes like a yoke over the back of a pair of oxen.

Oarlocks:

The keystone in any frame is the oarlock. There are many different systems for attaching an oar to a boat. Shun those that require drilling a hole through the oar. This weakens the shaft at exactly the point where it needs to be the strongest. It also limits the movements you can make. The oar cannot be "feathered"—turned at the end of a stroke so that the blade rests nearly parallel to the water—or drawn into the boat. It can also be easily broken should you catch a downstream oar on the bottom of the river—the biggest single oar-buster of all.

The best system is a conventional oarlock with an opening between the horns that will accept the oar at its narrow part, above the blade. The lock should be so sized that the handle of the oar is too large to pop out when rowing.

To keep the oar from sliding out into the water should you let go of it for a moment—very embarrassing—you will need to attach a collar just above the fulcrum point. Although you can buy an oarlock that has a pin or bolt, a piece of an old fan belt held in place with plenty of black plastic tape serves the purpose just as well.

Paddles:

A second way to propel a raft is with paddles. One advantage of paddles is that you obviate the need to build a rowing frame. But that is a negative consideration. There is only one positive advantage to paddles, but that may be enough to carry the day for many of us. A number of outfitters, particularly in the southeastern United States, give paddles to all their charges. With five or six paddlers on a side straddling the pontoons, one foot in and one foot out, flailing away like so many galley slaves at the command of the boatman at the stern, a big raft going down the New River, in North Carolina, is a sight to behold and a caution to hear: "Altogether now, portside, dig, dig, dig!" No question, this makes for a thrilling ride, if for no other reason than that you are always charging forward rather than pulling backward against the current as in the rowing technique—but it is safe to do with amateurs only on certain rivers. It takes a highly trained team of paddlers to match the pinpoint maneuverability of a rowed raft.

So, unless the river is an easy one and togetherness is your prime concern, stick to oars—you can always take turns.

Sweeps:

Two other steering methods should be mentioned: sweeps and outboard motors. Sweeps have a certain antique charm. They are great big long-handled affairs that look like oversized hockey sticks. Supported on tall stands, they are pulled by one or sometimes a pair of standing boatmen. Rafts on Mark Twain's Mississippi were often guided by sweeps. You can forget them except as curiosities.

Outboards:

You can also forget outboards. They are used occasionally—mostly as tools to get across large bodies of still water or to steer the huge pontoon boats that carry twenty or thirty people at a time through popular tourist rivers like the Green, a tributary of the Colorado, and the Upper Snake. But the noise outboards make, their stink, and their unreliability when you most need them are antithetical to everything river running is about. Highly *not* recommended.

Life Jacket:

You will need three other essential articles of equipment before you set out on a river, even for a day: Coast-Guard-approved life jackets for every member of the party, some kind of waterproof shoes, and at least fifty feet of strong rope. On all federally and most state-controlled rivers, life jackets are required by law. For example, in national parks like the Grand Canyon, you must wear one at all times in the boat or raft, or suffer a fifty-dollar fine. For the rest, common sense dictates. If you are a good swimmer and there are no rapids in sight or earshot, obviously you need not don a jacket. But do not be fooled by rapids; they can tug a strong swimmer under as easily as a crocodile takes a duck—and hold you there. If your raft flips or you go over the side, you will need all the flotation you can get. In fact, one of the best ways to appreciate the power of a river is to put on a life jacket, jump in, and float along with the boat. You will feel the river tugging and pulling at you like a blind giant playing with a doll. The best jackets for river running are those with high collars that will keep your head up even if you are knocked unconscious.

A short personal note on this score: When researching this book, I was knocked on the head twice— once when our dory turned over on the Snake River and an oar hit me on the back of the head, and another time on the White River, in Vermont, while learning to kayak. I was cut rather badly both times, even though in the kayak mishap I was wearing the mandatory protective helmet. The point is, it is easy to be hit on the head, and should you be stunned, which fortunately I was not, a jacket with a collar is the only thing that will save you. Vest-type jackets are more comfortable. They will keep you afloat but not hold your head above water. The choice is up to you.

Footwear:

Shoes are something that too often are taken off on river runs. When rafting, you can count on getting your feet wet at the outset of the trip and having them constantly wet thereafter, so there is a strong temptation to take your shoes off. In rapids, after your life jacket, shoes are your best protection. You cannot swim in a rapid with or without shoes, so having your feet free is no advantage. All you can do is flow with the river, lying on your back, looking ahead, with your feet thrust out in front of you to steer around any rocks. That is where the shoes come in. You may also find yourself, if worse comes to worse, with a long walk home over rocky and thorny ground. You will want shoes then, too, however wet they may be.

ROWING TECHNIQUES

I have said that rowing a raft with a frame is just like pulling a rowboat. That is not quite true. In a rowboat the oarsman faces aft. In a raft he faces forward, although on rafts without rockers the distinction is not always a clear one. There are two reasons for facing forward. First of all, it is absolutely essential that the man at the oars going through a rapid have a clear view of what lies ahead. Second, when rowing, it is much better to pull a boat than to push it—though both strokes will come into play. Pulling backward against the current is the basic maneuver in navigating a raft.

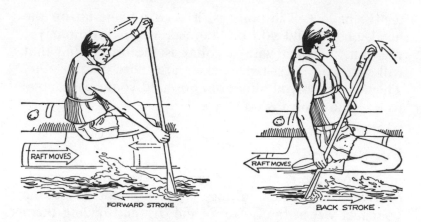

Basic raft strokes

Skill at rowing comes only with practice. Obviously, if you have had no experience rowing even small boats, you had better start your rafting career on flat water. And unless your hands are already toughened, you had better wear a pair of cotton or soft leather gloves. Otherwise you will quickly raise blisters. The same goes for paddling.

Let us assume, then, that you have learned to handle the raft—to pull astern, really getting your back into the stroke, to push ahead, to spin the boat right and left. Now, in your mind's eye, position yourself above a small rapid. You are in smooth water, the current carrying you toward the line of froth where the river bends perceptibly downhill. The drop is not so steep that you cannot see over it from a sitting position. There are a few protruding rocks to miss and a deep hollow behind a barely submerged boulder. A wave is pouring upriver into the hole. It is big enough to hold the raft. So you will definitely want to avoid that. Beyond the hole the rapid plays out in a diminishing confusion of waves and wavelets. Nothing here to worry about. This one is not a rapid that needs to be scouted.

THE IDEAL RUN

But this is to be a picture-book run. Everything will be done just right. You position your passengers—let us say there are four of you in a fifteen-foot raft—two in front and one behind. Contrary to boating instinct, it is best to keep more weight in the bow than the stern. These craft ride so high and light on the water that one of the dangers is of being flipped over backward by oncoming waves, or, in some extreme cases, having the raft bend backward on itself—a situation sometimes known as a "Colorado sandwich." This is the way most rafts go, quite unlike canoes or kayaks that roll easily but have almost perfect fore-and-aft stability.

The aspect of the raft on your approach should be across the current, pointing slightly downriver. Your work will be almost entirely pulling—or pushing—across the current. The water is carrying you forward —let the river do that work. Your job will be simply to move left or right to miss any and all obstacles in your way—the rocks, the breaking wave. Just about the only time you will row in the same direction as the main current is to punch through or climb over an extra-steep standing wave.

Now you position the raft to slide down the tongue of smooth water that points the way into the rapid. Below it, slightly to the right, is the hole with its breaking wave. You will want to pull away from that, so you point your bow at the hole. Remember, seated as you are—facing the bow—you are positioned to pull the boat astern. In rafting—as in life—the same advice applies: Face your dangers and pull away from them if you can. When danger is unavoidable, meet it head on with a strong forward stroke.

You are committed to the rapid now. You slide over the lip and accelerate quickly. Take two fast strokes, pulling the boat backward, toward the left, away from the hole. The current whips you past. Ahead lies the line of standing waves. No way around these. They are not big enough to stop you, otherwise you would want all the momentum you could muster at this point. As it is, the slower you are going when you meet these waves, the drier you will keep the passengers up front. You pull on your left oar, swinging the bow directly downstream, now a pull on both oars, counteracting the current. You are up and over the first wave. The rest of the waves are sloppy, coming at you first off the port quarter, then from starboard. Showing off a little now, you swing the bow first right then left, to meet each wave head on. The motion is not unlike a skier doing a series of quick parallel turns through moguls.

Ferrying:

Time now to introduce the word *ferry*. "To ferry," you will not be surprised to hear, is the verb boatmen use to describe the action of moving a raft across a river. When, a moment ago, you were pulling your boat away from the deep hole, you were ferrying left. A back ferry is the ordinary rowing stroke used to counter the force of the current. You may not actually move backward relative to the riverbank—unless the current is weak or you are very strong—but you will slow your forward progress while you move laterally. A forward ferry is made with a push rather than a pull of your arms.

Why do boatmen speak of ferrying rather than simply saying row right or row left, forward, or back? The term *ferry* implies a current. If you want to move laterally across a strip of still water, you need only point your stern toward your destination and pull on the oars. Add current and you will need to head for a point upriver from your intended landing spot. The stronger the current, the farther upriver you must head. Once the current reaches a speed that is faster than you can row your boat, it becomes impossible to row straight across. This is ordinarily the case in white water. You will have

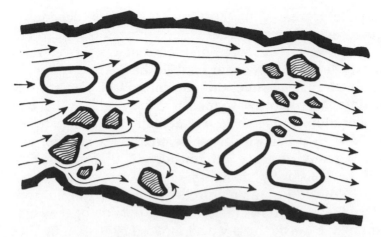

To ferry a boat in fast water, angle the stern toward
the side of the river you want to make for, but keep at
about 45° to the current. Then back row against the current.

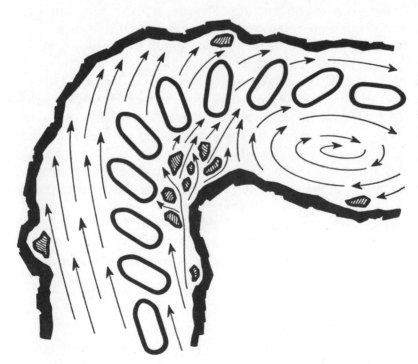

To ferry a boat around a bend in a river the most
important thing to remember is the angle of the boat to the
current. The boatman must maintain a 45° angle to
the current if he is to get where he wants to go.

to yield ground to the current—how much depends on your angle of attack. That is ferrying.

However, the force of a current on a river rarely if ever flows evenly from bank to bank. Even in a perfectly straight channel the current will be fastest in the middle, with slower water on either side, while back eddies along either shore are actually moving water upstream. In other words, when crossing a stream, even without any obstacles to consider, your ferry position will be constantly changing.

Now add to the picture a simple bend in the river. Here the water flows fastest on the outside of the curve, just as the outside of a wheel moves faster than the hub. The faster the water, the greater the turbulence. If there is nothing in the way, you will want to hug the inside of the curve. The river, all the while, will be trying to swirl you to the outside. So you will have to hold a ferry position relative to the current, pulling now and again to hold yourself perpendicular to the flow, while you sweep around the bend.

If the river makes a series of meandering S curves —and they almost all do—you are going to have to ferry across the current from one side to the other to keep on the inside of each bend. If you are swept to the outside, you can usually count on reflexive waves bouncing off the bank to keep your boat clear. Occasionally, however, these reflexive waves may be so great as to be dangerous themselves. In big water the full force of the river rebounding off a cliff face may create huge curlers that could swamp you. You will know them by their size and redouble your effort to keep to the inside of the curve.

Eddies:

We have already talked about eddies and eddy fences. Piloting a raft across them can be tricky, though not nearly so tricky as piloting a canoe or kayak, where your boat is more firmly in the grip of the river. The trick is to anticipate the sudden change of forces that will try to spin you like a pinwheel. No amount of discussion can prepare you for this twisting jolt any more than you can explain to someone the sensation of stepping on or off an escalator or moving train. You have to experience it yourself. So find a safe piece of water with a strong eddy and try crossing and recrossing the fence. You can go around and around this way on the same stretch of river indefinitely. Good practice.

Holes:

Avoiding trouble spots is the safest way to float a river; but you are there for fun, so sometimes you will want to take the rough-and-tumble route just for kicks. At other times the river may dictate the choices, confronting you with a low fall across its entire width, or it may draw down into a single narrow chute. In either case, you still have a choice. You can meet it head on, or you can stop, row to the bank and carry, or portage, your craft around the place if you deem it too dangerous. In order to decide intelligently, however, it helps to analyze the danger that rapidly falling water imposes. Even a short fall of a couple of feet can stop a big raft, often with uncomfortable consequences. The tumbling water creates a deep steep hole with strongly defined boundaries. Water will be rushing in from upstream and out the bottom of the hole, while the surface water on either side and downstream will be pouring into it as if down an open drain. If you do not get past this oncoming water on your first dash over the drop, you run the risk of being stuck there. You will probably be pushed back under the cascade, your raft will fill with water, and your chances of getting out become even smaller. When this happens, there is nothing to do but abandon ship, get a line to shore, and try to pop the raft free that way. The lesson is that if you are going to run over a steep drop, you should forward ferry with all your might right at the top to clear the falls behind you and get through the hole on the first dash.

Chutes:

When going down a chute the same advice applies. At the bottom you will inevitably meet a wall of water curling back at you. If the chute is so narrow that you cannot use your oars at this critical point, you may want to think twice about making the run.

Fall or chute, the larger the raft, the bigger the drop you can safely attempt. A general rule of thumb—very general—is not to try a fall that is greater than one third the length of your craft, nor face waves over half the length.

RAFTING MISHAPS

All of which brings up the subject of possible rafting mishaps. The most common trouble you can get into in a raft is to have it fill with water. You won't sink, but your boat will be transformed from a jaunty, easily steered craft into a lumbering behemoth with a will of its own, usually contrary to yours. So the first rule of rafting is, *Whenever you ship water, get it out*. There should be at least two bailing buckets—ideally, one for every passenger—in your boat. Ordinary plastic buckets with bails for the big work and Chlorox bottles with their bottoms cut out for the rest. Use a lanyard with a thumb clip to attach the bailers to the boat when not in use. Otherwise you will lose them just when you need them most, when a ton or two of water is pouring over the gunnels and carrying everything moveable away. You do not have to tip over in a raft to start losing gear. Everything, not just your buckets, should be tied down if you are going into rough water. More about stowing gear in the last chapter of this section.

Sometimes the only way to get the water out of your boat is to slash the bottom of it with a hunting knife. You might have to do that in the situation just described, when you are pushed under a falls. With tons of water pouring in every second, bailing becomes impossible, and you find the raft is too heavy to pop free, even with all hands tugging on a line from shore.

Another classic rafting setback is to be pinned on a rock. It happens to even the most cautious and well-trained boatmen. Sometime or other he is not going to spot that sleeper just below the surface and the raft will fetch up on it. Ninety-nine times out of a hundred, by rowing or by shifting weight, it is possible to break free around one side or the other; or, if the water is deep enough, to bounce over the top. But that one hundredth time the forces of the river may be such as to wrap the raft around a rock and hold it there like a barber's towel on a shavee's face. Then, should the current force the upstream gunnel under, the raft will fill and the chances of getting it off will be that much diminished. Again, it is time to resort to a line on shore. And if that does not work, put a knife to the bottom of the raft. The act of final recourse is to abandon the thing and wait for a change in river level—hours later, or perhaps weeks.

Some larger rafts are self-bailing, made with open bottoms to alleviate just this sort of danger and the nuisance of bailing. Passengers and gear are supported on a grillwork frame hung on the tubes. Grills are also installed on rafts with bottoms, to protect this most-often-ruptured tissue from wear and tear.

Slashing the bottom, incidentally, is not so drastic an act as it might at first seem. If you have the proper repair supplies with you—and you should—it is fairly easy to patch.

A minimal repair kit would consist of scissors, a yard or two of neoprene/nylon, contact cement, duct tape, bailing wire, pliers, drill, nails, bolts, and sail-maker's needle and thread. You should also have at least one, and better two, extra oars lashed to the gunnels. I have said that left to its own devices a raft will eventually get down most rivers by itself. This is true. But you wouldn't like the ride. Going down a river with just one oar can be a tedious, frustrating, and dangerous experience. Beter not try it. Oars are most often lost by being broken. Sometimes they just snap. You would be surprised how hard you can pull when the adrenalin is surging through you at some critical moment. The classic break occurs when you catch the downstream oar on the bottom or on an unexpected rock and the raft rides over it. Snap! No matter how much repair gear you carry, it is almost impossible to fix a broken oar.

Perhaps the most serious threat to life on any river —certainly the greatest danger on water below about 60° F.—is hypothermia. Hypothermia is the result of a cumulative loss of body heat. I will talk of this more in Chapter 6. But rafters must take special precautions. If the boat is being rowed, only one of your party will be keeping warm by exercising—and most often he will be the leader. In this case he must pay special attention to the passengers who have been sitting, perhaps for hours, cold and wet. Should you tip over in a rapid in cold water, the man who has been rowing may be able to survive for some time while those who are already chilled to the bone may be in serious danger in minutes. So, if there is any risk of cold, don't run that last rapid. Instead, pull over and find a camping spot, build a fire, and wait for tomorrow.

Do not try too much in one day. To extract maximum enjoyment from a rafting trip, take it at a gentle, relaxed pace—punctuated by moments of high tension. They will seem all the more exciting for the contrast. Leave plenty of time to explore the riverbanks and side canyons. Your raft is a vehicle for entering, quietly and without a trace, some of the continent's most astounding country. Rafting is a very special experience. Don't rush it.

CANOEING

Toward the end of a long winter evening spent talking about rivers and how to run them, I asked a cousin of mine, who is a professional guide, what craft he liked best—raft, canoe, or kayak.

"A canoe," he answered without hesitation. "You can do more with a canoe."

Canoes combine the best features of a raft and a kayak. They carry a lot, yet can themselves be carried. You can stow enough camping gear in a canoe to make you independent in the wilderness for weeks, even months, at a time. You can move canoes across lakes and reservoirs and maneuver them down rapids, and when the water runs out, you can turn amphibian, pick up your boat, and carry it on your back turtle-fashion. You can even sleep under a canoe.

Yet when you are on the water, you don't have to wear it the way you do a kayak. You can change positions, scratch your toe, reach for an apple among your supplies, jump out and push off a rock, or fish.

"Except for carrying it," I said, "you can do all those things in a raft."

"Not *in* a raft," he answered, "*on* a raft." There's the difference.

Rafts are merely platforms to sit on—and, too often, bounce off. It is hard to work up any rapport with a raft. Rafts have no personality, no roots. The difference between a raft and a canoe is the difference between a blunt instrument and a finely honed tool.

Short of hiking boots, the canoe, particularly in its modern incarnation, is the most useful tool there is for sampling the wilderness. Canoes open more boating options to their owners than do kayaks or rafts. So if it is versatility you want on a river—and grace—a canoe is the way to go.

EVOLUTION OF THE CANOE

The first canoes were wooden dugouts—logs, pointed at the ends, hollow in the center. The refinement of this simple craft took thousands of years, resulting eventually in boats of marvelous thinness and natural hydrodynamic lines. An early breakthrough was the discovery that hot water softens wood. Dugouts were filled with water, and red-hot stones dropped in. The sides became pliable enough to be spread without splitting. Thwarts, or crosswise bars, were inserted, giving the boat tensile strength, greater volume, and a more seaworthy shape. Eventually, in quest of lightness, boatbuilders hit upon the concept of rib and skin construction—wood, or sometimes bone, for the ribs; bark, animal hides, and, more recently, painted canvas over thin planking for the skin. Henry Rushton, of Canton, New York, working in the late 1800s, carried the art of building canoes of natural materials to its outer limits. He used very thin cedar planking for his skin, and so finely joined was each plank to the next that only varnish was needed to seal the boat. Rushton built his masterpiece for the Adirondacks sportsman George Washington Sears. It weighed merely 10.5 pounds. Just looking at a Rushton canoe, according to one modern-day enthusiast (there is a grand collection of Rushton boats at the Adirondacks Museum at Blue Mountain Lake), is enough to make you "hear loons calling." Such workmanship, alas, is not for sale anymore. During the first half of the twentieth century, wood and painted canvas became the materials that almost all canoes were made of. With their smooth, shellacked interiors and painted sides, they, too, exhibit an antique grace and charm. In the eyes of serious canoeists today, such boats light the same spark that afflicts auto buffs when they spot a Model T Ford cruising down the road. But who would take a Model T on an African safari?

CHOOSING A CANOE TODAY

Material:

What should you consider, then, before buying a canoe? Start with the material. Modern river running is hard on boats. Today's construction methods take advantage of a post–World War II boom in the development of synthetic materials. Synthetics, stronger pound for pound and cheaper when mass-produced, have all but eclipsed the market for wood and canvas boats. You can still buy wood and canvas canoes, but they are heavier than the new models and will not take punishment. They absorb water (and therefore weight), require yearly upkeep, and are more expensive.

Aluminum is not technically a synthetic, although it was the first innovative material to radically change the industry. The same technology that produced aluminum wings and fuselages for the aircraft manufacturers during the war lent itself in peacetime to the production of aluminum-hulled boats. The leader in the industry today is Grumman, which began as an aircraft manufacturer. Aluminum canoes still command a big piece of the market, since they are relatively inexpensive and will take an enormous amount of thoughtless punishment—an important factor in river running as it is practiced. In fact, it was aluminum that opened up thousands of miles of our rivers to white-water canoeists, miles theretofore portaged. One would never think of taking a wooden canoe through the rock gardens that today's novice canoeists regularly run with plenty of bumps and scrapes but without serious damage to their craft. One drawback of aluminum is that it has a tendency to stick on rocks, partly because it dents so easily. You can avoid this by rubbing the bottom of the boat with paraffin. But the real advantage of aluminum is that any dent can be easily pounded out again.

A more serious complaint against aluminum is aesthetic. There are those (myself among them) who harbor a prejudice against metal as a boatbuilding material in somewhat the same way we consider tin cans as belonging to a lower order of objects than glass containers. The feeling is not entirely unwarranted. Aluminum is also noisy when hit with a paddle, when slapped by windblown waves, when walked on or bumped against. Its thermal properties, too, are displeasing. It gets cold when it's cold and hot when it's hot. And when it's new it is so *very* bright and shiny. A lot of the pleasure of taking a canoe into the wilderness is lost when the craft is made of aluminum.

Fiber glass, the next material to be adapted to the manufacture of modern canoes, eliminates many of aluminum's faults. It is inherently strong, no elaborate skeletal structure is needed to support it, and yet, from the outside at least, it can be made to look like a traditional wood and canvas canoe. With fiber glass there are not, or ought not to be, any sharp edges. The variety of hull shape is virtually unlimited. And if fiber glass punctures and cracks more easily than aluminum, it can also be mended more easily. Moreover, its hard outer surface tends to slide over rocks.

Fiber glass has dominated the modern pleasure-boating industry—from canoes to oceangoing yachts—for nearly a generation. Now, a couple of new products threaten to make it obsolete—for canoes, at any rate. One is ABS (Acrolonitril Butadiene Styrene), the material Tupperware is made of. As used in canoe construction, ABS is made into a sandwich, with hard rubbery outer layers over a buoyant foam core. Canoe builders buy ABS in sheets, which they heat and vacuum-mold according to their own design. One advantage of ABS over fiber glass is that it floats. Fiber glass boats have to be fitted with some sort of flotation —usually consisting of blocks of styrofoam inserted bow and stern. More important, ABS is harder than fiber glass—harder to break, that is. It will dent like aluminum, but with the application of heat, the dent can be made magically to pop out again and the hull returned to its original contour, almost without blemish.

This slightly spongy quality of ABS, however, makes it perceptibly slower through the water. I have never heard a good explanation for that, since the skin seems as hard and slippery as fiber glass, but with a paddle in your hand you can definitely feel the difference.

An improvement on ABS is Kevlar, a Du Pont product. Kevlar does everything that ABS can do, but it is harder, faster, and weighs about twenty pounds less for an ordinary seventeen-foot canoe—roughly fifty-five pounds versus seventy-five pounds—a big advantage if portaging is to be part of one's canoeing program. By the inescapable laws of compensation, however, a Kevlar boat costs about $150 to $250 more—$250 versus $400 to $500. My cousin, who among his other enterprises runs a canoe livery outside Boston, uses Kevlar to replace the bows of his rental fiber glass canoes after they have been bludgeoned by a season of misuse.

Shape:

The shape of a canoe governs performance. Consider the two extremes: the V-shaped hull and the flat-bottomed hull. The term *V-shaped* is somewhat misleading; actually what is meant is a shallow angle, its apex running the length of the center line of the hull. The sharper the angle, the better the boat will track, meaning it tends to follow a straight course through the water rather than slewing from side to side with each stroke of the paddle. The disadvantages of the V-hull are that it draws slightly more water than a flat-bottomed boat and is harder to steer. For these reasons flat-bottomed canoes, by and large, make better white-water boats. Only if you are anticipating a great deal of flat-water paddling in windy places need you consider the V-shaped hull.

To give the flat-bottomed hull a bit more tracking capacity, a small keel is often attached. This also acts as protection and as a runner for sliding over rocks. Its disadvantage, again, is that it makes the boat harder to sideslip, to be pulled or pushed laterally with a draw or pry stroke, of which more later. Nearly all aluminum canoes are made with a seam down the center, which acts like a shallow keel. Because this makes them less maneuverable, in white-water races the aluminum canoes often compete in a separate class to make up for their handicap.

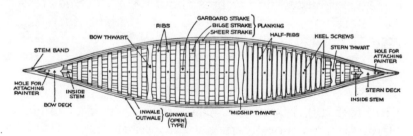

The anatomy of a canoe

Obviously, a wide, flat-bottomed canoe is more stable than a narrow, V-shaped one—more stable but slower through the water. There are other trade-offs as well. Freeboard, the distance between the waterline and the boat's deck, for instance. The more freeboard you have, the drier your boat will be. However, you pay a price in weight and wind resistance. Taper is another example. A long tapered bow and stern make a boat that knifes through waves rather than one that rides up and over them; it is faster and easier to hold on course, but more apt to ship water.

Two other terms need explanation: "rocker" and "tumblehome." A rockered boat is slightly banana-shaped and pivots like a top. This makes it easy to turn, especially by a single paddler seated near the center. Rockered boats go well, therefore, in rapids where quick maneuvering is demanded. The trade-off this time is a boat that tends to fishtail with every stroke and is difficult to keep on course. It can also be the devil to paddle into the wind, slewing first this way, then that.

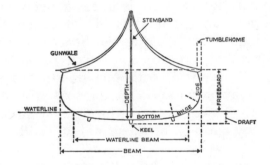

Tumblehome describes the inward slant of a boat's gunnels, which gives it a slightly pear-shaped cross section. Tumblehome is a comely word, and boats with it are pleasing to the eye. Its purpose becomes obvious if you pull an imaginary paddle beside your hip. If the gunnel is tilted in toward you, you need not reach so far outboard with your upper hand, for the paddle to clear the side of the canoe. In narrow, finely tapered canoes this is not an important consideration, but in wide canoes it can be. The disadvantage of tumblehome is that the shape does not slap down waves as well as a vertical or outward-slanting side does. Most modern designs, putting practicality above aesthetics, are without tumblehome.

Length:

All these shapes can be found in boats of varying lengths. And length is the third major factor you will want to consider in choosing a canoe. Again the trade-offs: the longer the boat, the more weight it can carry. But it will also cost more, weigh more, and be more difficult to handle in white water—to a point, that is. Shorter than about thirteen feet, canoes become skittish, difficult to manage, and slow through the water. Over eighteen feet in length, they enter the cruiser class. A fairly wide sixteen-foot boat or a narrower seventeen-footer makes a good compromise. A sixteen-foot canoe can hold four people—without gear—two people with gear. The carrying capacity is in the range of six hundred to eight hundred pounds in flat water. In white water the load limit should be cut nearly in half. What that means is that two people in a sixteen-foot canoe on an extended river trip, with one hundred pounds of gear or so, may have to portage their kit around certain rapids and then take the canoe through. Needless to say, if there is any question of capsizing, this is the strategy to follow.

One can get into difficulties with the manufacturer's load ratings, which are invariably optimistic. A good rule to follow when loading a boat for a camping trip—whatever the water you are expecting—is to have at least six inches of freeboard. Less than that and you risk swamping, either in white water or wind-driven waves.

PADDLES

Having chosen a canoe, you now need paddles. Wooden paddles, like the old wooden canoes, have a natural beauty that for some is irresistible. If you are so minded, there is no reason not to use a wooden paddle. Fiber glass paddles and various combinations of fiber glass, aluminum, and other synthetics, some with wooden shanks, are apt to be cheaper, certain to be lighter to handle, and if they are any good at all, they will be stronger. But the joy of pulling a beautifully shaped ash paddle through the water may overcome all those considerations.

Wherever you buy your canoe, you will most likely find a variety of paddle shapes and sizes. The general rule of thumb for paddle length is from the floor to about your chin or nose. Some people say to your eyes. Some like paddles that are as tall as they are. The latter will be too long for most modern boats, but they have the advantage of working well when the paddler is standing, which he may want to do to get a good view of an upcoming rapid. But until you have established your own preferences, you might as well start out with a paddle that reaches to your nose and has a grip that feels comfortable to your hand. Without actually having water to push against, the balance of the paddle will be hard for you to judge. Two basic blade shapes present themselves: spoon and spatulate. The oval spoon-shaped blades vary greatly in surface area. The bigger the blade, the harder it is to pull. The squared-off spatulate blade takes a bigger bite of the water than the oval and lends itself best to the quick, choppy strokes used by racers. White-water canoeists may also favor the squared tip for the same reason. In wood, the squared tip tends to split more easily than the rounded paddle. Fiber glass is the material you will usually find associated with this design.

The top grip of a paddle is almost more important than the shape of the blade. This must feel comfortable in your hand or paddling can become a blisterful nightmare. The so-called pear-shaped handle of the typical wood paddle gives a good grip, and can be filed and whittled to an exact fit. An even better grip—the one you will see most racers using—is the T. Again, less aesthetic, perhaps, but more practical.

PADDLING TECHNIQUES

Forward Stroke:

It is possible, of course, just to sit down in a canoe and start paddling. The motion is a natural one, and sooner or later anyone who does much canoeing will work out an easy and effective stroke for himself. At first, however, most novice paddlers will do too much pulling with the lower hand and not enough pushing with the upper. It helps enormously to think of the stroke not as an act of pulling the blade through the water but rather one of anchoring the blade and using

FORWARD STROKE

Forward stroke: Place paddle close to the boat, with the blade two-thirds of the way in the water. Push forward with the upper hand, but keep the lower arm straight as long as possible before lifting the blade.

it to lever the boat forward. In actual practice, of course, the blade does move through the water, but to the degree that it does, you are losing efficiency.

Assume, then, that you are paddling on your left side. Grip the paddle with your left hand a few inches above the blade. Because the paddle is going to be used as a lever, with your lower hand as the fulcrum, the closer to the water you grip the paddle the easier it will be to push your right hand forward. But the higher the hand grip, the more the paddle can reach ahead. It is your right hand that will be doing most of the work. Start the stroke by reaching forward and anchoring the blade in the water. Your right hand should be just about at a level with your chin. Push it straight

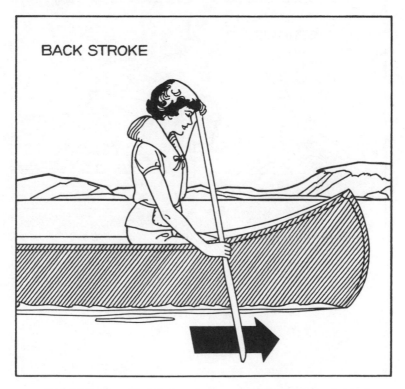

BACK STROKE

Back stroke: Hold the shaft vertical. Pull backward with the upper hand using the lower hand primarily as a fulcrum.

out, as if you were a boxer executing a right jab. When your arm is fully extended, rotate the right thumb forward and down. That will bring the blade up out of the water, and turn it parallel to the surface, bringing both hands to the same horizontal level. Now swing the feathered blade forward in a wide arc. Insert the blade, which should bring your fist back up to your chin again, and you are ready for the next stroke. Repeat a few thousand times, and you will find yourself well on the way to becoming an easy and efficient paddler.

Paddling on the right side is just a mirror image. That's for going forward in a straight line, with paddlers in both the bow and the stern. Even so, the stern pad-

J-stroke: The stern paddler pushes the paddle away from the boat by forming a J at the end of a forward stroke. This maneuver will keep the boat traveling on a straight course.

dler has more effect on the direction of the boat than the man up front, and if he paddles continuously on one side, the boat will tend to turn the opposite way. Two remedies: he and the bow paddler can change sides every few strokes, or he can twist his paddle at the end of the stroke and push it slightly away from the boat.

Backstroke:

Even more useful is the backstroke, in execution essentially the reverse of the forward stroke. Instead of pushing with the upper hand, you pull. When properly done, the backstroke can be every bit as powerful as the forward stroke. It is used to slow or stop the boat

C-stroke: The bow paddler pulls the paddle outward and back, as if forming the letter C. This stroke is used to accentuate a turn.

or to turn it even more abruptly than can be done with the C-stroke. When the bowman C-strokes on the right and the sternman backstrokes on the left, the boat can be made to spin like a top. Perhaps even more important than the tight turn is the opportunity a backstroke gives one in white water to slow down and take stock of the situation ahead. Is it the stroke you will use most often to ferry across the current when it becomes necessary to jog from one side to the other.

J-Stroke:

The twisting movement gives this stroke the shape of a J—hence, J-stroke. The amount of the J depends

PADDLE AS A RUDDER

Paddle as a rudder: The stern paddler finishes her stroke by letting her paddle trail in the water like a rudder. By this method she can force a turn or correct for any lateral movement of the bow to keep on course.

on the balance of the two paddlers. When executed properly, the boat should follow a true course. Another method for effecting the same compensation at the end of a stroke is to feather the blade while it is still in the water and let it act for a second or two against the flow of water, like a rudder. This creates a small amount of drag, and may not be quite as powerful a stroke, but it can be kept up for hours on end without tiring the paddler.

C-Stroke:

The sweep, or C-stroke, is used to turn a boat by pulling the paddle through a wide arc. When both bow and stern pull a C-stroke together on the same side, the boat will turn in a tight arc while maintaining most of its forward motion.

Brace:

For white-water paddling, there is one more important motion you can perform with the paddle—the brace. Manuals on canoeing speak of the high and low brace. In practice, braces are performed high, low, and in the middle, whatever the situation demands. It is enough to know that you can use a brace to steady your boat. Practice will do the rest. The reason paddles have wide flat blades is so they can exert maximum drag against the water and minimum resistance when they slice through the air. In normal paddling the blade is used to grip the water and push the boat forward. The blade can also be used to steady the boat—almost like a pontoon or outrigger. To do this, lay the blade flat on the water or slightly below the surface. You can then apply considerable pressure against it. The effect is as if you leaned far out of the boat and grabbed onto something to steady yourself. A timely brace by the bow or stern paddler can make the difference between capsizing and getting through a difficult stretch of rough water. The difference between the high and low brace concerns the position of the inboard hand. In a low brace, which is the one you should be using nine-tenths of the time (leave the high brace for kayakers and "hot dogs"), your inboard hand will be roughly at chest level, and you will be pushing up with it. The more tippy a boat, the rougher the water, the more need for the brace. Consequently, the brace is an even more important part of the kayaker's repertoire.

PRACTICE MAKES PERFECT

These are the basic strokes. Practice is the only way they can be mastered. You should start on flat water. Work through the repertoire until you can maneuver with assurance. From there on it becomes a matter of choosing increasingly difficult stretches of white water to practice on. By using eddies to help you slip upstream against the current, it is perfectly possible to run the same stretch of white water over and over again. This is a particularly good way to practice. But do not go too far too fast. The most common error for novice canoeists is to take on water that is too difficult. You are not learning then, just fighting to stay afloat and not wreck your boat. It is not enough to be able to execute a stroke perfectly when you want to. On a challenging rapid you must be able to do the right stroke at the right instant and do it without taking time to think. If there are two of you in the canoe, the problem is both easier and harder. You will have more power and control over the boat, but you must learn coordination. In white water experienced paddlers always talk to each other— "draw right" or "brace left," and so forth—but they also must work instinctively together if they are going to get the most out of the boat. Practice again.

When gathering material for this book, I was treated one cold and raw weekend in early April to a grand example of the value of experience in white water. The Westfield (Massachusetts) River Races, sponsored by the Westfield Wildwater Canoe Club and the Chamber of Commerce, is a gathering of white-water buffs, nuts, and serious competitors who convene each spring when the river is high. Now a quarter century old, it boasts being the largest race of its kind in the country. Last year there were more than three hundred entries. Canoeists compete in three classes: expert, intermediate, and novice. The race committee, as usual, issues the following warning: "The novice race is not for beginners. Only experienced white-water paddlers should participate. The water at this time of year is frigid, and the river will be running near flood levels."

Most of the novice paddlers, therefore, had been on white water a number of times before racing. Even so, the crowd that clustered at the Hill and Dale Rapids to watch them shoot by on Saturday morning anticipated spills and chills. And they were not disappointed. Every five minutes or so a boat would swamp and overturn. The occupants would go floating by, unnaturally high because of the life jackets all wore (an absolute rule in white water, whether it is frigid like the Westfield in April or not), puffing out their cheeks in silent outrage—no water had any right to feel so cold.

The next day the experts ran the course, their oversized spatulate paddles—tablespoons to the ordinary paddler's teaspoon—catching the sun in rhythmic precision, hardly missing a beat as they flashed down through the foam and protruding rocks. And there were no spills.

Races like the Westfield can be found throughout the country, usually on a smaller scale, wherever canoeing is popular. They represent the competitive side of canoeing, a sport with a following that is growing by leaps and bounds. The Westfield stewards judge that their entries have increased during the past decade by 10 to 20 percent each year. Within the three major classes—novice, intermediate, and expert—there are a number of different subcategories, depending on the type of boat (aluminum canoes, for instance), sex of paddlers (men, women, mixed), age (juniors and seniors), number of paddlers (one or two). The race committee has been able to keep track of all those boats in different classes, and in different races, only by employing the talents of the computer and a local computer expert.

TO PORTAGE
OR NOT TO PORTAGE

On Cars:

Canoes fit easily on cars. Their streamlined shape presents minimum wind resistance even at high speeds. Any ordinary two-bar car-top rack will do. Simply turn the canoe over and lash it securely to the front and rear bumpers. Two canoes should fit comfortably side by side on most cars.

On Your Back:

A canoe also fits easily, if not so comfortably, on a person's back. When you have portaged a forty-to-sixty-pound canoe for a quarter mile and are beginning to wish you had taken a seaside vacation instead, just remember the voyageurs from Chapter 2. On their portages, and there were many, most of the paddlers carried the cargo. No more than five were allotted to carry the long canoes, which often weighed upward of a thousand pounds.

There are two tricks to portaging in the easiest and most efficient manner. Both have to do with yokes. If you are going to be doing a lot of carrying, it may well pay you to buy a yoke that fits your boat. Otherwise you can improvise by lashing two paddles to the thwarts. You will then probably want some additional padding. A life jacket hitched up over your shoulders works well.

To get the canoe up on your shoulders, you can either prop one end in the crotch of a tree and walk under it or you can use a flashier method. Gripping it by the gunnel amidships and bending your knees, raise the boat up until it is resting on your thighs. Now reach one hand across to the far gunnel and both lifting and ducking your head at the same time, turn it so that the yoke rests on your shoulders. It is not as hard as it sounds.

The yoke should be positioned so that the balance of the boat is just slightly to the stern—so that when you are walking, the bow is at an angle in the air and you can see where you are going. How far you can carry a boat without resting depends on practice as well as such obvious variables as the terrain, your own strength, and the weight of the canoe. If there are two of you and the distance is not far, one can carry the gear and the other the boat. On longer distances, trade off. If you have a lot of gear, you may need to make two trips.

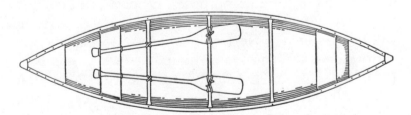

There are times when a canoe must be portaged, or carried over land. This is done by inverting it and hoisting it onto one's shoulders. An improvised carrying yoke such as the one shown above can be made by lashing paddles to the thwarts.

Lining or Tracking:

Many portages can be avoided by lining or tracking your boat through rocks that are too numerous or too shallow to allow you and your gear to paddle through. The situation will dictate whether you should leave your gear in the boat or carry it along the shore. In any case, you will need two lines of between fifty and one hundred feet. With one man at the bow and the other controlling the stern, you will find that you can use the force of the current to maneuver the boat with extraordinary precision through narrow passages between the rocks while you walk along the shore or wade in the shallows. When lining a boat downstream, keep the stern farther out from shore than the bow. The opposite is true if you are working your canoe upstream.

Poling:

Another method of working a boat upstream through shallow rapids is with a pole. This can be tricky at first, but it is a time-honored method for controlling a canoe up- or downriver. To begin with, you will want a pole twelve to fourteen feet long. Ash or some other hardwood is preferred. You may be able to find a sapling for this purpose, although cutting any live wood along most wilderness waterways is, or soon will be, prohibited. Next, you will have to become accustomed to the balance of your boat while standing. Plant the pole on the bottom of the river—an iron "shoe" fitted to the end helps grip slippery rocks. Where the bottom is mucky, some polers attach a "duckbill" shoe to the end; it opens automatically when pressure is applied and keeps the pole from sinking too deep into the mire. Now push the canoe forward until you run out of pole—just like any Venetian gondolier. The main use of poling is to work your way up swift currents where the water is often too shallow to take deep full strokes with a paddle and the back eddies are not helpful. A pole can also be used as a brake going downstream by holding it against the bottom and bearing down.

SAFETY PRECAUTIONS

Finally, a word about canoe safety. In the end it all comes down to this: Always prepare for the worst—that you are going to tip over and will have to spend some time in the water. If you are in warm, slow water without rocks and drops and you are a strong swimmer, you may not need to wear a life jacket. On almost all other occasions you would be foolish not to. The rules on many rivers, in any case, require you to have one with you at all times, even if you do not wear it. If you do tip over in rapids, you should try to stay with your boat and guide it safely ashore. The same caution applies as for rafting: Never get on the downriver side of a swamped canoe because you may get pinned between it and a rock. A canoe full of water becomes an incredibly heavy and awkward object. All canoes should have enough flotation to keep them up. In difficult rapids you may want to wear the sort of helmet kayakers use. Most rapids fit for canoeing, however, do not demand this.

As for the danger of cold water, and it is perhaps the biggest danger canoeists face, get out of it as fast as you can, even if it means leaving your canoe. Never paddle in freezing water without a life jacket. Once out, take all possible measures to get warm. The threat of hypothermia and how to deal with it are covered in Chapter 6.

Another danger peculiar to canoes is also dealt with there—overloading. It is quite possible to start out on still water with what appears to be plenty of freeboard, only to find that in the first rapid or encounter with wind-driven waves you begin shipping water faster than you can get it out—especially if the space for bailing is filled with gear. Slowly you sink deeper, more water pours in, and before you know it, the canoe is swamped and you are sitting in the river with little control of what lies ahead.

Paddling a canoe for the first time is not a difficult affair—providing the conditions are tranquil. Paddling a canoe through Class III or IV rapids is possible—by those who have trained long and, usually, hard. Between those two extremes lie years of canoeing pleasure (or if you are a quick learner, perhaps a matter of only a few summers). But if you are going to make that trip, remember one point: go slow. A canoe is an exquisite tool. In the hands of an expert it can perform extraordinary feats through moving water, but only when, as any accomplished craftsman knows, both tool and medium are treated with due respect. Go slow.

KAYAKING

IN northwest Maine, near the New Hampshire border, there is a river, the Rapid River, that drains the Rangely Lake district, down to the Androscoggin, down to the Atlantic. A century ago it was a route that logs went down, but little else. According to Louise Dickinson Rich, who lived beside the Rapid for a time back in the 1940s and wrote with understanding about the final days of the river loggers in her book *We Took to the Woods* [The Rapid] "is not navigable, being the swiftest river east of the Rockies—it drops 185 feet in three miles, with no falls, which is some kind of a record. . . . Cluley's Rip, a mile below us, is the most vicious piece of water I have ever seen. . . . Cluley, whoever he may have been, drowned there. That's how you get things named after you in this country."

If reading a description of such a river makes you want to get a boat and prove Louise Dickinson Rich wrong, you probably have the makings of a white-water kayaker. Don Wilson, a New Hampshire doctor, was tempted, and I am indebted to an article he wrote in *Down River* magazine about the doing of it—in all, as fine a description as I know of what it feels like to run a fierce rapid in a kayak, pound for pound the most waterworthy craft ever created. It has to be.

Here is Wilson describing Mrs. Rich's "not naviga-ble" river: "The rapid is a paradigm of New England whitewater, running clear, fast, bone-cold and boulder-strewn; hidden pine, white birch, and maple creeping right to the edge; dropping suddenly into clear trout pools under a sapphire sky, by low mountains, hazy in the distance, shining in the sun."

And here is Wilson describing what such a river can do to a boatman, even an experienced boatman, who makes a mistake:

A few years ago in the confidence born of . . . ignorance, I had failed to scout Island Rip. I let the brute force of the cataract hurl me into the outside curve *(note: keep to the inside curve of a rapid you don't know. It is slower and you have time to maneuver)* and into the hole, a horrifying surprise. I was over, inside the caldron, banging on the rocks. My heavy helmet cracked. The noise was like a sledgehammer inside a boiler. I panicked, pulled the rip cord, and shot out of my kayak. The grab loop jerked out of my hand and the boat smashed its way down a staircase of boulders and holes on the outside bank. I was right behind, jolted, gasping, bruised, bounced, turning. I tried desperately to keep my knees bent ahead of me but more than once I found myself tumbling head down in a backward somersault over a boulder and into a hole below. My paddle was torn out of my hand. I tried to reach the bank, only a few yards away, but there were no eddies and I was just a light ball of bruised flesh in the blasting run. When I finally reached the bottom and hauled myself half out of the water, completely uncaring, I knew I had lived through the afternoon of the long knives. I should have stayed in my boat and tried to roll until I was almost dead. The penalty for a flush in heavy rapids is too great.

That is one side of the coin, the dark side. But without the threat, the challenge, kayaking would be no

more than an agreeable pastime—not the thrilling sport
it is. And lest that description discourage anyone who
has never been down a river even in a plastic tube, here
is Wilson back again on a perfect day in October making the same run.

I took Island Rip sideways with my back to the
outside bend. This gave me room to shoot to the
inside fast. However, Ed McClure was just ahead
of me, back-paddling and I was almost on top of
him. Desperately I pushed to the inside curve. My
bow entered an eddy, and flipped me down the
race backwards. I remember Walt Blackadar's
confident, nasal voice saying, 'Lean downstream;
there's no way in hell you can flip if you lean
downstream.' So I leaned backwards over the next
wave, dug my paddle into it, and hauled the boat
sideways again, then a quick backferry, and I shot
past Ed and out into the wide, battering water of
Wing Dam Rip below the island.

EVOLUTION OF THE KAYAK

No craft other than a modern kayak handled by someone schooled in modern techniques could have made
it down such a river. In 1941, when the National Kayak
Races were held on the Rapid, the kayaks took the form
of foldboats—canvas stretched over a skeleton of fold-
ing wooden ribs. The boats ripped apart even in the
quieter water of the lower river. Today's boats are
tougher, all of a piece, and made of fiber glass or another of the new synthetic materials. And today's kayakers are much more skilled. In 1973 a young daredevil
successfully ran Cataract Canyon on the Colorado when
it was flooding at 65,000 cfs. He had to sneak onto the
river, which at that level had been closed to all craft,
including the huge commercial pontoon rafts.

The development of the kayak has been explosive. Modern kayaks bear no more resemblance to the original boats made by Eskimos than do plastic skis to their ancestors, twelve-foot hickory boards. The parallels with skiing go even further: Though kayaking relies on power from the arms and shoulders and skiing primarily on power from the legs, balance is the key to both. There is the same challenge, of an individual accepting the dare of nature, using muscle, guile, and good design to harness awesome power. Both sports involve a kind of duel with gravity fought on water— the one liquid, the other frozen.

No one quite knows when the first Eskimo kayaks came into being. They were made of skins, especially sealskins, stretched over a frame of wood so as to cover it completely except for an opening in the middle for the paddler. They did not ship water, they could be taken onto the open ocean, and they could be tipped over and righted again without the paddler's being dumped (the so-called "Eskimo roll"). Being dumped in the Arctic Sea was unthinkable, far worse than being dumped in the Rapid River. For the Eskimos the kayak was a matter of survival—a way of life. But for men like Don Wilson and the estimated thirty thousand kayakers in the world, it is sport. And like all sports, kayaking can be played at many levels. Wilson and his party were experienced, but not all expert, kayakers. And if they could turn over and turn up again, it was because they had practiced for many hours on many days.

On the Rapid the challenge was to get down it as gracefully as possible. Not all did. For others the challenge might be to get down some perhaps less demanding river or slalom course faster than anyone else. Kayaking is growing by leaps and bounds. Skiers, particularly those who enjoy cross country, are taking to it with a passion.

The evolution of the modern kayak began in Europe—mostly in Germany—during the 1920s and 1930s. In the 1938 Olympics kayakers competed in the same type of foldboats that the Rapid would chew up three years later. The early foldboats owed more perhaps to canoe design than to the Eskimo kayak. Modern builders, as they continue to adjust and refine, are discovering lines that hark back to Eskimo design. The boats remain, however, much smaller, lighter weight, and structurally stronger.

The remaining basic difference between Eskimo design and the modern kayak is the paddle that is used. The Eskimo blades are not turned at right angles to each other and so there can be no feathering on the return stroke. When an Eskimo pulls one blade through the water, he is pushing the other forward through the air, flat against it like a fan rather than the cutting edge of a knife. Hard work, especially in a strong headwind. It is difficult to imagine that the Eskimos would not have hit upon the principle of the modern paddles. A fair guess is that they did and then abandoned it. They carved their early paddles out of tree trunks, and these probably had turned blades. But when the flotsam in their remote corner of the world began to turn up sawn planks, they found these easier to carve than solid hunks of wood. The price they paid for the convenience was blades in the same plane. A different explanation for the Eskimo design is that when the blades lie in the same plane, the kayak is easier to roll because both blades can be used to grip the water at the same time. Therefore, one has double the purchase, double the push. And when your life depends on a quick roll, that may be the final consideration.

TYPES OF MODERN KAYAKS

Like all seafaring people, Eskimos built different kinds of boats—big, small, and in-between—depending on the job. In the same way, sports kayaks fall into three general categories: surfing, downriver, and slalom.

Surfing:

A surfing kayak has a flattened hull, like a surfboard, with lots of rocker so the blunt bow will not take a nosedive. Paddling down the front edge of a huge comber can be as thrilling as any outdoor sport imaginable, but it has little to do with rivers. One may, if one is clever, surf a slalom boat on certain standing waves in rivers. And that can be quite exciting in itself if the wave is a big one. Further, it provides a peculiar feeling, since one essentially stays in the same place while seeming to speed over the water.

Downriver:

Downriver kayaks, like downriver canoes, are strictly racing machines. Built for speed, they are tippy and hard to turn. For the average beginner, they have little to recommend them.

Slalom:

Slalom boats are made for maneuverability, and that, in essence, is what river kayaking is all about. The boat to start with, then, is a slalom boat, or at least a boat with slalom lines (see diagram). The trouble is, in recent years slalom boats, in order to slip more easily through the gates, which hang from cables above the course, have been pared to the absolute minimum. They are small and getting smaller—four meters long and barely over a half meter wide (13'2" and 23")—and of not much use for touring. There is barely room for your legs, and little space to store gear. If you intend to tour rather than race, you may want to consider a larger boat, possibly a hybrid between a slalom design and a downriver boat. A better solution might be to do your touring in a canoe, or, if the river is too rough for that, use a raft as combined cargo boat and mother hen for a fleet of kayaks. A sensible beginner's boat is one with slalom lines but with enough volume to give it stability and extra carrying capacity.

CHOOSING A KAYAK: TO BUY OR TO BUILD

It is premature to consider acquiring your own boat until you have tried the sport a time or two—either with kayaking friends, at a livery, or by making contact with a local kayaking club. Assuming that you have done this and are sufficiently motivated to want your own boat, you face a decision peculiar to kayaks: to buy or to build? For it is possible without the investment of an inordinate amount of time to build your own kayak, using fiber glass laid up on a mold.

But let us examine the simpler proposition first. Assuming your kayaking friends have not provided a good lead, seek out the sort of sporting goods store that caters to bicyclists and backpackers. If you live in country where there are suitable streams, these stores will undoubtedly carry kayaks, and the staff will be glad to discuss the relative merits of design with you. Lacking such outlets, get hold of a copy of *Down River* magazine or *American Whitewater*. Both list builders who supply catalogs. The cost, if you buy, will be in the $250 to $300 range.

Fit:

When you buy a boat you are, in a sense, taking a leap into the unknown. For general recreational paddlers—which is what you will be when you start—you want a boat with a responsive hull, one that is stable and easy to handle. It should be comfortable in heavy water, which simply means that in calm water it should float with at least a couple of inches of freeboard. Be sure the boat fits. The combination of kayaker and kayak becomes that of an aquatic centaur. In any case, the boat should feel like an extension of your body. This will not happen right away. But it can never happen if the boat and you do not mesh at the start. The foot braces and knee braces may have to be adjusted, but you still must be able to slip out easily. So slide in and out a couple of times.

Material:

As for materials, fiber glass is the most common, though Holoform (a major United States manufacturer) is now building boats out of the same material that Tupperware and Frisbees are made of. It is probable that all boats of the future will be made of some sort of specialized plastic. Until then, here is what to look for in a fiber glass boat. The weight should be in the neighborhood of twenty-five to thirty-five pounds— over that indicates the builder used too much resin. Under it, the boat will be weak. The seams should be neat and well finished. There should be no sharp edges. Most glass boats are finished with a jell coat. This makes a hard outer surface, but it does not add strength, per se, and it does add extra weight. The jell coat will help absorb the nackers, bangs, and dings that you are sure to get, and for an all-around boat it is probably best to have it, despite the added weight.

Building Your Own:

A way to save money—roughly half the price of a store-bought kayak—and still get a good, strong, well-designed boat is to buy a kit. These will provide the hull, deck, seat, and the resin to put them together. Even for someone who has never worked with fiber glass before, the instructions should suffice.

Not so if you are going to build your own boat from scratch. In this case, you will need help from someone who has done it before. And you will need a mold. This pretty much requires that you join a club or similar facility. The relative cost of buying a kayak outright, buying a kit, and building one yourself will be roughly in the ratio of $300, $150, $100. A thing to remember, no matter how clever you are, is that the homemade boat will not be as strong, pound for pound, as the other two. But it will be all yours, and there is something about the mystique of kayaking that makes this a consideration not to be scoffed at.

EQUIPMENT

Spray Skirt:

Once you have a boat, you are only partway there. You will need a spray skirt that fits over the cockpit lip like a drumhead, with you in the center. It can be bought with the boat or made out of neoprene rubber, the same material wetsuits are made of. The skirt provides a watertight seal between your body and the boat. It must fit snugly around the combing, but still come off easily when you want it to. It will have some sort of elastic hem. It is usually a good idea to attach a loop of the same material at the front of the skirt so that when you want to exit you can give it a tug and the skirt will come free. Otherwise, you may find yourself upside down and running out of air while you frantically try to get a finger under the hem and hold onto your paddle at the same time. This, of course, is before you have learned to roll.

Flotation Bags:

You should also have flotation bags for your boat. It is hard enough to get the water out of a swamped boat even with flotation. Innertubes will do. But if you are ever planning to tour, it makes sense to invest in the sort of bags that will accommodate gear. After they are sealed and put in place, they are inflated with a tube. Whitewater Sports of Denver makes these flotation bags at a cost of around thirty dollars.

Paddle:

You will need a paddle. There are literally hundreds of different designs and material combinations. Curved or cupped blades are better than flat blades, though you will still see expert kayakers using the latter. If you do get curved blades, you will be committing yourself, if you have not already done so, to paddling with the right or left hand as your control. The right hand, even for left-handed people, is usually the control hand, so if you are beginning, it makes sense to start that way—of which more in a moment. Paddle length should be such that you can stand one end on the ground and, reaching above your head, just curl your fingers over the top—another similarity to skiing. Paddles are often made of a combination of materials. Plastic or fiber glass is strong and long lasting. Wooden paddles are lighter weight and more beautiful, but also more easily broken.

Life Jacket:

Almost as important as a paddle is a life jacket or PFD (Personal Flotation Device, in bureaucratese). As the name implies, they come in many designs. Some are Coast Guard-approved and some are not. Certain controlled rivers require a Coast Guard-approved jacket, and that alone should dictate that you buy one. But even if the law were not a consideration, it is folly not to have as buoyant a jacket as is practically possible. It is true that the large Mae West type with a high horse collar to keep one's head out of the water in case of being knocked cold can be constricting. But good paddlers can manage it, and so should you. The dangers inherent in kayaking are too severe to risk using any cut-down version. A good rule to follow when choosing a life jacket is that it should support at least 20 percent of your weight. Another quote from Don Wilson about another river—this time the Chattooga, in Georgia, of movie *Deliverance* fame—illustrates the importance of a PFD. At the time Wilson was comparatively new to kayaking, and so had sensibly chosen to ride a particularly difficult section of the Chattooga on a raft. He and three companions flipped going over a fall. Three of them were spit out at the bottom into an eddy. "As we scrambled onto the rocks, we turned and saw Sanborn below us, holding onto the back of an overturned raft and heading for another and bigger waterfall. Then the raft was wrenched out of his hands, and he was alone, in big trouble. He shot over the lip of the waterfall and down, down into the biggest, most terrible hole I have ever seen. Our fingers dug into the rocks as he disappeared into the furious backlash of Jawbone. When his orange-jacketed body popped up 100 yards below, we cheered ourselves hoarse. We ran to him and dragged him to shore. He was limp and dazed. Later he said, 'It was a total blank. I don't remember anything after looking into that hole.' "

Helmet:

Next to a life jacket, the second piece of safety equipment you should never be without in white water is a helmet. The price range is extensive; you can pay anywhere from ten to seventy-five dollars. Points to look for: a helmet that covers the temples but not the ears, so you will be able to hear that waterfall ahead, and a foam lining rather than suspension straps. Sporting goods stores carry helmets, or you might try a motorcycle supply house. Wherever you go, get a good strong one. When you are hanging upside down from your cockpit bouncing down the river, your head is apt to be the first thing to hit bottom. The first time I went kayaking, despite the fact that I was wearing a first-class helmet, I received a five-stitch gash over my left eye.

With a boat, paddle, flotation, spray skirt, helmet, and, if you are going to be kayaking in cold water, a wetsuit or wetsuit top (the kind surfers use, with short sleeves, may be adequate), at last you are ready to start. If you have made contact with a kayaking club, it should have some sort of program for beginners. Or you may want to sign up with an outfit that offers concentrated instruction. You will find these in the periodical literature of the sport. If you are intending to learn the rudiments by yourself, make sure you never do it alone. In practicing all that follows, you must have someone standing by, even if he is also a beginner.

PADDLING TECHNIQUES

Getting In and Out of a Kayak:

Find a shallow, warm, quiet body of water, a pond or swimming pool. To get into the boat, lay your paddle at a right angle to the boat just aft of the cockpit, with one blade flat on the bank, or poolside, and the other projecting over the far side of the kayak. Take hold of the paddle with your outboard hand, which should then support most of your weight. With the other hand behind your back grab the part of the paddle shaft closer to shore but still over the boat. This way you can lower yourself into the cockpit the same way you would wearily lower yourself into a deep armchair or into a full bathtub. Your legs will be thrust out in front and unable to take any weight.

You can forget the spray cover for the moment because your first maneuver is turning over and getting out. Tip the boat this way and that to feel the balance of it. Finally, let yourself go all the way over. If you can, resist the initial panic. Keep your head as far forward as possible, your nose up close to the deck. This is the safest position when you roll over in a rapid and the one from which you will later learn to initiate your roll. Now, come out of the boat by pushing with your hands on the sides of the combing (the lip around the cockpit) and execute a forward somersault. Repeat this exercise until it feels comfortable. Next, try it with the spray skirt on. Once in, slip the spray cover, which will already be around your waist, over the back of the combing first, then the front and finally the sides. Be very careful pulling off the spray cover. It rips easily, and if you are not in the habit of freeing its front first and then the sides, you may find yourself someday far from civilization without a skirt to keep the water out.

Forward Stroke:

The decision you will have to make when you start paddling is which hand will be your control—that is, which hand is going to hold the paddle firmly and which one allow it to turn. As mentioned earlier, most paddlers use a right control, and therefore most curved paddles are right-handed. So unless that feels overly awkward to you, you might as well conform. Using the right control, then, grip the paddle in both hands above the right-hand blade so that your right wrist is perpendicular to the plane of that blade. Hand and blade will hold that relationship, while the left blade will pivot in your left fist on each stroke. Now position your right forearm so that it is perpendicular to your right leg. Bring your right hand up, wrist tilted back by your ear. The left blade should be in the water, in the pulling position. Pull on the left and push out on the right—not as if you were throwing a punch but rather pushing something with the palm of your hand. Every stroke is a combined push and pull. The hand that is pushing will be up in front of the face, the blade in feathered position. Alternating from side to side, that is your basic forward stroke, and all other strokes lead from it.

Back Stroke:

A backstroke is simply the reverse, pushing with the lower hand, pulling with the upper. If you are using a curved blade, you do not turn it so that the curve faces forward, you merely use the convex side to push with. It will give you all the purchase you need.

Drawstroke:

Drawstrokes are those that pull or lever the boat sideways. In using a draw, particularly in moving water, be sure to take the blade out of the water before it gets too close to the side of your boat so that you will not "trip" over your paddle. A general principle of maneuvering on a river is that if you want to get someplace, the best way is to paddle there with forward strokes. Drawstrokes are useful in avoiding hazards that are already upon you. But they are no substitute for pointing your bow, if you have the time, and paddling in that direction.

Quick turns are made with a sweeping motion of the blade, which describes a semicircle on the opposite side of the boat from the direction of the turn.

Brace:

Beside the propulsion strokes, there are the bracing strokes, made to stabilize the boat. You anchor the paddle by pulling the blade against the water. Leaning on it, you use your body to tilt the boat any way you want. Bracing strokes are the means by which you catch your balance in a kayak.

There is a fancy bit of handwork called the high brace, of which the beginner should beware. In the high brace the hand opposite the side on which the brace is being made goes up and over the back of the head. When done with know-how and muscles that have been trained to the awkward position, the high brace can be a classy asset to a kayaker's repertoire. It sets the blade in a more upright position than the low brace, so the paddle can be used more as a pivot for tight, hard turns. It can also dislocate a shoulder, and until one is well out of the novice class, it is just as well to leave the high brace alone. A well-executed low brace should serve all purposes, save showmanship.

Eskimo Roll:

When you have learned to move your boat forward, backward, and sideways, and have learned to lean far out to either side, supporting yourself with a brace, it is time to start thinking about acquiring a roll. For this you will need an instructor. The drawings here will be useful in helping you picture in your mind's eye the sequence of positions you will be following in getting yourself upright. Those who can picture it, and those who are used to moving their body around, gymnasts for instance, learn the roll quite quickly. For others it may take hours of practice. This, of course, should be done in quiet water or a swimming pool, and always in pairs so that the person practicing the roll can be helped up if he fails to make it.

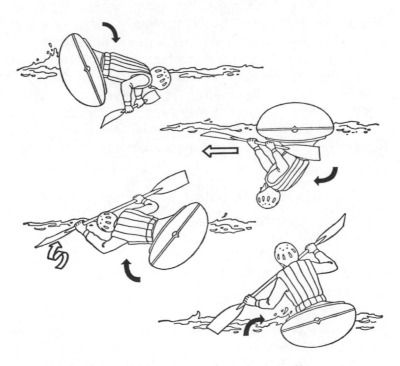

Using a technique called the Eskimo roll—a combination of paddle strokes and body movements—a kayaker can right his capsized craft.

MANEUVERING ON THE RIVER

With these skills you can start. You can, of course, take on a river without having mastered the roll, but you are going to get sick and tired of bailing out of your upside down boat, pouring the water out, and starting all over again. The essence of river running in a kayak or any craft is being able to read the water. Once you learn what surface features indicate drops, rocks, eddies, falls, and holes, you can anticipate what is coming, and your job will be much easier. Someone who can read the river does not need the power or even the skillful strokes to get himself out of trouble.

Rivers are alive, and every spring when they flood, they carve a channel that is generally clear of rocks. If you can follow the path of most of the water, you will generally avoid bad rocks and unexpected shoals. As a kayaker, however, you have one special handicap —your level of vision is little better than a crocodile's. Nor can you stand up the way canoeists and rafters are able to do. So if you suspect there is danger ahead, the best strategy is to stop and take a look—from the shore.

Waterfalls and Eddies:

The biggest hazard of all on an unfamiliar stream is a waterfall. Keep two things in mind: waterfalls are noisy, and they make a line across the river—a line beyond which the river disappears. Usually you can expect some slack water or back eddy above a falls or other dangers. You will want to be able to get into these with assurance. That is the first thing you should concentrate on when running white water—how reliably to get into an eddy and how to get into any eddy you pick. Eddies are your safety valve, your way out. When things start getting too rough and life looks unpleasant and the river starts throwing up waves that are bigger than you are and you are not enjoying yourself anymore, if you can duck into an eddy at the side of the river then things become all right again. The river is going downstream, but the eddy is holding still. And there you are, able to make a rational decision about what to do next.

Whenever you bring your boat into an eddy, you are bringing it inch by inch from fast current into a slow current, or one that may be running in the opposite direction. As you move bow-first into an eddy, your bow will stop while your stern is still out in the stream. This will throw you into an abrupt turn. The maneuver is called a breakout or eddying-out. As you breakout, you must lean to the inside of the turn, using a low brace to control the tendency to fall in. The more powerful the current is next to the slow eddy, the more sharply you will be spun around. On a big river you can be whipped around in a fraction of a second, and you must be prepared for this.

Once in an eddy, you will have to get out. The problem is similar. If you move too slowly, your bow will be caught by the faster moving water and you will be turned back. A little faster, and you will peel off into the current. Here again, you must lean to the inside of the turn, and you want to use your low brace on the inside to keep upright.

In getting into and out of an eddy, you are learning how to get yourself into a safe place. You are also learning how to let the water do the work for you, and that is half the secret of kayaking. The other half is to remember to lean downstream. Lean downstream, as Don Wilson pointed out, and your troubles are over. Of course, it is not that simple. Lean upstream, however, and you are sure to be in trouble. The river will catch your gunnel and push it under. Over you will go. So, if you are wondering what to do next, out in the middle of a river when you are feeling tippy, lean downstream.

A corollary to the caution not to lean upstream is not to execute an upstream brace. You will find your paddle swept under the boat, and over you will go again.

Ferrying a kayak is much the same as ferrying a raft or canoe. You paddle against the flow of the stream at an angle that takes you across the current.

THE REAL TEST

As you perfect your skills, you may want to begin to think about testing them not only against the river but against other kayakers. There are competitions at every level, novice to expert. All over the country you will find "citizens'" races on weekends when the water is high. The way to plug into these is, once more, to contact your local kayaking club.

You may also want to go off on weekend or week-long cruises. Depending on the size of your boat and the size of you, you will be able to carry more or less gear. Generally, a kayak should be able to carry the necessities for about a week in the wilderness. Forty pounds of gear is an average load.

The final word on kayaking and how to do it should go to my mentor Sandy Campbell, whose advice was invaluable in writing this chapter. Campbell, a medical student and former United States Olympic kayaker, has taught the sport to many beginners, including his wife Jean, presently ranked at the very top of United States women slalom kayakers.

One learns to kayak, says Campbell, "by cagily watching other people—preferably those who are better than you—and practice, practice, practice."

TRIPPING

RIVER running can be done in short spurts. And there is fun in that. An afternoon rafting on the Upper Snake guided by a professional boatman through Grand Teton National Park has given hundreds of thousands over the past decade a glimpse of the power and beauty of a wilderness river. In spring a wild dash down a swollen New England stream in an open canoe is a splendid way to raise the heartbeat. Kayaking anywhere, anytime, is grand sport.

But the unique attraction of rivers is as conduits out of our workaday lives into wilderness, into history, into geology—and, often, into calm backwaters of our own selves that we had forgotten existed. To gain that return, we must invest days at a time, weeks if possible, before our hyped-up rhythms begin to blend to the beat and song of the river. Spend the time and you will learn what river running is all about.

The rivers profiled in the second half of this book are designed to give a newcomer to river running a broad sampling of the most interesting streams across the breadth of the continent. Consider them sketches, not blueprints. Their purpose is to help you make a choice, for that is where every river trip begins.

Having picked your river, it is possible to leave the rest to a commercial outfitter. This is not a bad way to make your first river trip. If you are attentive, you ought to be able to learn all you will need to know to go by yourself the next time. On the other hand, you will be spending money to have someone else do for you what can be nearly as much fun as the actual running of the river itself. You will also be abdicating the responsibilities and worries that, when met, make any trip that much more memorable.

Generally, the character of the river you decide to run will dictate the necessary type of craft—crafts, in the multiple, one ought to say, for it is an imperative of wilderness touring that you not venture off alone. A possible exception is the two-man canoe—when one is running water that is not too "white" or on streams where one can expect to encounter help. Maine's Allagash, for instance, in the summer sees enough traffic so that a pair of paddlers in a canoe can expect help to come by if needed. When boats do go out together, some thought should be given to compatibility. Rafts of greatly different size will not move at the same speeds. Kayakers of varying abilities will not want to run the same stretches of river. Some canoeists may want to paddle all day, others for just a few hours. On the other hand, a raft and several kayaks make a viable combination. The kayaks can spurt ahead, act as guides, play in the eddies until the raft catches up, while the raft can carry enough extra gear to make a long river trip by kayak less of a Spartan affair. Members of the party can trade off between the raft and the small boats, widening the experience of all.

And, finally, in planning a trip, you have the pleasure of going twice—first in your mind's eye and second in actuality. The two experiences will never jibe completely. So you will be getting two trips for the price of one.

PLANNING A RIVER TRIP

Planning begins with the selection of a leader. If you are all good friends and relatively evenly matched in experience, choosing a leader may seem superfluous or may even be studiously avoided for fear of hurting someone's feelings. Such niceties are a great mistake. Whether the trip is demanding or easy, a leader is needed if only to save endless time in deciding where to camp at night. Under conditions of stress, the ability of a group to act quickly and without discussion nine times out of ten is more important than reaching a perfect decision, alas, too late. Of course, party members should feel free to give advice or make their preferences known. So even if you have to draw a name out of a hat, designate a leader.

At the same time you may also want to appoint a navigator-secretary to procure all the necessary maps, descriptive material on the river, and permits. This last point cannot be stressed too strongly. The most rewarding wilderness rivers in the country remain so only because some sort of regulation on their use has been imposed. As the sport of river running becomes more popular, the demand for reservations grows apace. On some rivers one must literally make reservations years in advance. So be prepared for disappointments and a change in plans. And do not forget fishing licenses and shuttle arrangements from the put-in to the take-out points.

Another useful appointee is a commissary agent to coordinate the meals, of which more later. As for the state of the equipment, every item you take with you should be checked thoroughly to be sure it is in serviceable condition. This can be done by the leader of the party or the individual owner, preferably by both. If the equipment is rented, it should be checked carefully before you set out.

On any kind of river trip there are certain basic facts you need to know about camping in the wilderness, things that apply whether you're climbing Mount Everest or on a walking tour of the English lake district. It is impossible within a single chapter to relate it all. There are many good books on the subject; one I find useful is Richard Langer's *Joy of Camping,* a Penguin paperback. What follows here, then, is advice peculiar to river trips.

WHAT TO BRING

Tent:

If you are touring by kayak, you will be limited to what a backpacker can comfortably carry, and the general choice of items will also be about the same. For instance, should you bring a tent? The answer is generally yes. As to the kind of tent you need, if you are rafting or canoeing, you can take a larger one than you might care to carry on your back.

Tents serve two purposes: shelter from the elements (cold, rain, and sun) and protection against bugs. Cold is rarely a problem during the seasons when most river running is done. However, you can expect to find bugs on most United States rivers. Delightful exceptions are the rivers of the Southwest.

Besides the luxury of a large tent, a special pleasure of river tripping is that you can take along enough gear to make a really elegant camp. Where this pays off most is in the kitchen and in what, for lack of a better word, one might call the library. Specifically, you can carry an iron skillet, a Dutch oven, a certain amount of fresh foods, and enough books to answer the hundreds of questions that pop up around every bend. You can also pack a good reading lamp.

Food:

There are two schools of thought on camp cooking, characterized by those who eat to live and those who live to eat. For the eat-to-livers, convenience is the operable word. This dictates that meals be prepacked and labeled—Tuesday breakfast, Thursday supper, and the like. This is a perfectly laudable procedure and requires less work at mealtime on the river, though perhaps more work beforehand. It is not a system I favor, simply because I care too much about food, and there is no way that I can predict a week or more in advance what I am going to want to eat for supper next Thursday. Trips can be overplanned, and this, it seems, is an example. The extra carrying capacity of a canoe or a raft permits you to load a varied supply of staples: flour, baking powder, sugar, salt, dried milk, cornmeal, granola, tea, coffee, dried beans, nuts, raisins, dried fruit, oil, vinegar, butter in tins (the only concession to canned food you need make), jerked beef, bacon, oranges, lemons, potatoes, onions, carrots, turnips, beets, bouillon cubes, chocolate, biscuits, and even some more delicate vegetables and fresh meat for the first few days. In short, take whatever food you like so long as it is relatively nonperishable. Watertight plastic pickle barrels make excellent, inexpensive food containers; smaller items can be packed in "ziplock" bags. The pickle barrels also make fine garbage cans after they are emptied, since you will be bringing out with you all refuse you cannot burn.

With such a larder, and a competent fisherman along, a party can exist for weeks in the wild and eat sumptuously and imaginatively every day. Mushrooms (if you know them), berries, fiddlehead ferns (in season), and the rest of the Euell (*Stalking the Wild Asparagus*) Gibbons menu will add authenticity to any wilderness meal.

It is possible, if the budget permits—and be advised that it will have to be highly permissive—to buy fully prepared freeze-dried meals at any camping store.

These are palatable and easy to pack, and if there is no one on your trip who enjoys cooking, they make an acceptable, convenient, and flexible alternative. It is just that all those little foil wrappers seem ludicrously inappropriate in a wilderness setting. Every time I rip open a packet of beef Stroganoff or chop suey—which is oftener than I care to admit—I am unpleasantly transported back to a roadside fast-food restaurant.

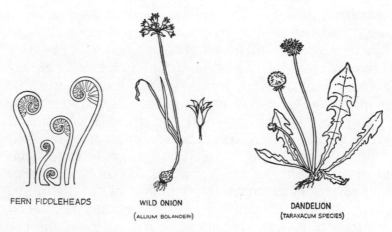

FERN FIDDLEHEADS

WILD ONION
(ALLIUM BOLANDERI)

DANDELION
(TARAXACUM SPECIES)

Fern fiddleheads, coiled young fronds of various ferns, are considered a delicacy. Generally, they are boiled in a little water before being eaten.

Wild onions can be identified by their round, spikelike stems, which sometimes have flower clusters at the ends, and by their characteristic odor. They are found mostly in rich, moist soils. The bulbs can be collected and stored for future use; the stems, called chives, can be cut up and eaten.

Young dandelion leaves may be eaten raw or boiled. Older leaves may lose their sometimes bitter taste if they are boiled in several changes of water.

Water:

A word about drinking water: the vast majority of streams in North America that are large enough to float a boat are polluted. There are exceptions, notably in Alaska and western Canada. But it is always best to take your water from springs or small tributary streams.

In planning your trip, you should consider the availability of water to judge how much you will have to carry at a time. One- to five-gallon collapsible plastic containers, obtainable in any camping store, serve this purpose well. Unless you are sure the water you are getting is potable, boil it or use halazone tablets or drops (as directed on the vial). They are available at drugstores or camping stores.

Wood:

On most rivers there is usually enough driftwood for at least a cooking fire. (The day is coming when even this commodity will be in scarce supply and all cooking will have to be on gas or alcohol-fueled stoves.) However, wood is often hard to find around favored campsites, and it is a good idea to pick up some in the afternoon before you reach camp.

Housekeeping Hints:

A simple metal grill large enough to hold several pots at a time should be all you need for a store, though some rafting parties carry iron stove boxes to cook on rather than build a rock fireplace each night. If finding wood is a problem, the firebox does conserve fuel. If you are camping at a site where there are fire pits provided by the Parks Department or other agency, use them. At least build your fire where there is evidence of one's having been before. A large part of the fascination of river running, particularly on some of the more remote western rivers, is the sense of pioneering. Without much effort one can imagine what it would have been like to be the first human being—or at least the first European explorer—to travel your river. A messy campsite, dotted with fire pits, is the quickest way to dispel that grand illusion.

Provided you do not use detergent—and you should not—dishes, pots, and pans can be scrubbed with sand in the river. The bit of refuse that comes off eating utensils is biodegradable. But never use the river as a latrine. On many rivers with designated campsites, you will find existing latrines. Otherwise dig your own, well away from the camp. Toilet paper should be burned. Leave a large coffee can beside the latrine to collect it and burn the contents when breaking camp in the morning.

The list of dos and don'ts for river camping might run indefinitely. In sum, however, it all comes down to this: Leave any campsite cleaner than you found it, with less sign of human presence, and you will always be welcome in the wilderness. If not, there soon will be no wilderness left to welcome you.

THE WILD SCENE

Sitting, yarning, and singing around a campfire at night are certainly among the great pleasures of camping, but they can be overdone, and blessed relief may come in the company of Thoreau, Lewis and Clark, or the incomparable Major Powell (see Chapter Two). Try to pick books about the country you are traveling through; they will increase your enjoyment of it immeasurably. The Peterson Field Guide series is particularly good for natural history, providing information on the local flora, fauna, geology, and history.

Rivers are especially fine locations to study geology. Cutting down through successive layers of rock, they are a graphic history of millions of years of evolution. The Grand Canyon is a prime example, but nearly all riverbanks tell the story of their evolution. It is usually possible to find a guide or scholarly work that speaks specifically to the river you are on. A good way to locate one is to write to the geology department of the nearest university. Reading the rocks as you float by becomes a fascinating addition to a trip.

Rivers are excellent places to observe birds. Bring a pair of binoculars and a field guide (the Peterson guides to American birds are in several volumes; be sure you have the appropriate one). Water acts like a magnet to birds. You will find the expected ospreys, ducks, kingfishers, herons, and geese. Besides that, the combination of cover along the bank, openness over the water, and the advantage of a silent moving platform brings you closer to shy species than is usually possible on land. Overhead, raptorial birds and buzzards soar on canyon updrafts.

Under these conditions, four-footed wildlife is also more approachable. Just as it is possible on the game preserves in Africa to move quite close to grazing antelope or snoozing lions if one does not get out of his Land-Rover or truck, just so can one sneak up on deer, bears, elk, bobcats, and foxes that come down to the river to drink. Otter are frequently spotted swimming or playing along the bank. Often animals that would flee at the first sight of a man on foot will stand transfixed as you float by.

Large mammals are usually easy to identify, but what about salamanders, newts, insects, and fish? For them most of us need field guides.

Still another book that makes an entertaining guide is one for the stars, because if you have any luck with the weather, you may spend a lot of time at night staring up at them from your sleeping bag. Also, journals of early exploration through the part of the country you are crossing become infinitely more meaningful when read *in situ*. The account Lewis and Clark made of their famous reconnaissance of the Upper Missouri across the Rockies to the Pacific is perfect reading while traveling any of the rivers of the Northwest. Powell's expedition on the Colorado is a must for anyone running the Grand Canyon or the Green. The Southwest abounds in accounts of early Spanish explorers.

If you are traveling in midsummer, when it does not become dark until nine o'clock and the dawn breaks at four thirty, the chances are that you will spend most of the hours of darkness sleeping. But early in spring or in September and October night falls too soon, and a good reading light is necessary so you can while away the hours with a good book.

BEWARE!

Bears and Snakes:

Having spoken of the pleasure of observing wild-life, it must be added that in direct contact there can, on occasion, be pain. The only serious danger from animals in the wild is from bears and snakes. Bears should never be fed, and precautions should be taken in bear country to keep camp food out of tents and sleeping bags. When in doubt, hang everything edible from the branches of trees.

Snakes, however, are a special danger for river runners because there is the strong tendency, against all advice to the contrary, to walk about camp barefoot. You should always wear shoes in the boat or on the raft because it is impossible to know when you might be called upon to walk, or, worse, steer around rocks in a rapid with your feet. A pair of old sneakers works well. But wet sneakers in camp are uncomfortable, and invariably they are taken off to let them dry. A solution is to have two pairs, or some type of ankle-length boot you can slip into while your sneakers are drying.

The only sound advice that can be given about snakes is to keep a sharp eye out for them. Given any chance, a rattler would rather retire than bite. In snake country, then, look before you leap—and always leap with your sneakers on. Beat thick underbrush with a stick before plunging in. A simple snake-bite kit should be part of every basic first-aid pack. Finally, if you do locate a snake, do not kill it. This is not the place for a lecture on ecology. Simply remember that the snake is part of the natural scene, as much as the river itself or the mountains it flows through. If it is living there, it has a purpose.

On river trips, you will be taking a lot of short, one- or two-hour-long hikes up tributary streams into hidden canyons, or up onto the heights above the river for a better view. Even if you are not planning to be gone long enough to carry food or water, it is a good idea to take a minimum survival kit with you in case you get stuck, sprain an ankle, or discover gold. This should include a plastic bottle for water—you will probably find someplace along the way to fill it. Halazone tablets, the snake-bite kit, matches in a waterproof container (or a flint and steel wool), and a jackknife complete the emergency gear. You might keep it all handy in a waist pack, to be strapped on whenever you set out to explore—even just down to the next grove of cottonwoods. The Siren song of the unknown too often calls one on a little farther, and then a little farther still.

Bugs:

Far more worrisome than bears and snakes, in point of their cumulative effect on river campers, are bugs—particularly mosquitoes and blackflies. The only sensible way to deal with these twin menaces is to go tripping during a season when they are not around, or at least when they abound in diminished numbers. That being often impossible, bring plenty of insect repellent and wear long-sleeved shirts and full-length trousers. If you are going into serious mosquito country—Canada in June and July, for instance—be sure you have netting for your tent. Rivers, at least the backwaters of rivers, are great breeding grounds for all sorts of insects that bite. During the day, out on the water, you will probably not be bothered much. Nighttime is a different matter. Mercifully, blackflies retire at night. But mosquitoes come on in droves. If you can, and if there is no chance of the river rising during the night from flash floods or the possible release from a dam, camp on bars out in the stream. Choose the side of the river against which the wind is blowing. Keep as far as possible from marshes and any still water. Or, as one book on canoe camping succinctly puts it, "If possible select a bug-free campsite."

Blackflies are a specialty of northern New England and Canada. Early to midsummer is their time. Some people are more affected by their bites than others. A constant threat is for the bites to fester and become infected. Do not take lightly the bite of the blackfly. Treat with disinfectant any bite that has become sore. And if you are a scratcher, tie your hands behind your back before you fall asleep at night.

For bug bites or allergic reactions, pack a supply of antihistamine with your medicines.

Out West, in dry areas, scorpions can be a problem. There are none that will kill you, unless you are supersensitive to their venom; but they can sting with the best of the venomous animals. Dump out your boots or shoes before putting them on in the morning. Scorpions are nocturnal, and boots are just the sort of nook they like to creep into at night.

Poisonous Plants:

After bugs, possibly the greatest danger to river campers comes from the three leafy witches—poison ivy, poison oak, and poison sumac. Of the three, poison ivy is by far the most prevalent. Along some watercourses it grows in such dense patches as to prevent landing. It is usually distinguishable by its glossy leaves in groups of three. Less well known are the sumac and oak, both of which are lovers of wetlands. If you know yourself to be susceptible to these scourges, you are most likely able to identify them. But no one should flirt with them. People who have never reacted to their poisons suddenly will. And few afflictions, short of a broken limb, can put a worse crimp in an expedition than a hideous, itchy rash. So study the sketches on the opposite page.

Sun:

Another easily overlooked danger of river running is the sun. Reflection off the water, repeated dousings (if in rapids) that keep you deceptively cool, lack of

COMMON POISON IVY
(RHUS RADICANS)

WESTERN POISON OAK
(RHUS DIVERSILOBA)

POISON SUMAC
(RHUS VERNIX)

Poison ivy can be a low-growing plant, vine, or shrub. It is common in all parts of the United States except California and sections of adjacent states.

Poison oak can be a shrub or a vine. It is found mostly in California and adjacent states, and also in the South.

Poison sumac is prevalent in the eastern United States. It grows as a shrub or a small tree, usually in damp places.

shade, the fact that many trippers go straight from their city jobs to the river, all conspire to make the beginning of a river trip high-risk days for sunburn. At any time of year, be sure to bring a hat. It should have a chin strap because on any white-water river worthy of the name, the moment when your hat blows off is not going to be a moment when it is convenient to turn back. In addition to a hat, bring plenty of sun-screen lotion and long-sleeved, loose-fitting clothes—pajamas, if the temperature is going to be hot.

PACKING YOUR BOAT

When packing for a river trip, two principles apply: keep it small and keep it dry. Whether you are tripping in a kayak or on a thirty-foot pontoon rig, your gear is more easily and efficiently stowed if it is packed in small bundles. As for keeping gear dry, a number of systems work in theory—almost none in practice.

For kayaks, a good pair of flotation bags is your best bet. For rafts and canoes the time-honored solution has been the black delousing bag. The originals of these were military surplus, along with the inflatable rafts that the early river runners used following World War II. They were *actually* delousing bags—the idea being that someone in need of delousing would take off all his clothes and put them in the bag along with a louse killer (some DDT compound, no doubt), seal the bag, and stand back. It has never been reported how well the neoprene-coated cloth bags performed their intended duty—one suspects not well, as there were so many of them on the surplus market. But when the tops are rolled, folded, and strapped, they prove marvelously watertight—gas-proof, in fact, which is what they were designed for—and therefore they float, which is another plus. The black bags are now no longer available in the surplus stores, but several firms are making civilian versions. William R. Donovan Company, 119½ Madison Street, Newark, N.Y. 14513, sells them by mail; the price is about $8. A black bag will hold about as much gear as a large backpack. Two bags per person should be plenty for an extended river trip.

A less expensive way to keep gear dry is with plastic garbage bags inside partially filled canvas duffles. If care is taken not to put anything in them that has sharp edges, they will not puncture—at least not right away. Large rubber bands are good fasteners for the tops.

For small items like binoculars, cameras, books, maps that one might want to keep both dry and at the ready, small shoebox-sized metal ammunition cases with rubber seals work well. It is a good idea, if you are running rapids, to tie these to the side of the raft or boat. In the spill on the Snake River reported in Chapter 1, the boat following us came to grief in the very same rapid that upset us. The passengers scattered, however, and swam to shore. The boat was too heavy for the boatman to turn over by himself. Consequently, when the next rapid came up, the boat was still upside down and unmanageable. Rocks smashed a great hole in the stern. Gear spilled into the river. Our first inkling that there had been trouble behind us was when we saw an orange-painted ammo can go bobbing by on the far side of the river from the place we had pulled into to camp. Camera, binoculars, wallet—everything valuable to the young lady whose can it was went down the river without her.

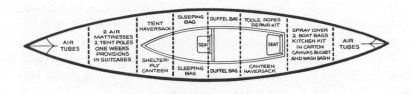

LOADING PLAN

One method of loading a two-man kayak for optimum balance on a week-long trip.

If you are canoeing and planning to make portages (or even if you are not planning, since conditions are not always predictable), you should have several pack frames with you. Another solution is the Adirondacks pack basket made of ash strips, available by mail order from L. L. Bean in Freeport, Maine. The latter, packed with a canvas bag and plastic garbage liner, makes a good river carryall—portable, waterproof, and easier to pack and unpack than a floppy sack.

SAFETY PRECAUTIONS

Safety on the water boils down to one serious precept: *Be prepared for the worst.* Take at least one extra life jacket for every four people and be sure they are buoyant. Wear them whenever there is the least possibility of flipping. In freezing water never take them off. Do not wear overly floppy clothes. Ponchos, for instance, are not advisable on the river because they can tangle you up if you go overboard. Do not have loose lines on your person or on the boat. Pack your boats so that in the event you lose one, you will have enough rations in the other boats to get you through. This does not mean to pack two of everything—only absolute essentials like first-aid kits should be doubled up on. But if you pack the flour in one boat, you might try to arrange matters so that the cornmeal goes in the other, and so on. Bring whatever materials you will need to repair a broken boat—bailing wire, epoxy resin, neoprene cement, neoprene patches, tools, nails, screws, and, above all, duct tape, the universal fix-it for all complaints on the river. You can mend a broken oar with duct tape, patch a leaky black bag, mend a tent, make a pot handle, and put labels on bags. Repair kits should be included on every craft.

When the broken dory on the Snake River finally was turned upright and pulled to shore, the boatmen patched it up the following morning with a piece of plywood found along the riverbank, some nails, and lots of duct tape. Thus mended, the boat was able to complete the remaining four days of the trip without any appreciable loss of maneuverability.

Duct tape is most decidedly something you do not want to be without. On the other hand, most parties go off with much more equipment than they need. David Farny, who runs an "Outward Bound"–type camp in Colorado and takes his charges on many river trips, is adamant on one point: do not overprepare. If you forget something or lose it in a mishap—as he has done on several occasions—do not lament. It may prove a blessing in disguise. Wilderness river tripping is a kind of make-believe in the first place, in which you place yourself in the shoes if not in the exact predicaments of the first explorers through those parts. They had to improvise, and often when modern trippers are forced to improvise it adds an element to the trip that can make everything more exciting and memorable. In Farny's case, a raft got loose and all the cutlery was lost, whereupon they whittled knives, forks, and spoons out of driftwood and made driftwood plates. The loss of convenience was more than compensated for by the sense of accomplishment at having overcome the difficulty. Therefore, prepare for the worst, but do not fret if you find yourself unprepared for anything less.

To return once more to the upset on the Snake, with two boats over, two heads bumped, some gear lost, a boat smashed, and a half dozen passengers rather rudely introduced to the power of big water, the trip was off to what turned out to be a superb start. The assemblage of passengers from different parts of the country and different walks of life, of different ages, in those few exciting moments were fused into a friendly, cooperative team. Adversity makes the best social glue. By the end of the trip we felt as close as a large family. That feeling comes on river trips, but it comes much faster when adversity demands it.

Mishaps can be anticipated. In extremis, however, certain rules apply. If you flip, stay with the boat. On the Snake those of us who did stay with the boat were able to right it and make it through the next rapid. The second boat, abandoned by all but its oarsman, was smashed. But be sure not to get yourself on the downriver side, for fear of getting squashed against a rock by the weight of the boat. An exception to the rule is when you flip in very cold water. It may then be more important to get out of the water as quickly as you can, even if this means abandoning the boat. The best thing is to try to get both passengers and the boat to shore as quickly as possible.

Hypothermia:

If you do flip in cold water there is extreme danger of hypothermia, a condition in which the body gets so cold it can no longer warm itself. Besides drowning, this is perhaps the greatest threat boaters face. Whenever the water gets much below 60°F., the potential is there. The human body is a marvelous mechanism, but it operates internally only within very narrow limits of temperature and chemical balance. It has many sensors built in that react to excess heat or cold. When these stops are run, however, the machinery may go haywire —or simply cease to function at all. Heat stroke is an example of one extreme, hypothermia is another. In the latter, metabolism no longer makes up for heat loss, and the body continues to cool down even though the person is once more dry and well covered.

Symptoms of hypothermia are a blue or white cast to the skin, uncontrollable shivering, and measurable loss of body temperature. A thermometer helps, but it is not necessary to judge when a patient gets that cold. If the body temperature goes below about 80°F. for any length of time, death occurs. If someone is stricken with hypothermia, it is not remedy enough to bundle him or her in blankets or a warm sleeping bag, because these simply retain the body heat generated by the person inside. Instead, put someone else in the sleeping bag with the patient, and at the same time administer a vigorous massage. Others should be getting a roaring fire going. Every possible means must be employed to raise the body temperature of the victim as rapidly as possible.

A FINAL WORD

Words of caution and notes on safety must, of necessity, find their way into a book like this, but they are not fit to be last words. The reason can be found in a talk I had with Dave Farny about the nature of professional river runners, those boatmen who conduct commercial trips. River rats, they call themselves with good-natured pride. They can be clean-cut (Dave's words) or long-haired, but all are fantastically strong characters—men and some women—who take charge. Their leadership is sensible, often deep-thinking. They care about other people, whether in teaching, guiding, or getting the group up in the morning to be off for the day. River running is not a lonely pastime. They are often musical, play the recorder, harmonica or guitar, and lead singing on the river and around the campfire at night. They are conservationists, preservationists, environmentalists, "but most important, river rats are optimists, in a free-thinking, adventure-dreaming way."

"Boatmen live to run rivers," Dave continued. "They will run the Omo in Ethiopia or rivers in Nigeria, Mexico, Peru. They have this dream of being the first down. Even on the Colorado they imagine themselves first, reliving the Powell expedition every time they go. And for them it is as if they were the first, for they share the same optimism of their one-armed hero, who a century ago plunged into the unknown gorge certain that he would get to the end of the river, to the bottom of the next rapid. Boatmen today show the same optimism, even if it is only that they will give their passengers an unforgettable trip.

"When a boatman wakes up and sees the river lapping at the shore, the clean sand, the smooth lines of river-worn rocks, the flowers open and dew-laden in the early morning, he is lifted by what he sees. And he starts the day off in a positive mood, so contrary to the effect of city life, the negative world of microwave ovens, telephones, cars, and the television media, with its news of disasters, murders, and befoulment. Sure, there are rapids ahead that might cause trouble, puncture a boat, flip you over, but you know that you are going to get through, that the camp you will reach that night will be even more beautiful than the one you are at right now. And I think that is why people come to run rivers."

Part 2
THE RIVERS

Editor's Note:

Part II, the section on rivers, like *Running the Rivers of North America* itself, is introductory in scope and depth of coverage.

Just as the previous chapters have provided a solid and general outline of the ways of rivers and river sports, this section will provide a general guide to the "wheres" for river recreation.

Concise maps illustrate 25 of the most popular runs on rivers across the United States and Canada, and some of the put-in and take-out points. However, both maps and word descriptions are intended as sketches. Their purpose is to characterize each river rather than to be used as actual guides in the field. Not every danger nor every pleasure is included.

Although the author has, as far as possible, graded the rivers as suitable for "novices," "intermediates," and "experts" (and "various" where all three apply), it is important to note that *seasonal and weather conditions make these general gradings subject to change*.

Where possible, sources for further information—both outdoor associations and specialized guides—are provided. Once you have decided on what river you are going to run, you will want to consult them for more details and seasonal conditions.

MAP LEGEND

CAMPSITES	▲
BOAT ACCESS	▷
PRIVATELY OWNED BOAT ACCESS	▷
STATE ROADS	———
PRIVATE ROADS	– – –
STATE LINES	–··–
DAMS	▮
RAPIDS	≋
FALLS	⌃
TOWNS	●
CITIES	■
PUT IN	PUT IN ➡
TAKE OUT	TAKE OUT ➡
BRIDGES	═
FOREST BOUNDARIES	∷∷∷∷∷
MOUNTAINS	⋀
FIRE TOWERS	▯
WATERWAY RANGERS	R
MAINE FOREST DISTRICT CAMPS	F
POINTS OF INTEREST	*
LEAN-TO	▫
CHECKPOINTS (ROAD OWNERS)	⊙
RAILROADS	┼┼┼┼┼
HIKING TRAILS	··········

NEW ENGLAND

ALL New England is divided into three parts. Maine—
as large as the five other states combined—is a king-
dom of lakes and rivers unto itself. Its widest, most
northerly, and most challenging river system, the St.
John, with its popular tributary the Allagash, caps the
state, running first northeasterly, then bending southeast to carve a part of the United States–Canadian
boundary. The Allagash and St. John flow through the
closest approximation to untrammeled wilderness that
the eastern United States can boast of. This is North
Woods country, where the forests of pine and spruce
once stood so close-shouldered and broad that the floor
was clear of underbrush and teams of horses could pass
at will. Heavy lumbering has laid low much but not all
of this colossal timber, and the flavor of the North
Woods remains—with no better way to sample it than
by canoe. Unfortunately for thee and me, thousands of
wilderness-hungry canoeists and kayakers (no rafting
allowed on the Allagash) test themselves on this offi-
cially designated Wilderness Waterway each season
(April to September). So if isolation is of prime importance to you, try some Maine streams of less renown.
There are hundreds. By and large, the rest of Maine's
water—the Penobscot and its branches and the Kenne-

bec—drains southward to meet the Atlantic along the state's rockbound shore.

Below Maine, two major drainage systems prevail, flowing eastward out of New Hampshire and Massachusetts to the Atlantic above Cape Cod, and south into Long Island Sound. Among the best of the eastward-tending rivers are the Saco, which rises on the slopes of Mount Conway and crosses southern Maine; the Androscoggin; and the Merrimack, made famous by Thoreau.

The southern drainage gathers in broad valleys that empty into Long Island Sound. The greatest of these is the Connecticut, flanked east and west by the Thames and the Housatonic. Each river has many tributaries worthy of a river runner's time and skill.

Except for areas of Maine, there is little wilderness left in New England. Nearly all the major rivers have been dammed for power. There are no fewer than sixteen dams on the Connecticut alone. Along the tributaries, deforestation has taken its toll, accentuating the natural swing to the seasonal pendulum of high water and low. Many rivers that are dangerously full in the spring dry during the summer to rocky pathways. April and May are the premier months for running rivers in New England. It is in the spring that the white-water canoeing and kayaking championships are held on rivers like the West in Vermont and the Westfield in Massachusetts. From June on, the water drops alarmingly—except where it is controlled by dams; then there may be water at certain times of the day.

Pollution and commercial waste have also ravaged many of New England's finest streams and rivers. To float or paddle them for any distance serves as an object lesson on how society has abused its most precious natural resource—its fresh-water supply.

But the gloomy side is only half the picture. Even in southern New England there remain literally hundreds of enchanting stretches of water—white water and still—to attract canoeists and, more recently, kayakers. Rafting is less popular there. The many portages make sizeable rafts more of an encumbrance than a delight, and the still water behind the many dams makes tough rowing. If you must raft in New England, consider the Connecticut above Hanover, New Hampshire, where there are fifty-three miles of gently flowing, undammed water.

The better way to go, the traditional way, is by canoe. The waterways of New England have been meticulously scouted by clubs and organizations. The most comprehensive guide to these waters is the *AMC New England Canoeing Guide,* compiled by the Appalachian Mountain Club, 5 Joy Street, Boston, MA 02108. In it you will find detailed directions for literally hundreds of river trips besides those of special interest listed here.

ALLAGASH RIVER

Wild and Scenic River; Maine Wilderness Waterway

Time of year: *late May to October*

Degree of difficulty: *intermediate to expert*

Craft: *canoe*

Character: *wild; semiwild*

Permit required: *For information write the Bureau of Parks and Recreation, Department of Conservation, Augusta, ME 04333.*

Rentals available: *yes*

The region of the Allagash in northern Maine was celebrated by Thoreau more than a century ago. "This prime forest and wild river should be preserved," he wrote. Nothing was done until 1966, when the state of Maine acquired control of the land abutting the river a mile wide on either side, declaring it a "Wilderness Waterway" and limiting the cutting of timber.

Betwixt times the river had become a major artery for flushing out the enormous stands of virgin pine that were the glory of the North Woods. Lumbering alters

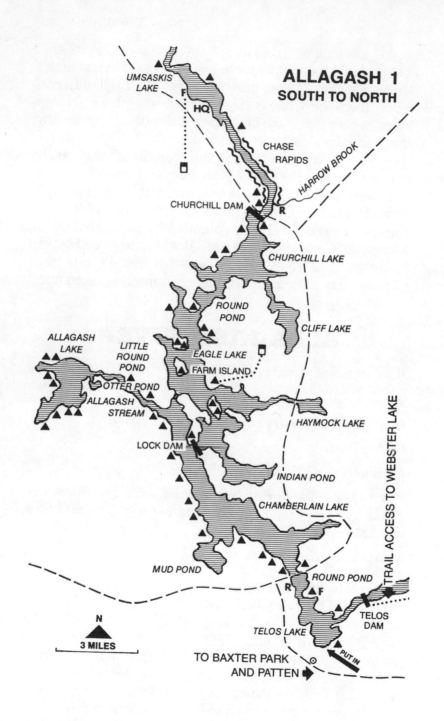

ALLAGASH 1
SOUTH TO NORTH

UMSASKIS LAKE
F
HQ
CHASE RAPIDS
HARROW BROOK
CHURCHILL DAM
R
CHURCHILL LAKE
ROUND POND
CLIFF LAKE
ALLAGASH LAKE
LITTLE ROUND POND
EAGLE LAKE
FARM ISLAND
OTTER POND
ALLAGASH STREAM
HAYMOCK LAKE
LOCK DAM
INDIAN POND
CHAMBERLAIN LAKE
MUD POND
ROUND POND
R
F
TRAIL ACCESS TO WEBSTER LAKE
TELOS DAM
TELOS LAKE
PUT IN
N
3 MILES
TO BAXTER PARK AND PATTEN

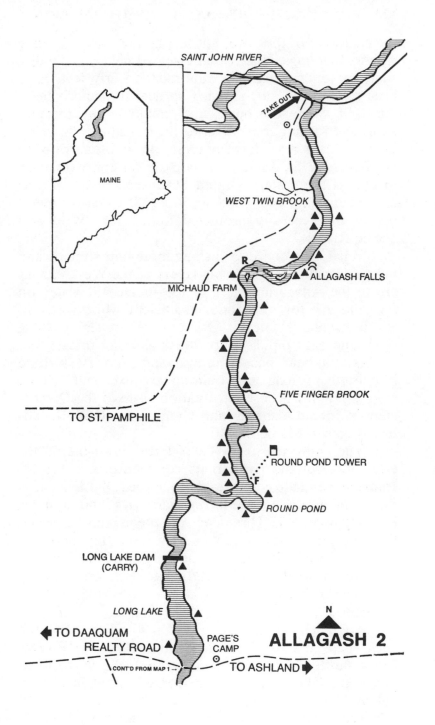

SAINT JOHN RIVER

MAINE

TAKE OUT

WEST TWIN BROOK

R

ALLAGASH FALLS

MICHAUD FARM

FIVE FINGER BROOK

TO ST. PAMPHILE

ROUND POND TOWER

F

ROUND POND

LONG LAKE DAM
(CARRY)

N

LONG LAKE

◀TO DAAQUAM
REALTY ROAD

PAGE'S
CAMP

ALLAGASH 2

CONT'D FROM MAP 1 →

TO ASHLAND ▶

the character of the land, but less so than does farming
with its buildings, fences, and cropped fields. The pines,
some of which reached a hundred and fifty feet, have
been replaced by fast-growing spruce; the land is heal-
ing itself. Some obvious scars remain in the form of
dams and logging roads. But to the casual eye the Allagash is again a wilderness river, or at least, with its
neighbor, the St. John, it is as close an approximation
to one as the eastern United States can boast. It was
an obvious choice to become, in 1968, a charter member of the federally protected system of "Wild and
Scenic Rivers."

What kayaks are to rushing mountain streams and
inflatable rafts are to the big rivers of the West, canoes
are to the Allagash. There is too much still water on
the Allagash for rafts, and insufficient white water to
stir a kayaker's interest. Ninety-eight miles of lake,
river, and easy rapids course through quiet forests that
are home to bear, beaver, moose, and deer. The birdlife
is rich, the fishing and hunting are excellent. (State
laws apply; for license information write to the Department of Inland Fisheries and Game, State Office Building, Augusta, Maine 04330.)

The entire trip from Telos Lake down the northerly course of the river to its confluence with the St.
John can be made comfortably in a week; but twice that
time can easily be spent on side trips and a more
leisurely approach. Three days are the maximum period
that one party may occupy a campsite. But there are
plenty of sites, although at the height of the summer
you are apt to find more fellow canoeists on the river
than beaver and moose. If you can, go early or late in
the season.

To reach the put-in at Telos Landing, take the
back roads out of Greenville, Millinocket, or Patten.
For a shorter trip, it is also possible to be flown in to
one of the lakes farther downriver, or to put in or take
out at Umsaskis Lake, where a private road (permit
required) crosses the waterway. The run from Telos to
Churchill Dam is mostly still water. The straight dis-

tance is something over forty miles, but many opportunities exist to explore lake shores and tributaries.

Most satisfying is a side trip up Allagash Stream into the fastness of Allagash Lake. The stream flows into the north end of Chamberlain Lake. Experience with poling a canoe is necessary to navigate the stream's six miles of rocks and riffles. The prize is worth the effort. No motorized transport or airplanes are allowed on the lake. The only way in is on foot or by canoe.

The preferred passage from Chamberlain into Eagle Lake is via a short portage around Lock Dam. You can also make the longer portage beside the tramway at the head of the lake, where logs were once hauled up by steam engines and cables from Eagle Lake into Chamberlain and thence, thanks to the high water backed up behind Lock Dam, up the Allagash and into the Penobscot River and on to Bangor. Relics of those pre-gas-engine days rust along the tramway.

Below Churchill Lake lies the Chase Carry, Class II white water that runs for nine invigorating miles. You do not have to be an expert but it helps. Ten more miles of lake-paddling lie below the rapids, and from there on it is mostly moving water, some fast, to West Twin Brook, where the official waterway ends. Another five miles of pleasant but inhabited river brings you to Allagash Village and the St. John River.

The upper reaches of the St. John are a wilder, less traveled, and more difficult version of the Allagash. The St. John boasts two truly challenging rapids, but it is harder to reach (airplane is the preferred method). A powerful torrent in May and June, it is apt to run out of water by midsummer. The St. John requires expert canoeists or strong backs to portage, or both.

Registration is required on the Allagash. Do this at Telos Landing, Churchill Dam, Umsaskis Lake, and Michaud Farm or at any ranger station. Parking areas are located at Churchill Dam and at the Telos and Chamberlain checkpoints. Camping is permitted—as on all Maine's public preserves—only at designated sites.

The trip should not be attempted before late May,

after the ice goes out. From then through October the river is usually runnable, except that there may be too much water in May and early June, and too little in the late summer. The blackfly season—a definite hazard to the thin-skinned and short-tempered—is at its worst during June. Drinking water is available from springs and tributaries and from the river itself, providing it is boiled or that halazone or other water-purifying tablets are added.

Anyone contemplating running the Allagash should write first for the brochure *Allagash Wilderness Waterway,* obtainable free from the State Park and Recreation Commission, State Office Building, Augusta, Maine 04330. Information on the St. John can be obtained from the same source. The Allagash brochure provides detailed information on the topographical maps you will need, access points that require permits and how to apply for them from the lumber companies that maintain the roads, and provocative photographs of the river itself.

Canoe rentals are available through Allagash Wilderness Outfitters, Frost Pond, Star Route 76, Greenville, Maine 04441.

AMMONOOSUC RIVER

Time of year: May to mid-June

Degree of difficulty: intermediate to expert

Craft: canoe, kayak

Character: pastoral

Permit required: no

Rentals available: no

The Ammonoosuc River rises on the western slope of Mount Washington. The snow melt from the Presidential Range, the highest peaks in New England, extends the season of runnability on the "Ammo" beyond that of many of New England's mountain rivers. May 1 to around June 10 are about the limits. After the first week in June the river shrinks until there is more rock than water. Two gauges tell the story: one at Bethlehem should read between 3.6′ and 4.8′; another, farther downriver, at Bath, should read between 3.6′ and 5′.

When the water level is right, the nearly fifty-mile run westward from below Ammonoosuc Falls to Woodsville, where the Ammonoosuc meets the Connecticut, is considered by many to be the finest piece of white water in New Hampshire. With several Class IV and numerous Class II and Class III rapids, it provides a keen test for intermediate to expert canoeists, and plenty of excitement for kayakers. The scenery, particularly along the upper stretch, is lovely, despite the presence of a road most of the way. The road does permit access at a variety of points and facilities several portages around dams.

The whole trip can be made in a couple of days or can be divided into several one-day excursions. As usual, the AMC guide is your best bet for planning a trip on the Ammonoosuc.

SACO RIVER

Time of year: April to October

Degree of difficulty: various

Craft: canoe, kayak

Character: semiwild; pastoral

Permit required: no

Rentals available: yes

The Saco has it all. Rising in New Hampshire, it dashes down the eastern slopes of New Hampshire's White Mountains into Maine, where, turning south, it flows clear and smooth for over one hundred miles to the Atlantic Ocean below Portland. The upper reaches of the Saco, steep and rambunctious, tear down from Crawford Notch above Conway and provide some of

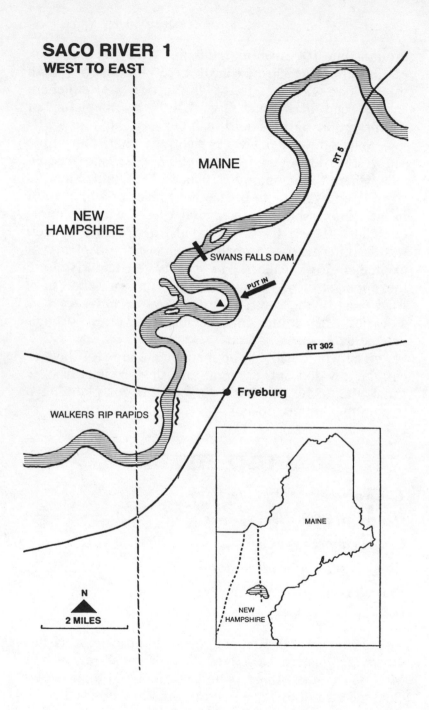

SACO RIVER 1
WEST TO EAST

MAINE

NEW
HAMPSHIRE

RT 5

SWANS FALLS DAM

PUT IN

RT 302

Fryeburg

WALKERS RIP RAPIDS

N

2 MILES

MAINE

NEW
HAMPSHIRE

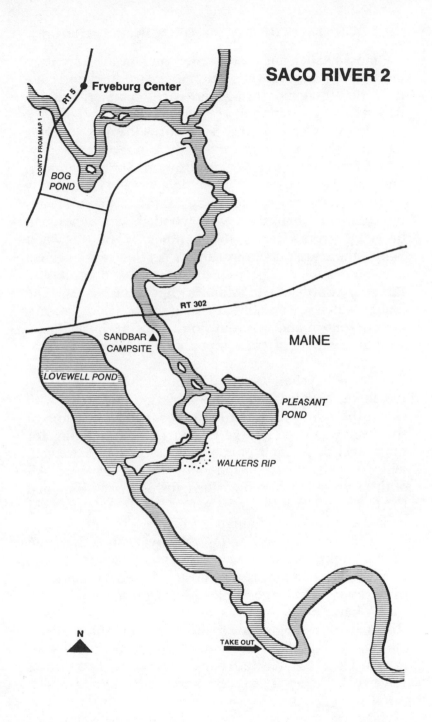

SACO RIVER 2

Fryeburg Center

RT 5

CONT'D FROM MAP 1 →

BOG POND

RT 302

SANDBAR CAMPSITE

MAINE

LOVEWELL POND

PLEASANT POND

WALKERS RIP

N

TAKE OUT

the most challenging white-water runs in all New England. The scenery, when one can pause to appreciate it, is breathtaking. Spring and early summer find the experts on this section of the river.

Below Conway, the Saco turns benign, offering near-perfect conditions for family canoe trips of anywhere from a day to a week's duration. Spring, summer, and fall, the Saco runs with sufficient water over sandy bottoms, with just enough easy rapids to make life interesting. The banks are well wooded with pines and broadleaf trees. During the summer, when the water is low, there are numerous sandbanks that make perfect campsites and havens from mosquitoes and blackflies, the only drawbacks to Maine's marvelous rivers. The amber water is irresistible to swimmers. There are numerous put-in and take-out points on the lower Saco, so that a variety of trips is possible.

The classic family trip is from the Swans Falls Dam near Fryeburg down to Hiram, thirty-three miles. It can be handled comfortably in two days, but with side trips may warrant three or four. This section of the river was once a large glacial lake, accounting for the gravel banks and ponds such as Kezar, Lovewell, and Pleasant, closed meanders of the former river. All of these provide interesting side trips. Lovewell is named for Captain Lovewell, who was killed there in a fight with the Pequawket Indians in 1725.

For the first five miles the river turns between sandy banks, outwash of the former glacier. At the Route 5 bridge there is a campsite owned by the town of Fryeburg. It is a good place to camp and park your car. A half mile below the Route 302 bridge is Walkers Rip, the only rapids worth the name on this stretch. Do not attempt it if you have no experience at all with rapids. Carry on the left bank. The river now grows somewhat deeper, narrower, and more intimate. The wooded banks press in. Gone are the magnificent vistas of the Presidential Range—in snow, if the season is still young. Instead, one senses a kind of warm conspiracy with nature, entering one of its most lovely green and guarded passageways. The normal take-out for this trip is at Hiram. But you can continue on down to the Atlantic, if you want. Carries will be necessary, and there are several challenging rapids. And, of course, the closer you get to the sea, the more urban becomes the Saco. If you do decide to continue past Hiram, take care early in the season to pull out well above Great Falls dam, three miles below Hiram. The current over the dam can be dangerous, and make a poor ending to a lovely trip.

CONNECTICUT RIVER

Time of year: May until late September

Degree of difficulty: various

Craft: canoe

Character: pastoral

Permit required: no

Rentals available: yes

When John Ledyard was a freshman at Dartmouth College in New Hampshire he hacked a canoe out of a large pine log and paddled down the Connecticut River to Hartford, just for the hell of it. That was in 1772, and Dartmouth students and non-Dartmouth students alike have been following the Ledyard's wake ever since, for pretty much the same reason. The Connecticut, New England's major waterway, cries out to be paddled on. Flowing due south from the Canadian border, it separates Vermont and New Hampshire for roughly half its four-hundred-mile length. It crosses the states of Massachusetts and Connecticut and pours finally into Long Island Sound at Old Saybrook. Of the New England states only Maine and Rhode Island are left out. Poor little Rhode Island. Where rivers are concerned, Maine can take care of itself.

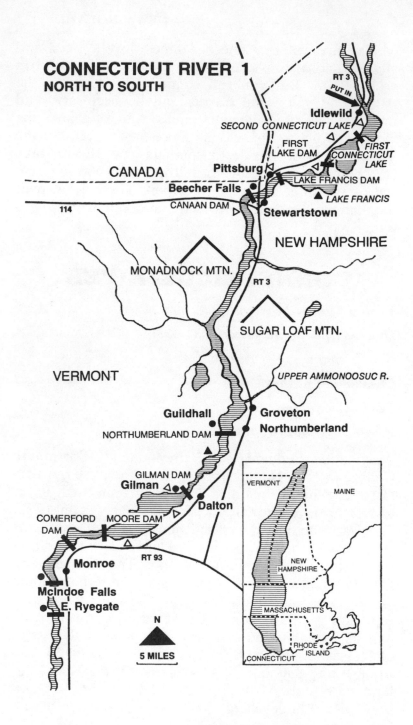

CONNECTICUT RIVER 1
NORTH TO SOUTH

RT 3
PUT IN

Idlewild

SECOND CONNECTICUT LAKE

FIRST
LAKE DAM

FIRST
CONNECTICUT
LAKE

Pittsburg

CANADA

LAKE FRANCIS DAM

Beecher Falls

LAKE FRANCIS

CANAAN DAM

Stewartstown

114

NEW HAMPSHIRE

MONADNOCK MTN.

RT 3

SUGAR LOAF MTN.

VERMONT

UPPER AMMONOOSUC R.

Guildhall

Groveton
Northumberland

NORTHUMBERLAND DAM

GILMAN DAM

Gilman

Dalton

COMERFORD
DAM

MOORE DAM

VERMONT

MAINE

Monroe

RT 93

NEW
HAMPSHIRE

McIndoe Falls

E. Ryegate

MASSACHUSETTS

N

RHODE
ISLAND

5 MILES

CONNECTICUT

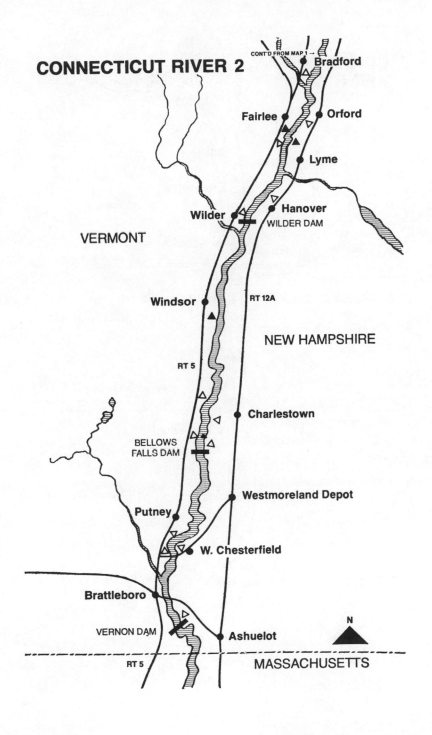

CONNECTICUT RIVER 2

CONT'D FROM MAP 1 → Bradford

Fairlee   Orford

Lyme

Hanover

Wilder   WILDER DAM

VERMONT

Windsor   RT 12A

NEW HAMPSHIRE

RT 5

Charlestown

BELLOWS
FALLS DAM

Westmoreland Depot

Putney

W. Chesterfield

Brattleboro

VERNON DAM   Ashuelot

N

RT 5   MASSACHUSETTS

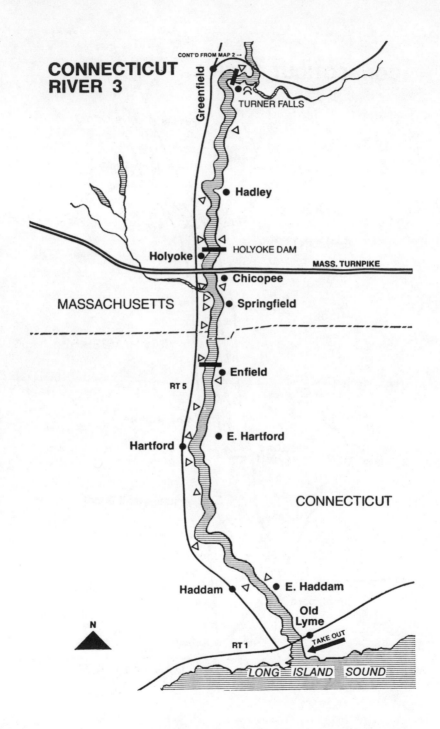

Each April the Ledyard Canoe Club, a Dartmouth affiliate, stages a rerun of its seminal event, from Hanover down to the Sound. The present record is thirty-three hours, fifty minutes, set by a couple of Dartmouth students. They knew what they were doing. They paddled night and day and jogged over the portages. Most of us, however, prefer to savor the favors of this regal lady at a more leisurely pace. She is the queen, after all, of New England's rivers—much soiled, to be sure, and constricted, but a grande dame, nonetheless. The camping is generally excellent. And although a great deal of the way is virtually flat water, stoppered by dams, there are exciting sections, too. Along the entire four hundred miles there are numerous entry and exit points, making possible dozens of different trips without ever repeating yourself.

For convenience's sake, the river may be considered in three sections: upper, middle, and lower. The first one hundred and sixty miles, between Pittsburg and Hanover, are generally the most demanding and pay the highest dividends in fast water and wild scenery. By late April the spring runoff has usually subsided sufficiently. On these upper reaches the river should be open for travel by early May. From June to late September, water conditions are at their best. A series of hydro-electric dams ensures a constant water level. Plan to spend the better part of a week on the upper section—more if you want to explore the lakes that are accessible by road. The river connections between the lakes are impassable above Second Lake, while the passage between Second and First lakes should be attempted only by experts. Below First Lake the stream can be canoed when the dam there is discharging. Times are posted daily at the dam site. Below First Lake the river is very rough for the first mile, then easier rapids follow into Lake Francis. Better scout this entire section, as changing water levels can turn the rapids angry. Below Lake Francis there is less than one mile of rapid river to the dam of Pittsburg, where one must take out and take care for the strong current over the dam.

From Pittsburg down to Hanover the way is blocked by seven dams, but no portage over half a mile, and there is plenty of white water in between (Class I and II rapids, with one Class III). Other than the dams, man's mark is light here and wildlife is prevalent.

The seven miles between Comerford Dam and McIndoe Falls Dam, continuous swift current and white water provide the most exhilarating on the whole river. The remaining fifty-three miles of the trip, from Ryegate Dam to Hanover, is free of portages. The river meanders through some of the most scenic country in the Northeast. An old farmhouse does swing into view betimes, a town now and then, but the feeling is strictly nineteenth-century pastoral.

Camping is on beaches and in the occasional field. Where tenancy is obvious, ask permission. Ordinarily it will be granted.

On the middle section of the Connecticut, six more dams hold back the river. The towns are larger and tend to smother the banks. Beyond them, though, the valley is wide and given over to pleasant farmland. The water is slow and placid; the views are of orchards, forests, and fields. A strong aroma of history rises from the exposed roots of New England.

Below Enfield, Connecticut, the river gradually widens, passing through towns like East Haddam, settled in 1670 and boasting the earliest church bell in the country. By the time one reaches the shipbuilding town of Essex, on the right bank, the river has become an estuary, nearly a mile wide. Tidal currents, waves, and wind rule here and must be considered on any trip.

A more detailed map of the river is published by the Connecticut River Watershed Council. This, with an accompanying guide, can be ordered at $4.50 per copy from the council at 125 Combs Road, Easthampton, MA 01027, or purchased in most camping stores. The *AMC New England Canoeing Guide* is also useful in planning a trip on the Connecticut.

CHARLES RIVER

Time of year: April to October

Degree of difficulty: novice

Craft: canoe

Character: pastoral; urban

Permit required: no

Rentals available: yes

The Charles—named long ago for England's Bonnie Prince Charlie—is to canoeing what Saratoga is to horse racing: more tradition than fierce excitement. During the nineteenth century, Norumbega Park, in Newton, Massachusetts, was the hotspot for recreational canoeing in the country. On Sundays, spring through fall, families by the hundreds came out on the trolley from Boston to rent canoes for a few hours' outing on the dark waters of the Charles, overhung with willows that grow there still. Rampant pollution and the rise of the family automobile changed all that.

Now the pendulum has swung back again. Sunday driving is no longer fun, while every year sees the Charles a cleaner river. At Cambridge goldfish can be spotted wallowing beneath the murk, almost as numerous as the rowing shells that put out daily from the Harvard and MIT boathouses. And on the sinuous eighty-five miles that the Charles travels between its rise at Hopkinton (a mere twenty-six air miles west of Boston) to Boston Harbor, increasing numbers of canoeists are making the acquaintance of this charming stream.

No wilderness experience this! But the Charles can nonetheless take pride in providing the finest urban canoeing in the country. From South Natick Dam down to Boston, the river runs almost entirely through parkland. It is a thoroughly managed river. Flood control dams ensure sufficient water to run the lower three quarters of the Charles, from Medway Dam down, at any time of the year. Above Medway, spring is the time to go.

The many ponds and easy carries make the Charles an ideal river for family canoeing. Rafting has no place on the Charles, and its still waters provide little challenge for kayakers. With the help of the AMC guide, canoe trips of several days' duration can be planned through country abounding in historic sites and fine New England scenery. But primarily the Charles, wherever one chooses to put in and take out, lends itself to a day's comfortable outing. Besides Norumbega Park, once again open for canoe rentals, there are liveries in nearly every town along the river.

PENOBSCOT RIVER

Time of year: mid-June until late August

Degree of difficulty: intermediate

Craft: canoe

Character: pastoral

Permit required: no

Rentals available: yes

The Penobscot drains central Maine. With its four branches (North, South, East, and West), it was once the prime transportation system for this vast and sodden country to big timber. Countless logs providing millions of board feet of lumber have come down the Penobscot. Where once a trip to the headwaters of the Allagash, St. John, or Penobscot was an expedition in itself, like climbing Mont Blac before skiing down, there are now a number of private logging roads into the area that are open for public use. A permit may be necessary on some of these, so check your route carefully before you start. (Write to State Park and Recreation Commission, State Office Building, Augusta, Maine 04330.) All these waterways now provide superb access to wild surroundings. Here and there one finds old dams, a tramway, reminders of past days of logging glory when guile, muscle, and occasional steam power got the logs out. Now the timber comes out on trucks—hence the roads.

The East Branch of the Penobscot is probably the most interesting. You can start as far north as Telos Lake—the same take-off place as for the Allagash trip —or you can put in at the dam below Grand Lake Matagamon, reached by gravel road out of Patten. The run from there is forty miles down to Grindstone, where the river meets Route 11. This is a rough stretch of water, which nevertheless can be run by intermediate paddlers. But they must have good maps and good sense, for there are some fearsome drops that must be portaged (or carried, as they prefer to say in Maine) around. Stair Falls, Haskell Rock Pitch, Pond Pitch, Hulling Machine Pitch, Grindstone Falls, are all boat-busters. In between, however, the East Branch is a magnificent wilderness river. Consult the AMC guide.

WEST RIVER

Time of year: mid-May to October

Degree of difficulty: various

Craft: canoe, kayak

Character: pastoral

Permit required: no

Rentals available: no

The West River slants southeast out of Vermont's Green Mountains to meet the Connecticut at Brattleboro. Big excitement on the West comes each year in mid-May when the Eastern Slalom Canoe Championships and the West River Slalom Races for canoes and kayaks are held. The little town of Jamaica, on the edge of Green Mountain National Park, hosts the event. There can be no better way for a would-be kayaker to gain an understanding of the sport than to visit Jamaica during White-water Weekend. In the hands of an expert, the maneuverability of these light semi-submarines is marvelous to behold. There was a time, in the early 1960s, when participants at Jamaica outnumbered the spectators. No longer. Today you may have to fight for a vantage point along the half mile of river festooned with slalom gates. As for motel or hotel accommodations, there will probably be none in a twenty-mile radius, so bring a tent and sleeping bag, like most of the other folks do.

On the other spring days the upper river can be canoed or kayaked from Londonderry down to Jamaica —but only by experts. Below Jamaica the river gentles for an easy thirty-mile run to the Connecticut. A worthwhile weekend for beginners might well start at Jamaica during the championships. After spending a few hours seeing how it should be done, you can try it yourself on the lower river on the two-day run down to Brattleboro.

THE MID-ATLANTIC STATES

THE Appalachian Mountain chain marches down the mid-Atlantic States like China's Great Wall. The region is amply endowed with the sort of high country that makes wild and scenic rivers. A fortunate condition, since the appetite for rivers in this, the most populous region of the nation, is great and growing.

At the northern end, hardest to reach and therefore least spoiled, lie the fabulous Adrirondacks, with a maze of lakes and streams that have provided canoe trails and white water for a half-dozen generations of campers and fishermen. The Adirondack water splits, some flowing north into the St. Lawrence Valley, some south to the Hudson. Like most river running in the East, a trip through this watershed becomes a voyage through history. Today, the region's most beautiful lakes are marred by the blemish of development, but there remain in the Adirondacks many wild and lovely corners to explore. To help you, the *Adirondack Mountain Club* canoeing guide is thorough, full of interesting historical highlights, and fairly well up to date. No one should try to canoe this region without it.

Moving south, there are the Catskills. The mighty Hudson provides drainage east of them. Along the western side runs the Delaware, surprisingly unspoiled for a stream whose headwaters lie only a few hours' drive from Times Square. Both these major rivers have tributary streams that make exciting white-water boating in the spring. Two excellent examples are Catskill Creek (put-in, South Cairo; take-out, Leeds) and the Normanskill Creek (put-in, Gilderland; take-out, Delmar).

In New Jersey and eastern Pennsylvania most streams suffer heavily from overuse. This condition, happily, is abating. Measures to ban the indiscriminate dumping of sewage and industrial waste, so long an assumed right of society and industry, are being felt. The Hudson is cleaner today than it was a decade ago —not clean, just cleaner. But even in New Jersey there are surprises for the canoeist. One such is Wharton Tract State Forest, part of the Pine Barrens in the southern part of the state, midway between Philadelphia and Atlantic City. Here you will find a quartet of clean, unspoiled small canoeing streams of rare beauty—the Batsto, Mullica, Oswego, and Wading—their waters stained brown by tannin from the cedars along their banks.

For a sense of deeper wilderness, there are western Pennsylvania and parts of Ohio to explore. On the Youghiogheny you can find white-water excitement to match any in the country. For a total change of scene, there is fine canoeing to be had in the creeks and bayous bordering Chesapeake Bay.

The message, then, is that, for all its urban sprawl, there is plenty of water for everybody in the East. And if on summer weekends the streams are sometimes crowded, there are compensations: no waters in the country have been more assiduously scouted or better documented. With a little research and a little planning, you can find boatable streams in some of the most unlikely places.

A second compensation is the number of available boat rentals. You will find well-equipped liveries on most of the popular streams and rivers. Usually this means canoes. But on rivers like the Youghiogheny, where rafting and kayaking are popular, you can find that equipment, too. Though if you rent a kayak, you may be asked to prove a certain level of competence.

HUDSON RIVER

Time of year: April to October

Degree of difficulty: various

Craft: canoe, kayak

Character: wild; pastoral; urban

Permit required: no

Rentals available: yes

One could write a book about the Hudson, and many people have. It is hard to imagine while viewing the enormous open sewer that flows back and forth beside Manhattan Island (the river is tidal all the way to Albany) that there could be anything about the Hudson to attract the river runner. Yet the Hudson River Gorge, according to one authority, "is certainly one of the finest [kayaking] runs in the entire East," with "utterly magnificent scenery, complete isolation from the daily routine and challenging rapids."

Complete isolation—sometimes! For it is on the Upper Hudson near the town of North Creek, above Albany, that the Annual Hudson River White-water Derby is held each spring. Besides the contestants themselves who compete a dozen different classes, including kayaks and both open and decked canoes, the derby ordinarily attracts well over twelve thousand spectators.

For the rest of the time—meaning spring and early summer, really, because the water may be too low after that—the Upper Hudson from its source at Sanford

Lake in the Adirondacks to Glens Falls, seventy miles, is a highly desirable white-water stream. Many enthusiasts begin a trip through "the Gorge," a mile and a half up the tributary, at Indian River, near the lower end of Lake Abanakee.

For less specialized sport, the river can be run from Glens Falls to Manhattan, a total distance of one hundred and seventy miles, by making several urban "portages." Expect to fight tides and winds below Albany. There are no formal campsites as of this writing, but a chain of them is being planned.

PINE CREEK

Time of year: *April to October*

Degree of difficulty: *novice to intermediate*

Craft: *canoe, kayak, raft*

Character: *semiwild*

Permit required: *yes*

Rentals available: *no; commercial float trips are available*

Pine Creek, on the northern border of Pennsylvania, flows out of one of the wildest regions of the Appalachian chain, cutting what enthusiasts delight in billing as the "Grand Canyon of Pennsylvania." The stretch they speak of is some nine miles long—put in at Ansonia on U.S. 6 and take out at Tiadaghton (which means "lost" or "bewildered" in the local Indian tongue), where civilization begins again. The well-wooded sides of the gorge rise steeply for hundreds of feet, but only occasionally in sheer stone faces. A Grand Canyon it is not, but it is an extraordinary piece of scenery to lie so close to what must be the epicenter of the industrial Northeast.

Pine Creek itself is runnable for some sixty miles, from a put-in on U.S. 6 near Wellsboro down to the town of Jersey Shore. The upper stretch that threads the gorge is runnable only in spring and early summer, when it runs swift and clear, creating rapids rated up to Class II. This makes an excellent warm-up stream for beginning canoeists and rafters. Camping in the bottom of the gorge is possible. The rest of the river is rather spoiled by accompanying roads.

Two commercial outfitters conduct canyon float trips: Edward McCarthy, The Antlers, RD 4, Wellsboro, PA 16901, and Kenneth Schlicher, RD 2, Center Valley, PA 18034. Both offer two-day trips with overnight stops in the canyon at reasonable rates.

LITTLE MIAMI RIVER

Wild and Scenic River

Time of year: *April to October*

Degree of difficulty: *intermediate*

Craft: *canoe, kayak*

Character: *semiwild*

Permit required: *For information write the Ohio Department of Natural Resources, Division of Natural Areas and Preserves, Fountain Square, Columbus, OH 43224.*

Rentals available: *yes*

The Little Miami River in Ohio provides a ninety-five mile run, with several short portages. Stretches pass through the Spring Valley Wildlife Area and Fort Ancient State Park. It has been nominated to become one of the growing list of Wild and Scenic Rivers.

The full trip (a distance of nearly one hundred miles) is from John Bryan State Park, near Clifton, in the west-central part of the state, down to Cincinnati, where the Little Miami joins the Ohio. Above Clifton, the headwaters meander through the flat farmlands of

Clark County. At Clifton, on the Greene County border, the river plunges into a steep, narrow gorge that extends for four miles, picturesque but not boatable. Put in at the John Bryan State Park, just west of Clifton, where the river takes on the character of a small mountain stream. Low water can expose too many rocks to make this section runnable in late summer. From Spring Valley to Waynesville the river valley is almost a mile wide, and although there are plenty of signs of civilization, a barrier of trees dominates the sides of the river.

The valley begins to constrict once more near the mouth of Caesar Creek. There is a canoe livery at Fort Ancient. Nearby Hills Creek forms a series of small waterfalls as it drops over the Ordovician limestone bedrock to meet the Little Miami. The river from Loveland to the Ohio is characterized by long, quiet pools separated by stretches of fast water.

LITTLE BEAVER

Wild and Scenic River

Time of year: *April to October*

Degree of difficulty: *novice to intermediate*

Craft: *canoe, kayak*

Character: *semiwild; pastoral*

Permit required: *For information write the Ohio Department of Natural Resources, Division of Natural Areas and Preserves, Fountain Square, Columbus, OH 43224.*

Rentals available: *yes*

The Little Beaver, on the eastern boundary of Ohio, runs into the Ohio River at Glasgow, just across the Pennsylvania line. Although it lies in the midst of one of the most industrialized areas of the country, and the valley was one of the first parts of the Ohio Territory to be settled, it contains some of the wildest and most scenic country in the state, according to a recent study made to determine how to preserve it. There are three forks: West, Middle, and North. Much of the Middle Fork runs through Beaver Creek State Park.

The Little Beaver is a pleasant and undemanding run of some forty miles through pastoral and semi-rugged country. In spring flood the North Fork can provide challenging water for canoeing.

The history of the valley is interesting. The eastern portion of the Northwest Territory became the state of Ohio in 1803. Virtually at its doorstep lay the Little Beaver Valley, a fair portion of it under water as a result of great beaver dams. Behind these, the silt of centuries had created a rich bottom land. By killing the beavers and destroying the dams, settlers gained for themselves pre-cleared and immensely rich fields. Almost overnight the area prospered. Later the river became part of a briefly used canal system that was put out of business by the railroad. Some of the stone locks still stand.

Put-ins are at Elkton on the Middle Fork, where the YMCA Camp road crosses the stream on the West Fork, and at the junction of Brush Run, about one mile south of Negley.

DELAWARE RIVER

Time of year: all year, depending on rainfall

Degree of difficulty: various

Craft: canoe, kayak, raft

Character: pastoral

Permit required: no

Rentals available: yes

The Delaware River has very little to do with the state of Delaware and almost everything to do with the state of canoeing in the metropolitan New York–Philadelphia

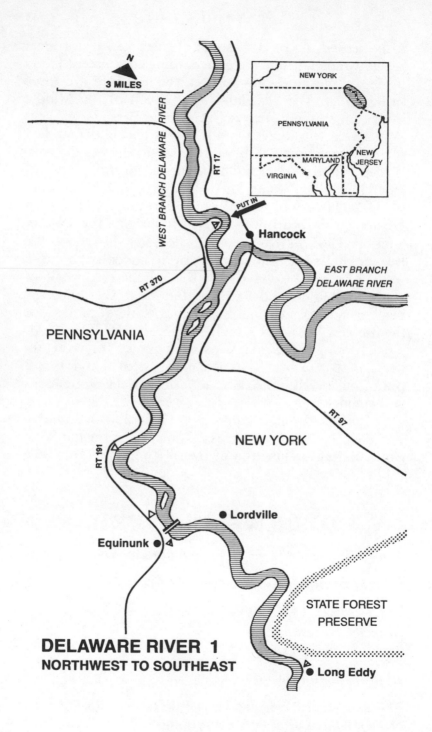

N

3 MILES

NEW YORK

PENNSYLVANIA

MARYLAND

NEW JERSEY

VIRGINIA

RT 17

WEST BRANCH DELAWARE RIVER

PUT IN

● **Hancock**

EAST BRANCH DELAWARE RIVER

RT 370

PENNSYLVANIA

RT 97

NEW YORK

RT 191

● **Lordville**

Equinunk ●

STATE FOREST
PRESERVE

DELAWARE RIVER 1
NORTHWEST TO SOUTHEAST

● **Long Eddy**

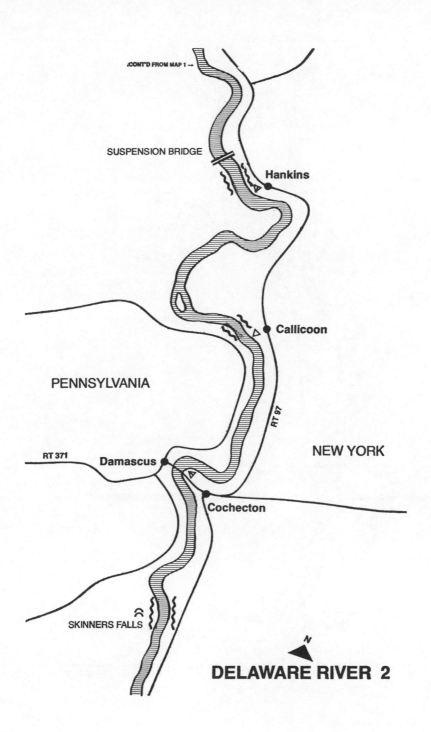

CONT'D FROM MAP 1 →

SUSPENSION BRIDGE

Hankins

Callicoon

PENNSYLVANIA

RT 97

RT 371

Damascus

NEW YORK

Cochecton

SKINNERS FALLS

N

DELAWARE RIVER 2

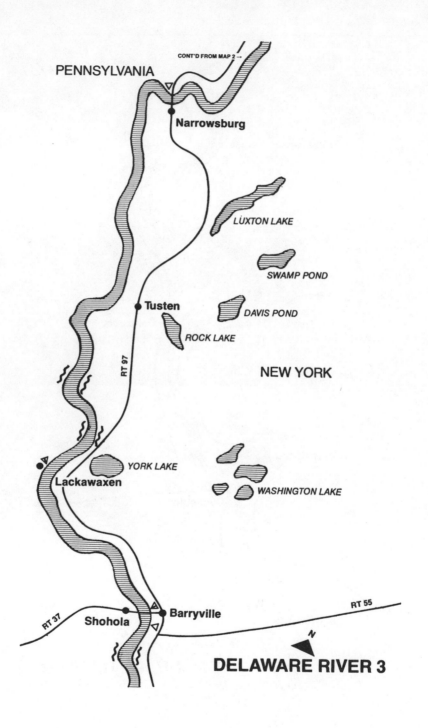

CONT'D FROM MAP 2 →

PENNSYLVANIA

Narrowsburg

LUXTON LAKE

SWAMP POND

Tusten

DAVIS POND

ROCK LAKE

RT 97

NEW YORK

YORK LAKE

Lackawaxen

WASHINGTON LAKE

RT 55

RT 37

Shohola

Barryville

N

DELAWARE RIVER 3

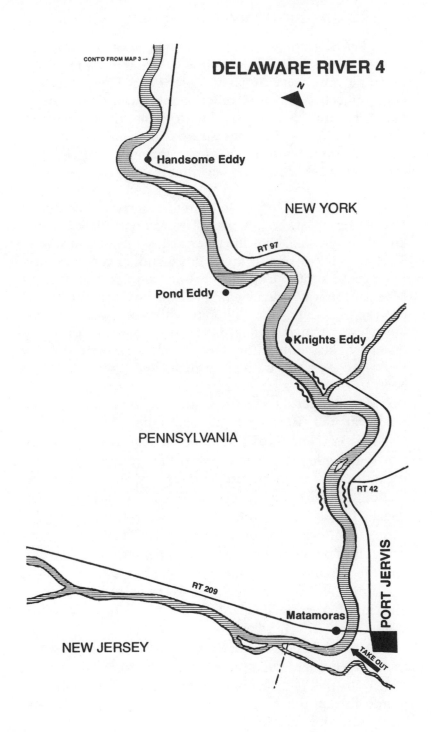

axis. The river begins at the confluence of its east and west branches in Hancock, New York, about a hundred ten mile northwest of New York City. From there it runs some two hundred miles along the eastern boundary of Pennsylvania. At Trenton the river becomes tidal—not tidy—and loses all appeal. You can, just to prove a point, continue on down through Philadelphia into Delaware Bay and eventually to the Atlantic Ocean.

But it is the Upper Delaware, from Hancock down to Port Jervis, at the juncture of New York, New Jersey, and Pennsylvania, that the river is at its most charming. This trip takes about three days and covers seventy miles, with a total drop of four hundred and eighty feet. Most of the way is easy going, fit for novices. But there are rapids. Some, like Skinners Falls, are well able to upset even expert canoeists. Rafters and paddlers in decked boats should have no trouble anywhere on the Delaware—except in high water—and then anything goes.

The Upper Delaware is one of the most scenic rivers in the East, carving its valley between the Catskills of New York, the Poconos of Pennsylvania, and the highlands of New Jersey. There are too many rocks for power boats, and many parts of the northern section are virtually inaccessible except by canoe or kayak. It may not be total wilderness, but it is the best you can find within a few hours of New York City.

The flow of water varies with season and rainfall, and the best time for white water is after winter's melting snows and the spring rains. But the river is navigable in all seasons, if one does not mind an occasional short portage during late summer dry spells.

There is access at nearly every town along the way, so the Delaware will accommodate almost any length trip. With this fact in mind, there are two basic philosophies for approaching the river. One, just get in a car some Saturday morning (we are talking now to people who live in the New York metropolitan area—all God-knows-how-many-million of you) and go. The chances are good that you will find a canoe livery near most towns along the river, and that some sort of shuttle can be arranged. Just bring money.

The second strategy is to plan the trip. In that case the first thing to do is to write for a detailed set of maps and explanatory information published by the Delaware River Commission, P.O. Box 7360, West Trenton, NJ 08628. The kit, called *The Delaware . . . and Outdoor Recreation,* costs two dollars. It contains all the information you could possibly want, and then some.

If you own a canoe, a good suggestion for boating the Delaware, made by someone who has done it often, is to run the river with parties of at least four people, two canoes and two cars. With trips of seventeen to twenty miles a day, it then becomes a simple matter to make your shuttles each morning and evening. In the evening you pick up the car you left behind that morning and the following morning you take a car ahead to the next stopping point. At the end of the trip you have only a short drive back to pick up your last car. You will usually find no trouble locating a parking lot, though probably a small fee will be levied. You can either camp on the river or stay in one of many hostelries along the way, ranging from ordinary motels to some of the region's finest inns. These are particularly prevalent in the area above New Hope.

One of the river's most interesting inns is Zane Grey Inn, at Lackawaxen. Once the home of the novelist and famed sports fisherman, it overlooks the river and contains his memorabilia. Make reservations well in advance.

There are numerous outfitters and hotels that provide canoes or Delaware float trips. For a partial list write to the Sullivan County Publicity and Development Commission, County Office Building, Monticello, NY 12701.

YOUGHIOGHENY RIVER

Time of year: May to October

Degree of difficulty: intermediate to expert

Craft: canoe, kayak, raft

Character: wild

Permit required: no

Rentals available: yes

About the Youghiogheny there is good news and bad news, and it can be summed up in one sentence: the Youghiogheny is the most popular floating river in the East for inflatable craft. Kayakers love it, too. The Youghiogheny (pronounced *yok-a-GAY-nee,* or simply *yok,* as in "Don't knock the Yough") is full-bodied white water, dam-controlled, and therefore seasonally relatively constant. It is runnable all summer and into the fall, which accounts in part for its enormous popularity. It is a sporty river, good for day-long runs full of thrills and spills. It is not a river for contemplative camping.

At its most difficult, the Youghiogheny pours over ledges and between huge boulders, dropping one hundred feet in a single mile. This series of rapids—Entrance, Cucumber, Railroad—is collectively known as the Loop because the river turns back on itself in a giant horseshoe. It is a section that, according to legend, stopped George Washington when he canoed the river more than two hundred years ago.

You will find the "Yough" in southern Pennsylvania's Fayette County, abutting the West Virginia and Maryland state lines. As if its challenge to the boat handler were not enough, the setting is wildly beautiful, should anyone have a moment to take a look. A seasoned river runner, Verne Huser, has described the great gorge of the Youghiogheny as the most verdant he has ever run, "decorated with flowering dogwood,

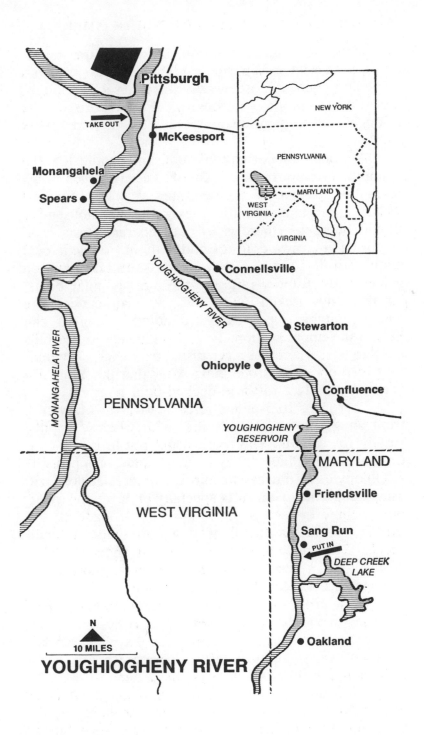

YOUGHIOGHENY RIVER

rhododendron, azalea, mountain laurel and trailing ar-
butus, with wild sassaparilla and New Jersey tea, wild
grape and cherry, gooseberries, witch hazel and mountain sumac, and alas, poison ivy." Few reports on the
"Yough" fail to mention poison ivy, so be particularly
cautious.

Although a reported nine thousand people float the
Ohiopyle-to-Stewarton stretch of the river each week
during the height of the summer season (July and
August, four thousand on weekends, one thousand a
day in between), there is to date no regulation. You
can bring your own craft, or find without trouble a local
outfitter well equipped to rent rafts or take you on
guided trips. Rubber rafts are the most popular boats;
kayaks, and decked one- and two-man canoes are
equally suitable. Open canoes paddled by experts can
handle the upper section, from Confluence to the falls
at Ohiopyle, where the river disappears over a magnificent forty-foot sandstone cliff. After that the Youghiogheny is strictly a raft-and-decked-boat river.

There is a 10.5-mile stretch of river in Maryland,
from Sang Run to Friendsville, with Class V rapids,
strictly for experts. The more usual put-in is either at
Confluence or Ohiopyle, in Pennsylvania. It is possible
at Ohiopyle for novices to join a commercial float trip
using neoprene/nylon rafts specially built for this river.
Four people in each boat, equipped with paddles, are
led like so many ducklings down the most difficult
rapids. The guide boat goes first to show the way
through rocks and rips, and, amazingly, most boats
manage successfully to follow the leader.

These professional boatmen are the most conscien-
tious of shepherds, ready instantly to come to the aid
of anyone in trouble. There is also a kayak in attend-
ance with each flotilla of rafts. There are bound to be
spills, but care like this defuses the danger.

A day on the "Yough" not only makes the nucleus
of a perfect outdoor weekend, it is an excellent way for
easterners to get a taste of tough white water while at
the same time paddling their own boats. This sort of

thing builds confidence, a very valuable commodity on rivers. An outfitter to write is Douglas Ettinger, Canoe, Kayak & Sailing Craft, 701 Wood Street, Wilkinsburg, PA 15221.

A note of caution if you are setting out by yourself. The run from Confluence to Ohiopyle is 11.5 miles through extremely rugged country, with no access between the two points. If you lose your raft, the walk out is no joke. So do not try this one alone. Follow the general rafting rule for big, strong rivers: two boats are an absolute minimum.

The run from Ohiopyle to Stewarton is just 6.5 miles. This is the roughest stretch that the Yough has to offer. No matter how good you are, you had better first scout the rapids.

From Stewarton to South Connellsville, 11.1 miles, the first rapid is the worst. The rest flows pretty smoothly, with excellent scenery along the way. Take out on the left bank at a waterworks about a quarter of a mile past a footbridge and about one hundred yards above the dam.

RAQUETTE RIVER

Time of year: *May to October*

Degree of difficulty: *various*

Craft: *canoe*

Character: *semiwild*

Permit required: *no*

Rentals available: *yes*

To taste the pleasures of canoe-touring through that sodden semiwilderness in upstate New York known as the Adirondacks, an excellent beginning is to spend a week or two on its rivers and satellite lakes. A most popular candidate is the Raquette. The possible combinations and permutations of trips in this heartland of sport canoeing is nearly endless.

RAQUETTE RIVER

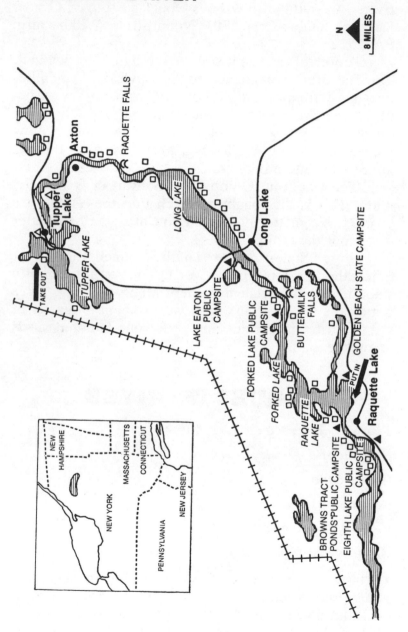

N
8 MILES

Axton
RAQUETTE FALLS
LONG LAKE
Long Lake
Tupper Lake
TUPPER LAKE
TAKE OUT
LAKE EATON PUBLIC CAMPSITE
FORKED LAKE PUBLIC CAMPSITE
FORKED LAKE
BUTTERMILK FALLS
GOLDEN BEACH STATE CAMPSITE
PUT IN
Raquette Lake
RAQUETTE LAKE
BROWNS TRACT PONDS PUBLIC CAMPSITE
EIGHTH LAKE PUBLIC CAMPSITE

NEW HAMPSHIRE
MASSACHUSETTS
CONNECTICUT
NEW YORK
NEW JERSEY
PENNSYLVANIA

The Raquette belongs to the Adirondacks' north-west watershed. It rises in a chain of lakes and ponds and flows for many miles across a flat, gently sloping plateau before tumbling over the rim into the St. Lawrence Valley.

Long before the Raquette became a vacation high-way, with too many private cabins along its banks and too much posted land, it was a major artery of travel between the St. Lawrence and the Hudson valleys. Much of the pleasure of a trip on the Raquette today is knowing its history. Take with you, or read beforehand, Charles W. Bryan, Jr.'s *The Raquette: River of the Forest* (1964). Some of the highlights you will find there are a description of the pioneer settlement at Long Lake; the invasion of the lumbermen; the feud on Eagle Lake between the dime novelist Ned Buntline and woodsman Alvah Dunning; the first luxury camps at Raquette headwaters; the tourist hotels; steamboat days.

You can also read about George Washington Sears's three summer cruises during the late nineteenth century in canoes he commissioned from Henry Rushton. Sears, who wrote about his trips in *Forest and Stream* under the pen name "Nussmuk," was a diminutive chap weighing only 105 pounds dripping wet—a not uncommon condition in the Adirondacks. Because of the many carries the terrain demanded, he needed as light a craft as could be made. On his third attempt Rushton came up with a ten-foot canoe made of white pine that weighed just 10.5 lbs. It now resides with a dozen or so other Rushton canoes in the Adirondack Museum, near Blue Mountain Lake, where the Raquette rises. It needs to be seen to be believed, which is another reason to start an Adirondack trip with the Raquette.

Canoes can be rented and provisions obtained along the way. Lodging is available but scarce in the forty-one-mile stretch between Long Lake Village and Tupper Lake. If you bring your own camping gear, you are free from this worry—but you will have a harder time on the carries. State-owned lean-tos are available along the route, though there never seem to be enough of them for the peak traffic of July and August, so it is wise to take a tent or tarpaulin.

Preparation for any boating expedition in this part of the world should include buying a copy of *Adirondack Canoe Waters Guide, North Flow,* written with enormous attention to detail and an obvious love of the region by Paul Jamieson. You can get the book by writing to the Adirondack Mountain Club Headquarters, 72 Ridge Street, Glen Falls, NY 12801, or you will find it in most eastern camping and sporting-goods stores.

In the section on the Raquette, Jamieson takes his readers step by step from the headwaters at Blue Mountain Lake down through Raquette Lake to Outlet Bay and the official beginning of the river. He comments on such matters as the origin of the name—*raquette* means "snowshoe" in Canadian French—and provides a thorough geological explanation for the lie of the land.

For the next twenty or so miles below Outlet Bay, the run is mostly through long narrow lakes. The Raquette is flowing down there somewhere under your keel, but you will not get much help from the current. Wind is the thing to consider here, and if it is blowing out of the southwest, as it most commonly does, you will get a welcome boost. Between Forked Lake and Long Lake the river drops abruptly through rocks and rapids. You may want to miss this part. It is possible with a few inquiries at Blue Mountain Lake to arrange for a truck to meet and transport your canoe and duffle down to Deerland, where you pick up Long Lake. Those who keep to the river will, in any case, have three carries.

Long Lake, according to Jamieson, "is really just a widening of the river in a fault basin probably enlarged by glacial action. The average width is about half a mile and the length is fourteen miles."

There is splendid scenery along this way, particularly on a still September day when the water of the lake reflects the blazing fall color. But there are many bordering permanent camps as well, to remind you that this has been a favorite vacation area for at least a century and a half.

It was the sons of early settlers on Long Lake who developed the concept and craft to build the Adirondack guide boats and then took the nabobs from New York and Boston fishing in them.

Beyond Long Lake, the Raquette becomes a languid stream, meandering over a wide, silent valley floor —until the river pitches eighty feet in a single mile, part of the drop over Raquette Falls. This calls for a mile-and-a-half carry, the most taxing of the trip.

At Axton it is possible to connect with the Saranac lake and river system by walking 1.3 miles over Indian Carry, a natural crossroads predating Columbus. If you stick with the Raquette, however, you will reach Tupper Lake. Be careful on this run, as the meandering channel is not always obvious. Tupper ends the lake section of the Raquette; from there on down to Carry Falls Reservoir, some fifty miles, the Raquette takes on the aspect of a more conventional North Woods stream. There are numerous carries—mostly around man-made obstructions. Much of the land is posted, and camping is limited. But it is quite possible to make the run, paying careful attention to the AMC guide directions. In midsummer, when the Adirondack lake regions are crowded, this section of the Raquette is the least crowded.

THE SOUTH

A strong feeling for moving water is characteristic among southerners. It is hardly by chance that timeless songs like "Ol' Man River" and "Swannee" speak of southern rivers or that the greatest writer the South produced, Mark Twain, should have taken his pen name and perhaps his inspiration as well from the great Mississippi.

Steamboat days of waiting on the levee are long gone, but the affinity southerners feel for their many and varied streams holds fast as ever. "Varied" is the operative word to describe southern rivers. Without splitting hairs too finely, three categories present themselves. There are, first of all, the rushing white-water roller coasters like the New River, the Gauley, and the Chattooga that come slashing out of the Blue Ridge Mountains of North Carolina and West Virginia to provide some of the most thrilling rides this side of sledding the north face of the Matterhorn.

Then there are the hidden and mysterious waters of the Okefenokee Swamp, in southern Georgia, and the moss-draped passage of the Suwannee River, which gathers its water from it to flow through Florida two hundred miles to the Gulf of Mexico. This is country of a thousand times a thousand backwaters and beckoning runs, through floating fields of water hyacinth and lily pads, leading the adventurous boater farther and farther into a wild maze. Here live tropical flora and fauna quite unlike anything to be found under your keel anywhere else on the North American continent.

Between these two extremes lie the easy meandering streams meant for float-fishing and camping. Forty years ago, during the Great Depression, many a Southern gent would leave cares and family behind and go off with a few "good old boys" for a week or two on one or another of the beautifully placid streams like the Eleven Point, the Buffalo, or the Big Piney that wind through the lush green limestone hills of the Ozarks. The water in these streams runs clear and cool, and the chiggers and mosquitoes won't get you if you camp out on the gravel bars. For as little as five dollars, back then, a man could actually buy an oak-planked scow, the so-called johnboat, and just abandon it at the bottom of the run when he was through. Days were spent floating and fishing for bass and catfish, cooked each night over a driftwood fire, like as not, a bottle of bootlegged white lightning to wash it down. And there are plenty who do it still—except that the johnboat, though not extinct, has largely been replaced by the canoe, and families are now more common on the streams than fraternal groups with stubbled beards and galluses.

Time marches on, and with it come certain perversions. On these same Ozark rivers today, alas, are also to be found businessmen and their clients, complete with outboard-powered commissary boats that precede them to camp each evening. By the time the big-bellied fishermen step ashore, cots and tables are already in place, a wood fire is burning and bacon fat spitting in an oversized frying pan, ready for the day's catch. Well, it beats conventions in a suburban supermotel.

The rivers listed in this section have been chosen as representative of each of the three categories of southern streams described above. To augment the information given here, you may want to write to the state capital of your choice. Most states have prepared booklets on float trips and canoe trails, and they will send them to you free of charge. Missouri alone, for instance, has catalogued hundreds of miles of swift white-water and spring-fed streams for year-round boating. A book of particular interest is *Wild Water: West Virginia,* by Bob Burrell and Paul Davidson, a lively and exhaustive account of the runnable rivers of that state—mile by mile and rapid by rapid—available in most southern sporting-goods stores or large bookstores.

Except for Florida and along the Gulf Coast, the best time of year for river running in the South is early summer. Most streams, however, can be run all year long. Florida waters are best tackled in winter, when the temperature and humidity are bearable.

NEW RIVER

South Fork: Wild and Scenic River

Time of year: *June to October*

Degree of difficulty: *various*

Craft: *canoe, kayak, raft*

Character: *wild; semiwild*

Permit required: *For information write Stone Mountain State Park, Star Route 1, P.O. Box 17, Roaring Gap, NC 28668.*

Rentals available: *yes*

There is nothing new about the New River. Along with the Ohio, Missouri, and Mississippi, it belongs to the oldest known river system in North America. Metamorphic rock visible along its banks dates back more than a billion years. The New has had time to cut its way into the very foundation stones of the continent itself, all of which provides food for reverie during the quieter passages down this southern stream but is quickly forgotten in the gut-wrenching rapids that make the New the most exciting big white water east of the Mississippi.

The New rises in the Blue Ridge Mountains of North Carolina. It marches north across Virginia into West Virginia, where it flows through a spectacular gorge before meeting the Gauley River at Gauley Bridge. The Gauley and the New join waters to make the Kanawha. It is on this last sixty-six-mile section, from Bluestone Dam down to Gauley Bridge, that the river makes its reputation. Here it has carved a magnificent gorge, inevitably called the "Grand Canyon of the East," which has effectively held civilization at arm's length. Rafting is thrilling, canoeing and kayaking for experts only. The stretch between Thurmond and Fayette Station is a fabulous piece of white water that boasts the heaviest flow in the East. The rapids, which bear names like Surprise, Railroad, The Keeney Brothers (triplets—Upper, Middle, and Lower), Double Z, and Greyhound Bus Stopper are full of stoppers, souse holes and drops (called falls in this part of America).

The top of the gorge, from Prince to Thurmond, can be handled by intermediate rafters. From Thurmond down to Fayette Station Bridge, you had better be good. For easterners who would like to experience the thrill of rafting on big water the first time out, Jon Dragan (P.O. Box 55, Thurmond, WV 25936) runs commercial float trips on the New from May through October. On these excursions each passenger wields a paddle. Lined up like galley slaves on either side of an eighteen-foot raft, under the command of an experienced guide, they pull as if their lives depended on it— which, in fact, they do. The run is thirty miles and takes two days. The cost, as of this writing, is in the neighborhood of eighty dollars, including a tent to sleep in at night. You will know for sure after two days on the New whether white-water rafting is for you.

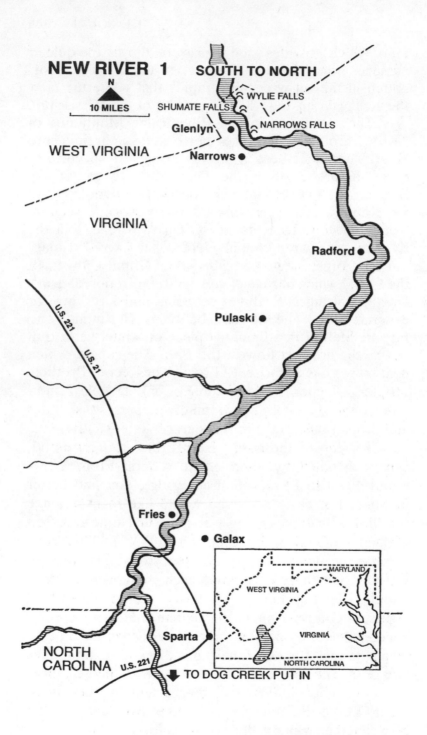

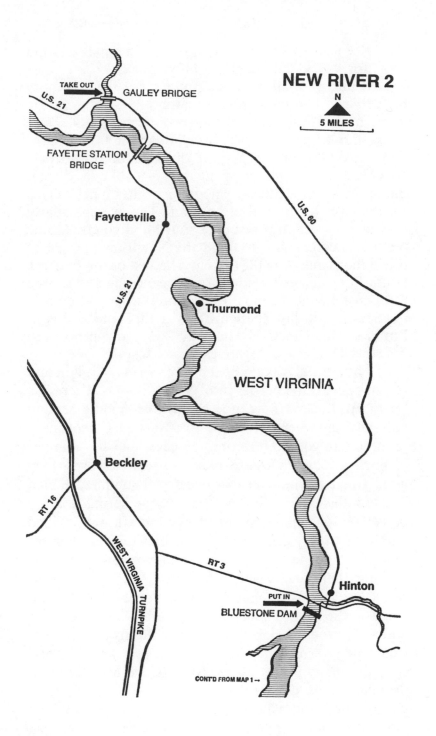

NEW RIVER 2

N

5 MILES

TAKE OUT

U.S. 21

GAULEY BRIDGE

FAYETTE STATION
BRIDGE

Fayetteville

U.S. 21

U.S. 60

Thurmond

WEST VIRGINIA

Beckley

RT 16

WEST VIRGINIA TURNPIKE

RT 3

Hinton

PUT IN

BLUESTONE DAM

CONT'D FROM MAP 1 →

Needless to say, this section of river makes good sport for kayaks and decked canoes.

If this were all, it would suffice; but there is more to the New than the gorge. Recently, 26.5 miles of the river, more specifically twenty-two miles of its South Fork, and 4.5 miles of the trunk stream in North Carolina, have been named as part of the Wild and Scenic Rivers system. This segment behaves like a typical mountain stream. It is not uncommon after a heavy rain for the river to rise a foot an hour. The average yearly flow on this section is just over four hundred cfs. (cubic feet per second). But in flood the New runs upward of thirty thousand. Stay off it then. The rest of the time the South Fork makes for comfortable canoeing and rafting through some of the most rugged and unspoiled land in the South, with just enough Class II rapids to add zest. Put in at Dog Creek off Highway 221 and run north to the state line.

The central section of the river spans Virginia and reaches across the border into West Virginia. There is a lot of river here. To canoe the whole middle section may take anywhere from one to two weeks, depending on how fast you go, the time of year, and the number of portages you choose to make—in other words, how good you are. The river can be run all summer, though it gets rather low in dry weather. In the spring it is too powerful for anything but decked craft and skilled paddlers. In any case, there are a half dozen big dams that must be portaged. Some make grueling carries. Rafting, therefore, is generally restricted to shorter runs between dams. What makes this part of the New worthwhile is the rugged mountain scenery. Towering cliffs and steep wooded slopes spring directly from the riverside. The river is wide and powerful, and when it flows over the many ledges of the Blue Ridge Mountains, it provides some challenging passages. The camping is good. Road and villages intrude along the way, but most of the river appears suitably remote.

ELEVEN POINT RIVER

Wild and Scenic River

Time of year: May to September

Degree of difficulty: novice to intermediate

Craft: canoe

Character: pastoral

Permit required: For information write Mark Twain National Forest, 401 Fairgrounds Road, Rolla, MO 65401.

Rentals available: yes

The Eleven Point, a charter member of the Wild and Scenic Rivers system, meanders purposefully through the picturesque Ozark hill country of southern Missouri. Its course is cut in the shadows of tall bluffs, beside gravel bars, through sloping forest valleys and flat pasturelands. River birch is abundant at the water's edge, and aged sycamores lean out to roof the river in a canopy of green. The water, gushing from many underground springs (this is limestone country) is crystal clear—so clear, in fact, that it is organically rather sterile and does not support a large fish population. Still, there is fishing for trout and bass and the possibility of seeing a large variety of wildlife, including foxes, raccoons, beavers, muskrats, turtles, banded water snakes, bobcats, coyotes, wild turkeys, blue herons, bobwhite quails, pileated woodpeckers, and kingfishers.

For all its wilderness setting, the first fifty miles of the Eleven Point, the portion protected by the federal government, lies within easy reach of five major metropolitan areas: Kansas City and St. Louis a day's drive to the north; Memphis about 150 miles southeastward; and on the south and west, Little Rock and Tulsa, respectively.

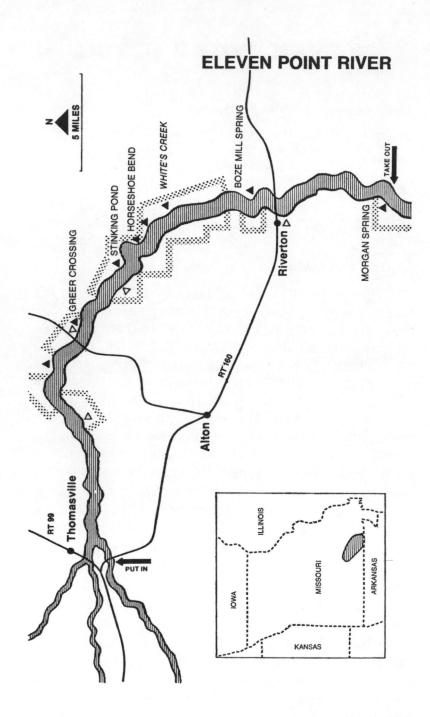

ELEVEN POINT RIVER

5 MILES
N

GREER CROSSING
STINKING POND
HORSESHOE BEND
WHITE'S CREEK
BOZE MILL SPRING
MORGAN SPRING
TAKE OUT

Riverton
RT 160
Alton
RT 99
Thomasville
PUT IN

IOWA
ILLINOIS
MISSOURI
ARKANSAS
KANSAS

When the river is in flood (sometime in April or early May), it can challenge rafters and paddlers in decked boats on a number of rapids above Greer Spring (the second largest spring in Missouri). The rest of the year, however, this is strictly a canoeing and camping river. The main season is from May to October. During the late summer and fall the water level is normally too low to boat above Greer Spring. The Forest Service Station (Eastern Region, Department of Agriculture, 633 West Wisconsin Avenue, Milwaukee, WI 53203), which administers the 631,000-acre Mark Twain National Forest, through which the river flows, will provide water-level information on request.

A number of national forest campgrounds lie within a few minutes' drive of the Eleven Point. Camping on the river itself is on gravel bars. A scenic zone— generally one-quarter of a mile wide—has been established on either side of the river to maintain as nearly as possible a sense of wilderness. By taking advantage of the great camping along the way, you can easily spend a week on this stretch of river. There are numerous take-outs, however, so that shorter trips can be arranged. Boat rentals are available at Thomasville.

BUFFALO RIVER

Time of year: April to October

Degree of difficulty: various

Craft: canoe, kayak

Character: semiwild; pastoral

Permit required: no

Rentals available: yes

The Buffalo, in northwestern Arkansas, is the Ozark river by which all others are judged, and the judgment is universally good. Some call the Buffalo the finest all-around family camping river in the country. The emphasis is on camping. There is so much to do and see

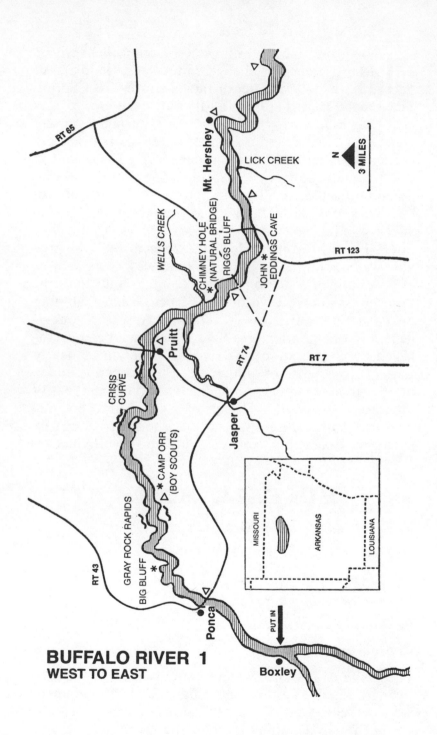

RT 65

N
3 MILES

LICK CREEK

WELLS CREEK

Mt. Hershey

CHIMNEY HOLE
(NATURAL BRIDGE)
RIGGS BLUFF

JOHN
EDDINGS CAVE

RT 123

Pruitt

RT 74

RT 7

CRISIS
CURVE

CAMP ORR
(BOY SCOUTS)

Jasper

MISSOURI
ARKANSAS
LOUISIANA

GRAY ROCK RAPIDS

BIG BLUFF

RT 43

Ponca

PUT IN

BUFFALO RIVER 1
WEST TO EAST

Boxley

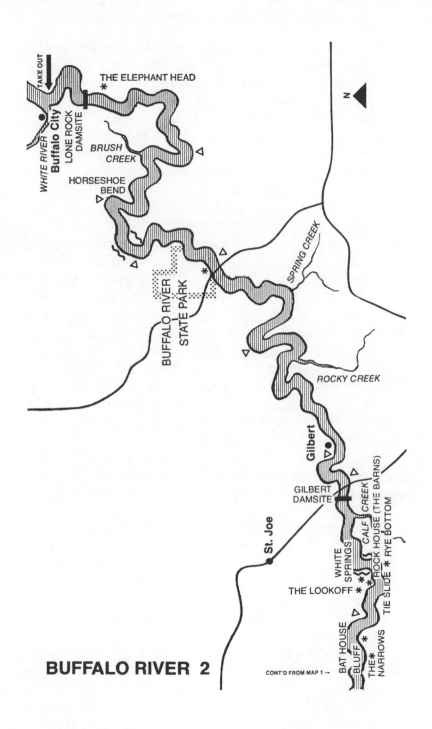

TAKE OUT

THE ELEPHANT HEAD
*

N

WHITE RIVER

Buffalo City

LONE ROCK
DAMSITE

BRUSH
CREEK

△

HORSESHOE
BEND

△

SPRING CREEK

△

*

BUFFALO RIVER
STATE PARK

△

△

ROCKY CREEK

△

Gilbert

●

△

GILBERT
DAMSITE

CALF CREEK

ROCK HOUSE (THE BARNS)

RYE BOTTOM

St. Joe

●

WHITE
SPRINGS

* *

THE LOOKOFF *

*

TIE SLIDE *

BAT HOUSE

△

*

BLUFF

THE *
NARROWS

BUFFALO RIVER 2

CONT'D FROM MAP 1 →

along the way that you should not plan on logging more than ten miles a day on the river. You may well travel that much more on foot on side trips. Or you may wish just to laze around the camp, fish, and swim in the deep emerald pools that lie under towering limestone cliffs.

In the spring there is good white water from Boxley to Pruitt—a challenge to kayakers and expert canoeists. The rest of the river runs fairly deep and riffle-free beneath towering limestone bluffs and wooded slopes. Opposite almost every bluff is a gravel bar that makes an ideal campsite, free of those southern camping pests, ticks, chiggers, and mosquitoes. It is, in fact, as though the river put them there just for campsites—washing them clean each spring and rearranging them slightly and stocking them with firewood for the campers to come. The problem of being caught by rising water when camping on a bar is slight. The bars drain readily in case of rain. The river may rise during the night if there are heavy rains upstream, but it will not come down on you like a wall, as sometimes happens on some western gorges. Just make sure you have an escape route back to the riverbank. Don't camp on island bars.

The Buffalo is some one hundred fifty miles long, and one hundred thirty miles of it, from Boxley down to its confluence with the heavily boated White River, is navigable in the spring. By early June, however, you will want to put in at Pruitt or below. This part of the Buffalo can be run year round. There are no portages. This is one river that seems to have beaten the threat of the United States Army Engineers to dam it.

There are some twenty access points, so almost any length trip—a day, a weekend, two weeks—is possible and rewarding.

The side trips you can make on foot are as extensive as your taste for exploration. The Buffalo is fed by numerous creeks and springs (this is limestone country and the land is full of surprises), streams flowing out of rocks or disappearing under them, caves, sinkholes, abandoned mines, ghost towns, Civil War sites, back-woods towns, wildlife. In spring, when the river is at its best, the blossoms of the redbud tree, rhododendron, azalea, and laurel turn the forest ablaze with rosy color. Waterfalls grace the region all year long.

The open canoe is the proper craft for the Buffalo. There is too much slack water for rafting; though, as noted, the spring floods turn the upper stream into a genuine white-water challenge for kayakers and paddlers in decked canoes. Beginners can handle the rest of the river with ease.

Though the Buffalo is now controlled, and during the spring and early summer is fairly heavily traveled, registration is not yet required, as it is on some western rivers.

Rentals are available in Pruitt, AR 72671 (see Bill Houston) and in Ponca, AR 72670 (Harold Hedges), where you can also park your car or arrange for someone to drive it to your take-out point. More detailed data and maps for the Buffalo are available for one dollar by writing to the Ozark Society, P.O. Box 2914, Little Rock, AR 72203.

The water is not potable from the river, but there are springs on the tributary creeks. Bring water containers, in any case. Fishing for smallmouth bass, perch, and catfish is excellent.

Just to confuse matters, there is another Buffalo River, to the east, in Tennessee, which, though not so remote as this Ozark stream, offers much the same attractions. So if you get on the wrong river, it doesn't really matter very much.

SUWANNEE RIVER

Time of year: *all year*

Degree of difficulty: *various*

Craft: *canoe, kayak, raft*

Character: *semiwild*

Permit required: *no*

Rentals available: *yes*

The government report proposing the inclusion of the Suwannee River in southern Georgia and northern Florida in the National Wild and Scenic Rivers system describes it well:

> The Suwannee River first appears as dark water intermingled with marsh vegetation in Sapling Prairie, deep in the great Okefenokee Swamp. Here at its source, 265 miles upstream from the Gulf of Mexico, it begins as a network of slender threads of open water flowing south to Billy's Lake. Then it moves beneath towering cypress and tupelo gum to the southwest edge of the swamp where it escapes from the wilderness into a well-defined river channel. Once free of the great swamp, the Suwannee River meanders through a broad flood plain densely wooded with bottom land hardwoods.
>
> A few miles south of the Georgia-Florida line, the channel deepens, the banks become higher and steeper, and occasional outcrops of limestone appear. At river mile 177, the river surges over big shoals on the limestone floor of the basin.
>
> Downstream, changes in the river are more pronounced. The flow of the river is nourished by clear, cool waters discharged from numerous

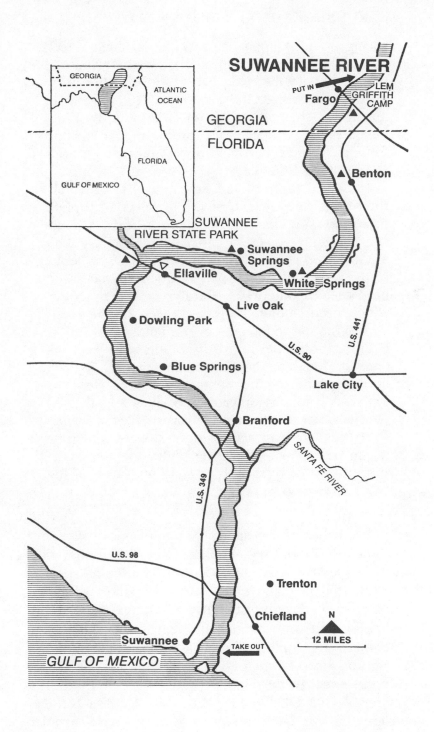

springs. The Alapaha and Withlacoochee rivers, two of the Suwannee's three major tributaries, add their waters to the river. Entering the upper coastal plain province, the Suwannee River flows in an eroded channel walled on either side by limestone bluffs, draped with pines and hardwood foliage. Springs become more numerous downstream from Ellaville.

Near Branford, the Suwannee River enters the broad, flat lowland of the lower coastal plain province. The channel broadens to form a wide, sluggish body of water—more like an estuary than a young and active coastal stream. The low banks of the river are bordered by frequent marshes and hardwood hammocks. Stately cabbage palms, which occur along the lower reach of the river, add to the natural beauty of the landscape. Below Branford, 66 miles above its rendezvous with the Gulf of Mexico, the Suwannee receives its last major tributary—the Santa Fe River. Near its journey's end, the Suwannee divides and distributes its water into the gulf by way of West Pass and East Pass and a myriad of tidal sloughs and runs which irrigate and drain the delta marshes. Offshore from the river and the shallow waters of the Gulf of Mexico.

The entire river is navigable by kayak or canoe, but too sluggish for rafting—not surprising when one is reminded that the average elevation of Florida is only one hundred feet above sea level. The most dramatic and rewarding section of the river comes right at the beginning, in the mysterious and legendary Okefenokee Swamp, a half-million-acre wilderness that supports vegetation and wildlife found nowhere else in the world. Administered by the United States Fish and Wildlife Service as the Okefenokee National Wildlife Refuge, the great swamp is fast reverting to the primeval wonder it was before loggers devastated huge sections of it. Under the massed canopy of cypress, maple, tupelo, and bay lives a wealth of birdlife, including the rare wood ibis, various egrets and other wading birds. Four-footed animals that frequent the area are deer, bears, and raccoons. Alligators also abound, and are harmless unless stepped upon. The snake population is high, but they will slither or swim from you, given half a chance.

For years the fragility of the Okefenokee eco-system prompted the Fish and Wildlife Service to ban overnight camping in the swamp. That policy has changed. Now certain water trails with designated camp-sites are available, but on a strictly limited basis. These camps are usually on platforms raised above the level of the swamp. For information and reservations write to the Okefenokee National Wildlife Refuge, P.O. Box 117, Waycross, GA 31501.

If you do camp in this intriguing wetland, there are a few essentials that may not be part of your usual river-running kit. Take a reliable compass. For all its beauty, the swamp is a miserable place to be lost in. Mosquito netting is a must any time of year, and you will want a portable stove. A jungle hammock is a good idea, particularly for camping farther down the river. Camp Cornelia has canoe rentals. For other liveries in the area, consult the wildlife service.

Downriver there are two shoals to watch out for during time of low water—White Springs and, below it, Blue Springs. It is best to scout the latter. You will want to pass it in any case on the southwest side, close to the bank.

Although the river can be run at any time of year, winter is best. Summer is too muggy, buggy, and hot.

The entire run down from swamp to gulf should take anywhere from two to three weeks. In all that, there is only a single portage—over the Suwannee River sill—constructed in 1960 to prevent excess drainage out of the swamp during times of drought.

CHATTOOGA RIVER

Wild and Scenic River

Time of year: *April to October*

Degree of difficulty: *novice to intermediate*

Craft: *canoe, kayak, raft*

Character: *wild*

Permit required: *For information write Chattahoochee National Forest, P.O. Box 1437, Gainesville, GA 30501.*

Rentals available: *yes*

The movie *Deliverance* has transformed a fierce twenty-two-mile section of the Chattooga River near Clayton, Georgia, from a popular white-water run into an idiot shoot. That is because most of the boating sequences for the picture were shot along its rock-ribbed course. Now, during the summer season, some fifteen hundred daredevils each week, many of whom have never set foot in the bottom of a canoe or raft, come from all over the country to prove their manhood on the Chattooga. During the three seasons after the movie was released (1972–1974), no fewer than eighteen people drowned on this short but challenging run. Nearly all those deaths could have been prevented, according to the United States Forest Service, which tries its best to regulate the river, if the victims had observed the most elementary safety precautions or recognized their own limitations. With a gradient many times greater than that of the Grand Canyon, and dozens of blistering falls and rapids, this part of the Chattooga is for experts only.

There is more to the river, however, than just the one taxing section of white water that the movie made famous. The Chattooga begins life on the crest of the

Blue Ridge Mountains in North Carolina and flows south for about fifty miles in a mostly primitive setting of national forest lands.

A seven-mile section along Georgia's border with South Carolina has been designated suitable for novices and beginners.

For more information, write for a brochure entitled *Canoeing the Chattooga,* U.S. Forest Service, Andrew Pickens Ranger District, Walhalla, SC 29691.

GAULEY RIVER

Time of year: April to October

Degree of difficulty: intermediate to expert

Craft: canoe, kayak, raft

Character: wild; semiwild

Permit required: no

Rentals available: yes

The Gauley is mecca for white-water thrill-seekers in West Virginia—and given the many choices there, that is saying a lot. The Gauley begins, tight and feisty, high up in the crags of Webster County. It drains a large watershed, however, and its many tributaries quickly turn it into a muscular brawler. The Three Sisters of the Monongahela National Forest called the Williams, Cranberry, and Cherry—all runnable rivers in the spring and early summer in their own right—join the Gauley in that order.

Along the border of the national forest there is a longish placid stretch, lovely to canoe though hardly worthy of the Gauley's fierce reputation. Below Summersville, however, the river makes its true character known with a vicious, unrelenting twenty-four-mile plunge to a place called Swiss, a dozen miles above its confluence with the New. This is the Gauley at its best —or worst, depending on how many years you have been running rivers. There must be a hundred named rapids—Lost Paddle, Five Boat Hole, Tumblehome, Pure Screaming Hell—between the dam and Swiss. This run is for experts only, and even they should go with someone who has had previous experience on the "Golley."

SOUTH FORK, CUMBERLAND RIVER

Time of year: April to July

Degree of difficulty: intermediate to expert

Craft: canoe, kayak

Character: semiwild

Permit required: no

Rentals available: yes

A wild, spectacular canyon on the Tennessee-Kentucky border roughly cradles the South Fork, Cumberland River. Float trips begin at New River or at Leatherwood Bridge and run down to Highway 92 in Kentucky. The entire trip can be made in three days. If one lingers to fish and explore—and the temptation for doing so is great—a week can easily slip by.

Over all, the upper section is the most demanding. There are several stout Class III rapids and one Class IV, at Jake's Hole. The longer, lower section from Leatherwood Bridge is rated only Class II, providing two falls are portaged. The put-in for the upper run is at the town of New River, on Highway 27.

You should have no trouble locating the many fine camping spots on this part of the Cumberland. A special attraction is the numerous Indian cliff dwellings underneath the canyon rims. To reach most of them, however, requires mountain-climbing gear. A powerful pair of binoculars makes a fair alternative.

EDISTO RIVER

Time of year: April to October

Degree of difficulty: novice to intermediate

Craft: canoe, kayak, johnboats

Character: pastoral

Permit required: no

Rentals available: no

The slow-moving Edisto River, in South Carolina, offers floaters a prime chance to view wildlife. Alligators, bobcats, otters, turkeys, white-tailed deer, and an uncountable number of bird species are among the river swamp's inhabitants. The Edisto is easily canoed, though the seemingly placid surface of its dark waters hides currents and snags that have brought swimmers to grief.

Camp along the river's many sandbars and high banks on the northernmost stretches of the river. Public and private campgrounds are available farther down.

Beginning on the North Branch at Orangeburg, South Carolina, there are sufficient access points so that the river can be run in a series of one-day excursions or several of those combined into longer floats. The craft to take are canoes, kayaks, or johnboats. Fishing is excellent for all freshwater species: largemouth bass, bream, crappie, catfish, and jackfish. Even shad and striped bass can be taken on the lower part during the spring months. But it is the rare redbreast sunfish for which the Edisto is most famous.

Because of the many roads in the area, the wilderness content of the Edisto is not high. On the other hand, roads mean easy access, and the flexibility of the runs is one of the strengths of this gentle, scenic river meant for contemplative canoeing, camping, and fishing.

SIPSEY RIVER

Time of year: April to October

Degree of difficulty: novice to intermediate

Craft: canoe, rowboat

Character: semiwild; pastoral

Permit required: no

Rentals available: no

A rewarding day can be had on the east fork of the Sipsey River, in northern Alabama. This shallow, narrow, slow-moving stream lends itself to float-fishing in canoes and johnboats, as it winds south through the hilly country of the William B. Bankhead National Forest. Here one moves through forests and under shoreline bluffs that rise a hundred feet and more. No motors are allowed on this part of the stream, and the peace and quiet of the place is hypnotic. A feeling of remoteness slips easily between you and the outside world. Yet access from the Sipsey River Picnic Area, about four miles west of Grayson, is simple. There is ample parking.

The take-out is at U.S. 278, making an eleven-mile run—just right for a day's outing. The fishing is excellent.

THE MIDWEST

THE river runner's Midwest divides nearly into two
halves: the rich northern crescent—Minnesota, Wisconsin, and Michigan—and the relatively impoverished
lowlands—Iowa, Missouri, Illinois, and Indiana. The
lowlands lack much in the way of boatable streams, but
the northern states more than compensate for that.
North or south, however, understand that this is primarily canoe water. Except during spring floods, there
is too much still water to make the offing of a raft practical, while white-water enthusiasts prefer decked canoes to kayaks. Camping is an important adjunct to
river running in the Midwest, and kayaks do not have
the carrying capacity of canoes.

Minnesota claims more fresh water than any other
state in the Union. True or not (who can tally all the
water in Alaska or even upper Maine?), its 1,900 miles
of trout streams, 13,100 miles of inland rivers, and
15,291 lakes make a good starting place. Minnesota
also abuts what must certainly be the richest canoeing
area in North America. The binational Boundary Waters Canoe Area combines the Superior National Forest
and Canada's Quetico Provincial Park, nearly half a
million acres of virgin forest, laced like well-marbled
beef with streams, ponds, and lakes. There is so much
water here that one may explore the region for years
without ever repeating a stroke. And much of it remains

virtually unchartered. For established routes, write for an excellent book called *Minnesota Voyageur Trails* (send $2 to Documents Section, 140 Centennial Building, St. Paul, MN 55101). Besides detailed directions about Minnesota's streams, you will find instruction on such matters as the need to carry Coast-Guard-approved life jackets for every member of your boating party.

Like Minnesota, Wisconsin recognizes canoeing as a sport and has established regular canoe routes outlined in *Wisconsin Water Trails* (write Department of Natural Resources, Madison, WI 53701). Michigan, sticking up like a mittened hand between Lakes Michigan and Huron, spawns interesting and, alas, heavily canoed rivers like the Au Sable, Pere Marquette, and the Manistee. There is enough varied canoeing here to last a lifetime, whether it is handling an open boat in tricky rapids or seeking after wilderness, solitude, and a mystic contact with the ghosts of voyageurs past. The best guidebook for the region is *Whitewater, Quietwater,* with excellent mile-by-mile maps of the wild rivers of Wisconsin, upper Michigan, and northeastern Minnesota. Bob and Jody Palzer are the authors, and it is published by Evergreen Paddleways, 1416—21st Street, Two Rivers, WI 54241 ($7.95).

The lower Midwest is flat land. The cold hand of the last glaciation has not lain so recently here as it has farther north. In consequence, the country is better drained—good for farming and settlement but poor for water sports. Much of the river mileage has been spoiled by pollution and the encroachment of cities and towns. What is left, however, affords some fine, if placid, canoeing.

Iowa publishes a booklet called *Iowa Canoe Trips,* in which you will find twelve runs described (write Iowa Conservation Commission, 300 Fourth Street, Des Moines, IA 50319). But if the topography is generally flat, there are compensations. This is largely limestone country, with towering bluffs, like those on the Upper Iowa, caves, clear water, and many springs. The fishing is grand. The trout of the north, which require colder water, are scarce, but bass and other riverine fish abound. Fishing licenses for each state are necessary.

There is an interesting distinction that Iowa makes between its rivers, which it lists as either meandered or nonmeandered rivers. Meandered rivers are state-owned. Nonmeandered rivers are the property of the abutters. These are usually farmers, and they are required by law to fence their streams to control livestock. So be careful, and do not take personally the spans of barbed wire you may have to duck under. Just remember you are on private land, and act accordingly. Ask permission to come ashore to camp or picnic. Usually it will be granted.

The rivers described here represent a cross section of midwestern streams.

SUGAR CREEK

Time of year: April to July

Degree of difficulty: novice

Craft: canoe

Character: semiwild; pastoral

Permit required: no

Rentals available: yes

There is both good and bad about Indiana's Sugar Creek. The good is that the westward-tending river that empties into the Wabash provides forty miles of some of the most pleasant canoeing in the Midwest. It is a fairly swift stream that winds between forested banks and under high limestone cliffs. There are no difficult rapids, a perfect stream for beginners. The bad is that there are an awful lot of people in western Indiana—beginners and seasoned canoeists alike—who are of a mind to sample the pleasures of Sugar Creek. To add to the weekend congestion, Sugar Creek is one of the few Indiana rivers with canoe rentals readily available.

Put in at Crawfordsville at Clements Canoe Rental, where Highway 136 crosses the river. There is a small fee for this, but it is worth it. If you rent a canoe, transportation will be provided from the take-out. The twenty-nine-mile trip to Turkey Run State Park is a two-day outing. The river is shallow and clear and averages some seventy-five feet in width; the bottom, sand and rock. Opportunities for camping are numerous.

AU SABLE RIVER

Time of year: May to October

Degree of difficulty: novice

Craft: canoe

Character: semiwild

Permit required: no

Rentals available: yes

The Au Sable River flows easterly through the Huron National Forest and empties into Lake Huron. The total run is 180 miles, but it is the top 75 miles of this famous trout stream that command the attention of canoeists and fishermen. Like all Michigan streams large enough to float a stick, the Au Sable was once a major conduit for logs. Today, people float down the river instead of logs. According to the Department of Natural Resources, the Au Sable is the most canoed river in Michigan, which makes it a top contender for the most canoed river in the entire country. Still, it promises wooded banks, enough campsites to accommodate the traffic, and, of course, excellent fishing.

The usual put-in is at Grayling, but many seasoned canoeists start twenty-five miles downstream, at Wakeley Bridge, to avoid the heavy traffic immediately below Grayling. Rentals are possible at both locations. The run from Wakeley Bridge down to Mio Dam is a three-to-five-day trip, depending on how hard you want to paddle and how much time you want to spend fishing. There are two quality trout areas that come under special fly-casting rules—8.7 miles from Burtons Landing down to Wakeley Bridge, and a 14.2 mile section in the Mio area.

THE UPPER MISSISSIPPI RIVER

Time of year: May to October

Degree of difficulty: novice

Craft: canoe

Character: semiwild

Permit required: no

Rentals available: yes

The Indians knew, and the voyageurs proved, that the Mississippi provided the canoe link between the Great Lakes and the Gulf of Mexico. But it was not until 1832 that Henry Schoolcraft actually pinpointed the source of the "Father of Waters," in north-central Minnesota. The point is Lake Itasca, and between it and Lake Bemidji wind eighty peaceful miles of river, through wilderness little changed from the days of the voyageurs. Settlement is sparse. There is only one portage (around Vekins Dam), and fishing and opportunities for observing wildlife are excellent. There are a number of developed campsites as well as fine possibilities for improvising. A road map of Minnesota should be all you need to find the major access points. But for a more detailed picture of the river write the Minnesota Department of Natural Resources, 658 Cedar Street, Centennial Building, St. Paul, MN 55155, for a brochure entitled *Mississippi Headwaters Canoe Routes*. For water level information on the Upper Mississippi—and in dry weather this can be a problem—write the Itasca State Park Forest Station, Lake Itasca, MN 56460.

Below Lake Bemidji the river maintains its wilderness quality for several hundred miles, describing a long arc to the town of Brainerd, 376 river miles, but only 70 air miles, from Lake Itasca. Below Brainerd, the Mississippi is a settled river.

PERE MARQUETTE RIVER

Time of year: May to October

Degree of difficulty: novice to intermediate

Craft: canoe, kayak

Character: semiwild

Permit required: no

Rentals available: yes

The Pere Marquette runs due west out of central Michigan into Lake Michigan. The river is a living example of the extraordinary recuperative power of nature. During the late 1800s down this stream during the spring flood each year came three and a half billion board-feet of lumber to feed the sawmills on the Michigan shore. Careless farming upriver further weakened the fabric of this great watershed. Yet today modern voyageurs are able to wonder at the "primitive and unspoiled beauty" of the Pere Marquette. With good reason, a sixty-six-mile stretch of the river as it appears in the full mantle of second-growth timber is under consideration for inclusion as one of our Wild and Scenic Rivers. An estimated nine thousand canoeists last year shared the Pere Marquette with wild turkey, river otter, and white-tailed deer.

From the put-in on Highway 37, south of Baldwin, the river winds through Manistee National Forest. This is not a loafing stream. There are many sharp turns, overhangs, and logjams. The rapids, however, are not above Class II, and most of them are just Class I. The longest is Rainbow Rapids, about an hour by car past Baldwin Bridge. Novices should portage this one, on the south side. Camping spots are numerous. Trout fishing is surprisingly strong this far south.

One can spend a weekend or a full week on the trip down to Lake Pere Marquette, adjoining Lake Michigan, where the development of the city of Ludington begins and the pleasure of canoeing ends. Canoes and supplies are available at Baldwin, Branch, Custer, Scottville.

THE UPPER IOWA RIVER

Time of year: April to July

Degree of difficulty: novice to intermediate

Craft: canoe, raft (only in spring)

Character: pastoral

Permit required: yes

Rentals available: yes

The Upper Iowa begins life, if not as an ugly duckling, at least as a very plain stream. It rises on the prairies of southwestern Minnesota, where it meanders unspectacularly through flat farmland. In the limestone hills of Iowa it becomes a swan. A tame swan, to be sure, but as beautiful a river as there is in the Midwest.

This is a stream for contemplative canoeing. Rafting is possible, but, except in the spring, the current is not swift enough to make inflatable craft much fun. During times of low water, from July on, at the head of the river you will have to drag from time to time over bars and riffles. Of course, rafts are useful as fishing platforms, and fishing is one of the particular strengths of the Upper Iowa.

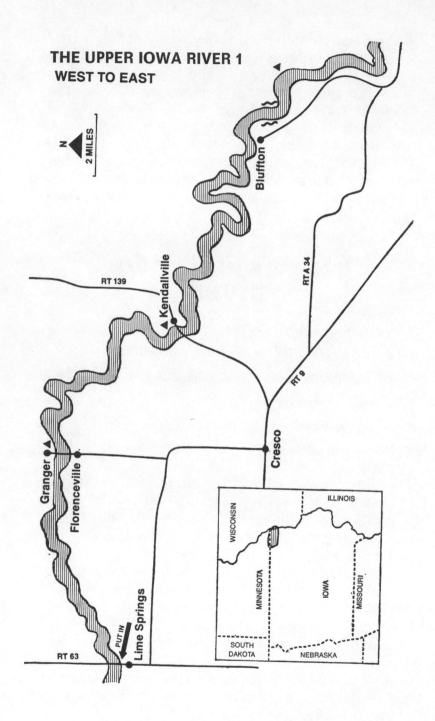

THE UPPER IOWA RIVER 1
WEST TO EAST

N
2 MILES

Bluffton

RT 139

Kendallville

RT A 34

RT 9

Granger

Florenceville

Cresco

PUT IN

Lime Springs

RT 63

WISCONSIN
ILLINOIS
MINNESOTA
IOWA
MISSOURI
SOUTH DAKOTA
NEBRASKA

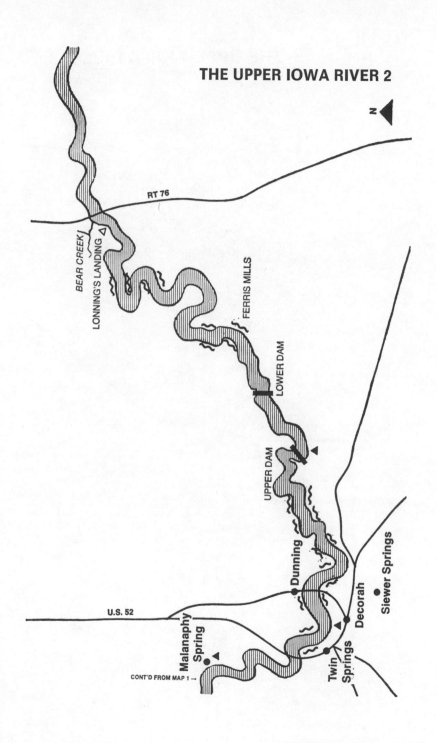

THE UPPER IOWA RIVER 2

N

RT 76

BEAR CREEK

LONNING'S LANDING

FERRIS MILLS

LOWER DAM

UPPER DAM

Dunning

Siewer Springs

Decorah

U.S. 52

Malanaphy Spring

Twin Springs

CONT'D FROM MAP 1 →

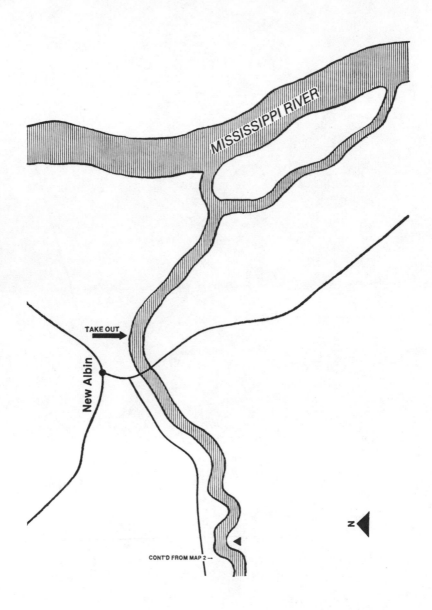

MISSISSIPPI RIVER

TAKE OUT

New Albin

CONT'D FROM MAP 2 →

N

Although its wilderness quotient is not high, this river is under consideration by the Interior Department for inclusion under the Wild and Scenic Rivers Act. Scenic it is! The beauty of the Upper Iowa is uncontested, while its watershed contains no major urban centers, little industry, and no superhighways. Agriculture is the principal land use and the mainstay of the economy in this part of Iowa. Population pressure is low, the water is clear, the fishing excellent. Entry and exit points are convenient. Trips of one day, a weekend, or longer are all possible on the Upper Iowa. The trip from Kendallville to Decorah is the most popular run. But some prefer to spend a weekend on the twenty-four-mile stretch above Kendallville. Though the scenery here is mostly flat prairie, fed by numerous springs and spring-fed tributaries, the fishing for smallmouth bass is at its best.

The put-in for the upper section of the Upper Iowa is one mile north of Lime Springs on a rocky point below the bridge on the right bank. About half way to Kendallville, the river passes between the towns of Granger, in Minnesota, and Florenceville, in Iowa. This is about the extent of the encroachment of civilization on this stretch of river. Just below the broken dam at Florenceville the stream divides. The left channel can be navigated without a portage. Below Larkin Bridge the character of the river changes. The flat prairie is left behind as the river enters the more rugged limestone rock country typical of the river below Kendallville. On this section one must be careful of cattle fences stretched across the river. The run from Kendallville to Decorah (two days, thirty miles) begins on the north side of the river above the bridge. Here spectacular limestone formations often flank the river. The halfway point is the small town of Bluffton, where one can find lodging if camping is not on the agenda. Below Bluffton the rock bluffs become infrequent, but the river environment continues to be attractive and undeveloped. At Decorah the valley widens. Farms can be seen. There are four highway bridges between Malanaphy Spring and Decorah. The last makes a good take-out. You will know when you have reached it by the buildings of Luther College, which can be seen on the high ground back of the river.

The section of the river below Decorah runs for about fifty miles before reaching the flood plain of the Mississippi, where it has been straightened and diked, losing all charm. Before that point, however, there are many miles of arresting scenery, limestone banks, and a few gentle rapids. The trip presents few surprises or difficulties, but considerable paddling through man-made lakes and portages around dams. For more detail on the Upper Iowa write for *A Guide to the Upper Iowa River,* c/o George Knudson, Luther College, Decorah, IA 52101.

ST. CROIX RIVER

Wild and Scenic River

Time of year: *April to September*

Degree of difficulty: *novice to intermediate*

Craft: *canoe, kayak, raft*

Character: *semiwild; pastoral*

Permit required: *For information write St. Croix National Scenic Riverway, P.O. Box 708, St. Croix Falls, WI 54024.*

Rentals available: *yes*

With the Bois Brule River, the St. Croix, in northwestern Wisconsin, provided a main link in the route the voyageurs took between Lake Superior and the Mississippi. These French traders of the eighteenth century used this natural road to travel between their northern province in Canada and New Orleans on the Gulf of Mexico while the British were establishing the thirteen colonies on the Atlantic seaboard. Burial mounds and other evidence of early Indian inhabitation are numerous along the watercourse, indicating that the voyageurs were not the first to value this trade route. After the voyageurs came the loggers—this is Paul Bunyan country. But even those terrible scars are largely healed now, and a canoe trip down the St. Croix through forests of balsam and cedar, past sandy islands touched by the footprints of deer and wading birds, is to float backward in time. The camping along the way is superb, the wildlife plentiful, the sense of seclusion profound. With good reason the St. Croix was chosen as one of the original Wild and Scenic Rivers.

Though it runs fast and clear, the St. Croix presents no special challenge to the white-water enthusiast. The strongest rapids are Class II, and that is only when the river is high in the spring and early summer. But for beginners there are just enough rough spots to make the St. Croix a fine introduction to the sport of river canoeing. For rafting, the St. Croix is strictly a relaxed run, but an enormously pleasant way to move through a fine wilderness area without having to shoulder a pack. And you need not leave any amenities at home. Although the river is navigable for 120 miles—from the forests of Burnett County all the way to the Mississippi —the wilderness section extends just half that distance, roughly from Danbury, Wisconsin, to Taylor Falls, Minnesota. Below Taylor Falls there are roads beside the river and numerous towns.

The usual put-in is just below Gordon Dam, three and a half miles west of Gordon, Wisconsin. It is thirty miles, two comfortable days, down to Danbury. Some twenty-two miles below Danbury the river divides into two channels. Here are the Kettle River Rapids, followed by Paint Pot Rapids, making some five miles of moderate rapids to add excitement to what is otherwise a peaceful and charming run through relatively unspoiled wilderness. White-tailed deer can be seen along the riverbank, and blue heron and bald eagles are sometimes spotted soaring above the forests.

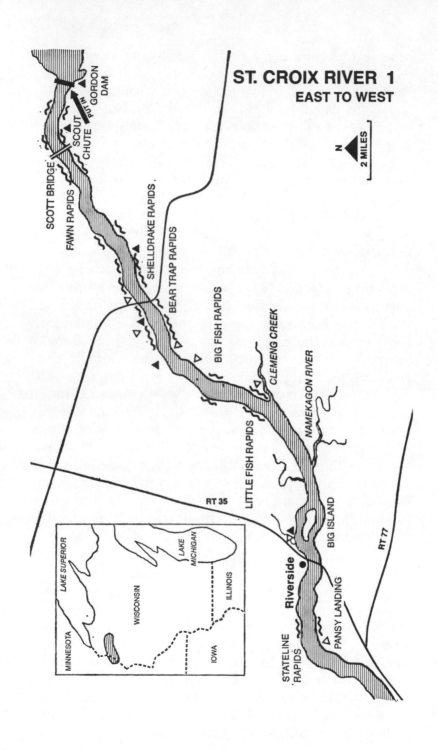

ST. CROIX RIVER 1
EAST TO WEST

N
2 MILES

GORDON DAM
PUT IN
SCOUT
CHUTE
SCOTT BRIDGE
FAWN RAPIDS
SHELLDRAKE RAPIDS
BEAR TRAP RAPIDS
BIG FISH RAPIDS
CLEMENG CREEK
NAMEKAGON RIVER
LITTLE FISH RAPIDS
RT 35
RT 77
BIG ISLAND
PANSY LANDING
Riverside
STATELINE RAPIDS

LAKE SUPERIOR
LAKE MICHIGAN
MINNESOTA
WISCONSIN
ILLINOIS
IOWA

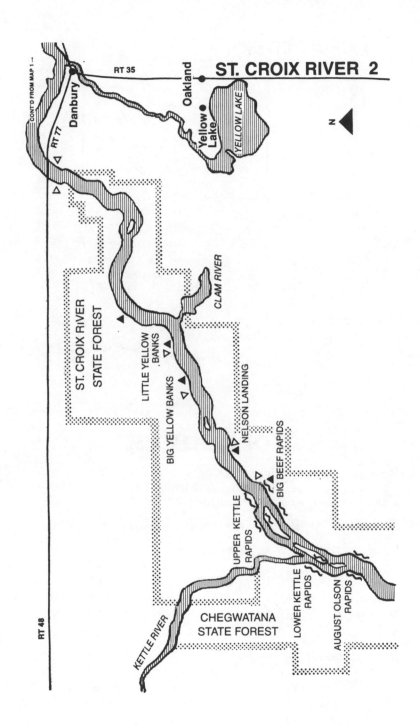

Yellow River.

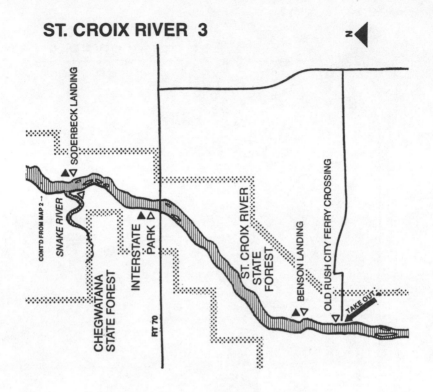

WOLF RIVER

Wild and Scenic River

Time of year: *May to October*

Degree of difficulty: *intermediate to expert*

Craft: *decked canoe, kayak, raft*

Character: *semiwild; pastoral*

Permit required: *For information write Menominee Restoration Committee, P.O. Box 397, Keshena, WI 54135.*

Rentals available: *yes*

The Wolf River in northeastern Wisconsin is known for its white water. For a combination of scenery and challenge to kayakers and paddlers of decked canoes, the eight-mile run between Pissmire and Big Smokey falls is one of the nation's finest. Rafting on the Wolf is also justly popular, though the river is too narrow and rocky for inflatables over about nine feet long. Sixteen-footers are possible during the spring runoff, though the river narrows in spots to barely more than twenty feet. Pull in your elbows.

There is a lot more of the Wolf to run than just this sporty section. In most water the thirty miles above Pissmire Falls are navigable in rafts by rank amateurs, especially those willing to take a dunking from time to time. The water is suitably boulder-strewn and narrow, with frequent thrilling drops that can be handled by the simple application of good sense. This is a good river for beginners to start on. Raft rentals are readily available in Langdale County. On the other hand, the Wolf has chewed up so many canoes and kayaks that one has either to demonstrate expert ability or put down a deposit big enough to buy the craft. A sturdy, two-person raft plus life jacket and paddles can be had for about twenty dollars a day for runs of up to 28.6 miles.

The rapid-free lower section of the Wolf on down to Lake Winnebago is cruised by houseboats. Canoeists are welcome, of course, but it is the upper section that is most interesting. To savor it all, put in on the right bank at the Lily River above the Highway 55 bridge in Lily. Highway 55 parallels the entire length of the Upper Wolf, making it a simple matter to hitch a ride back to get your car if a shuttle cannot be arranged. A half mile downstream from the confluence of the Lily and the Wolf there is a permanent logjam, usually open through the middle. For the next twenty-five miles the river alternates with rock gardens, rapids, and stretches of deep, calm water. The riverbanks are steep and rocky, sliced through bedrock of granite and other igneous rocks, which comprise the boulders in the river. In the quieter sections of water there are sand and gravel beds. The fishing for trout is excellent.

Some twenty-six miles below the put-in comes Boy Scout Rapids. This is the first really challenging rapids one comes to, and should be scouted. Two miles below

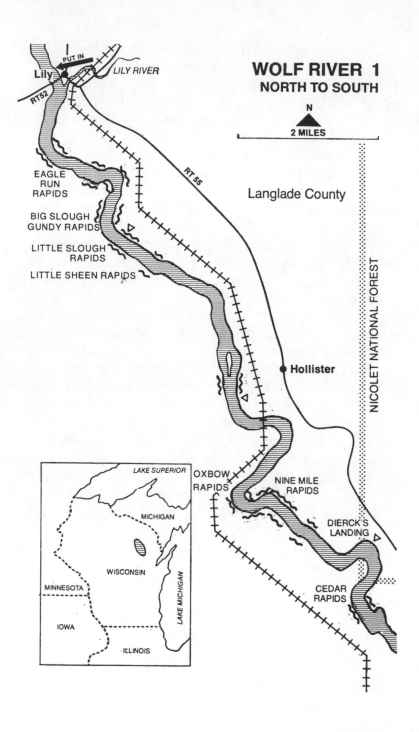

WOLF RIVER 1
NORTH TO SOUTH

N

2 MILES

PUT IN

Lily

LILY RIVER

RT52

RT 55

Langlade County

NICOLET NATIONAL FOREST

EAGLE
RUN
RAPIDS

BIG SLOUGH
GUNDY RAPIDS

LITTLE SLOUGH
RAPIDS

LITTLE SHEEN RAPIDS

Hollister

LAKE SUPERIOR

MICHIGAN

WISCONSIN

MINNESOTA

LAKE MICHIGAN

IOWA

ILLINOIS

OXBOW
RAPIDS

NINE MILE
RAPIDS

DIERCK'S
LANDING

CEDAR
RAPIDS

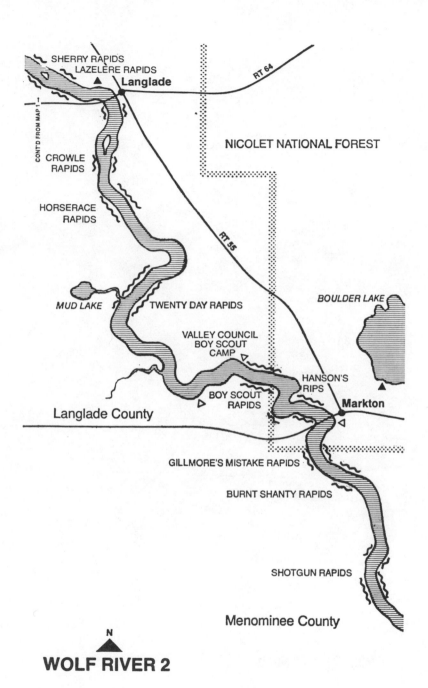

SHERRY RAPIDS
LAZELERE RAPIDS
Langlade

RT 64

CONT'D FROM MAP 1

NICOLET NATIONAL FOREST

CROWLE
RAPIDS

HORSERACE
RAPIDS

RT 55

BOULDER LAKE

MUD LAKE

TWENTY DAY RAPIDS

VALLEY COUNCIL
BOY SCOUT
CAMP

HANSON'S
RIPS

Markton

BOY SCOUT
RAPIDS

Langlade County

GILLMORE'S MISTAKE RAPIDS

BURNT SHANTY RAPIDS

SHOTGUN RAPIDS

Menominee County

N

WOLF RIVER 2

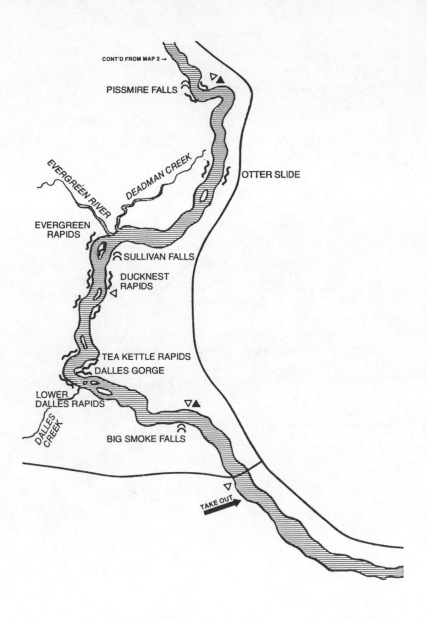

CONT'D FROM MAP 2 →

PISSMIRE FALLS

OTTER SLIDE

EVERGREEN RIVER

DEADMAN CREEK

EVERGREEN
RAPIDS

SULLIVAN FALLS

DUCKNEST
RAPIDS

TEA KETTLE RAPIDS

DALLES GORGE

LOWER
DALLES RAPIDS

DALLES CREEK

BIG SMOKE FALLS

TAKE OUT

N

WOLF RIVER 3

Boy Scout is the constricted sluiceway called Gillmore's Mistake Rapids. It is here that the river narrows to a mere twenty feet, between rock walls. Gillmore, the story goes, was a scout for a lumber company. When he reported the river at this point too narrow to permit logs to be floated through, the company failed to acquire timber rights upstream. Their competitors did. Then, using dynamite, they enlarged the pass and made a fortune. Hence, Gillmore's mistake. Most of us, one suspects, seeing the narrowness of the pass, even as it is today, can sympathize with Gillmore.

Shotgun Rapids, a few more miles downstream, is the longest one on the Wolf. This half mile can be run by competent canoeists in open boats, but should be scouted first. The next challenge is Pissmire Falls, with a hole at the bottom that can trap rafts and swimmers. Scout this one, too; it has flipped hundreds of rafts. And hold onto your glasses going over. Below Pissmire, the Wolf lives up to its name. There is nothing tame about it. The rapids are nearly all Class III, rising to Class IV in high water. There are several unrunnable falls and many sheer drops. When in doubt, scout. The rapid that epitomizes the Wolf and makes the whole trip worthwhile is a granite gorge with the profile of yon Cassius—it has a "lean and hungry look." The steepest drop comes right at the beginning. In high water there is a wave at the bottom of the drop that can trap rafts and swimmers. Scout along the left bank. About two miles below the Dalles is Big Smoke Falls. Above it the river splits in two. Neither channel is recommended, though experts have gone over the drop on the right. The sensible among us take out above Smokey. A dirt road leads from the left bank back out to Route 55. Or if you prefer, you can portage the falls and run a mile and a half down to a wayside picnic area where the highway runs close to the river.

THE
CENTRAL PLAINS

ONLY two entries for the Central Plains states merit attention, which is not to say that there is not plenty of running water here. It is just that the land is relatively flat—we are on the plains, after all—and the rivers are either without strong physical excitement or so plastered with the imprint of our industrial society that they have lost all attractiveness as wilderness roads. So generally scarce, in fact, are the streams that qualify as wild in this part of the nation that to expand the plains states as such—North Dakota, South Dakota, Kansas, and Nebraska, it was necessary to throw in Montana, which boasts some of the best wild water in the West—in particular, on the Upper Missouri.

For contrast, there is, among many candidates, South Dakota's Little White, a minor stream of major interest to wildlife enthusiasts. In fact, it is the opportunity to observe wildlife, particularly water birds, that is the main strength of the streams on the plains.

Eons ago, when Ice Age glaciers pushed across the flat, former seabed of the Dakotas, they gouged out depressions. On retreat of the ice, these "potholes" filled with water, making a land studded with ponds and marshes—a formation that geologists, with irreproachable logic, have named Prairie Pothole Country. By whatever name, it is a perfect breeding habitat for waterfowl.

Another phenomenon of this part of the country is the sandhills along the Nebraska–South Dakota border, for which the sandhill crane is named. These high, grass-covered dunes were raised up by wind blowing along the shores of a prehistoric ocean. Today they act as sponges, releasing rain and snowmelt in the form of crystal-clear springs, the source of streams like the Little White.

In western Montana you will find numerous fast, shallow streams pouring out of the Rockies. Prime among them is the Madison, which rises in Yellowstone National Park and is runnable all summer and into the fall. No special difficulty. Excellent fishing. As on all Montana streams, you must carry a Coast-Guard-approved life jacket for every member of your party.

A booklet to write for is *Montana's Popular Float Streams,* put out by the Montana Fish and Game Department, Helena MT 59601. Nebraska has a similar publication, *Canoeing in Nebraska,* which covers a dozen or more of its waterways. Write to Nebraska Game and Parks Commission, 2200 North 33rd Street, Lincoln, NE 68503.

In North Dakota you can canoe the Little Missouri from a few miles northwest of Amidon down to Medora, a sixty-mile run. This takes you through the heart of that state's rock-ribbed badlands.

In short, there are plenty of streams to be run on the plains, but with a very few exceptions it is gentle canoeing rather than white-water challenge.

THE UPPER MISSOURI RIVER

Wild and Scenic River

Time of year: mid-May to September

Degree of difficulty: intermediate

Craft: canoe, raft

Character: semiwild

Permit required: For information write Bureau of Land Management, P.O. Box 30157, Billings, MT 59107.

Rentals available: yes

Look at the map of Montana. The wall of the Rockies lies on the left, with the Continental Divide snaking its way northwestward along the ridge. From there the land descends eastward into prairie. With it comes the eastern drainage of the Rockies. Two trunk streams carry the water—the Yellowstone and its big brother the Missouri, the longest river in the United States.

The Yellowstone, closely hugged by highways, holds little interest for float trips. The same is true, alas, for most of the 2,448 miles of the Missouri, harnessed behind dams and fettered by levees. In their turn Indian canoes, buffalo boats, explorers' pirogues, keelboats, and, finally, large steamers made the Missouri the busiest waterway in the West. Lewis and Clark used it to explore the vast Louisiana Territory in 1805. The discovery of rich gold fields in Montana and Idaho during the early 1860s created a booming river trade. During the summer of 1866, thirty to forty river steamboats were plying the Upper Missouri at one time. They came up the river as far as Fort Benton, below Great Falls, where mule trains took over.

Then the railroad changed all that. By 1890 the river had become an artery of ghosts. Since then, dams, sewage from encroaching cities and towns, and roads

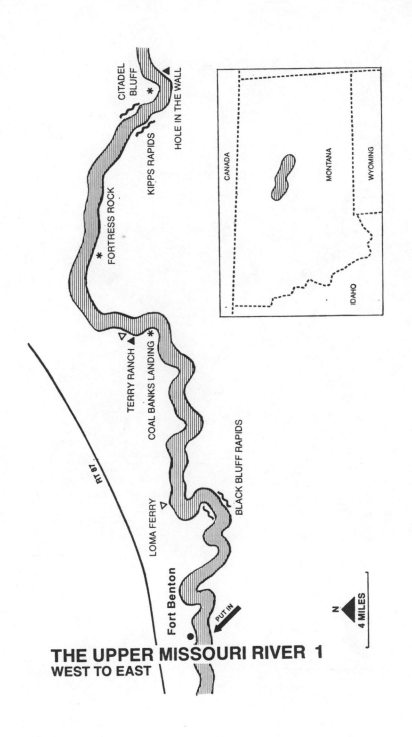

THE UPPER MISSOURI RIVER 1
WEST TO EAST

Fort Benton

RT 87

LOMA FERRY

TERRY RANCH

COAL BANKS LANDING

FORTRESS ROCK

CITADEL BLUFF

KIPPS RAPIDS

HOLE IN THE WALL

BLACK BLUFF RAPIDS

PUT IN

N
4 MILES

CANADA

MONTANA

WYOMING

IDAHO

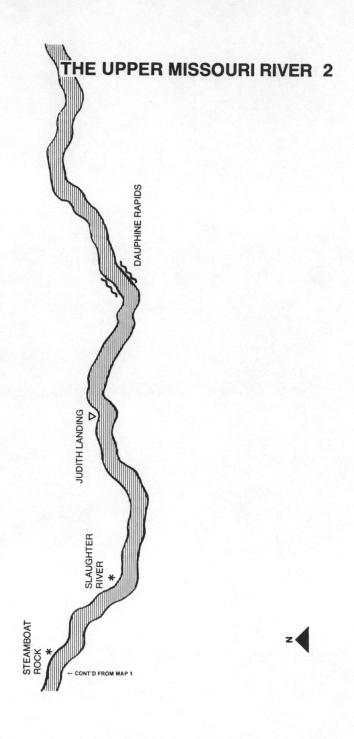

THE UPPER MISSOURI RIVER 2

DAUPHINE RAPIDS

JUDITH LANDING

SLAUGHTER RIVER

STEAMBOAT ROCK

← CONT'D FROM MAP 1

N

THE UPPER MISSOURI RIVER 3

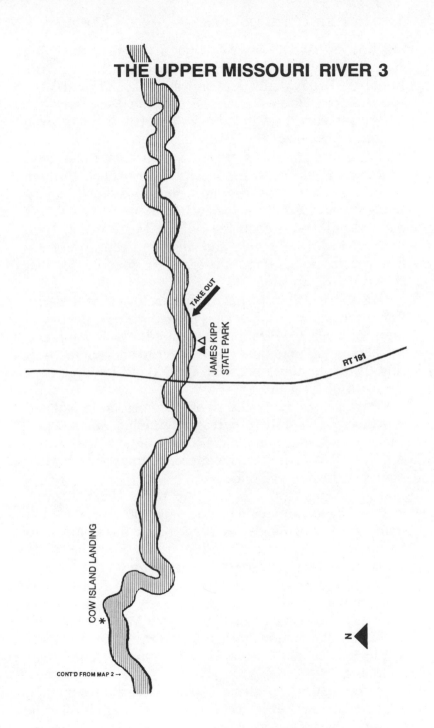

TAKE OUT

JAMES KIPP
STATE PARK

RT 191

COW ISLAND LANDING

*

N

CONT'D FROM MAP 2 →

and bridges have destroyed all but a vestige of the living river, known affectionately by boatmen as the "Big Muddy." Today, only 160 miles of the Missouri, between Fort Benton and the Fort Peck Reservoir, are left in any condition that Lewis and Clark might even remotely recognize.

But that 160 miles, traveled for a week to ten days in a canoe, makes an unforgettable trip back through history. There are no portages and no difficult rapids, though it is possible in low water to be forced to get out and pull. With good reason, the Missouri has been described as a mile wide and an inch deep. There are five access points (but no parallel roads), so that shorter trips can be made.

For the full trip, put in just below Fort Benton. For the next forty miles canyon walls slope steeply to meet the river. Civilization, though not overly apparent, is still close at hand, and if you want to shorten the trip, skip this section and put in at Coal Bank Landing near the town of Virgelle.

After Coal Bank the river becomes more isolated and the canyon walls progressively higher and steeper. Sheer white sandstone cliffs tower above the water. Ages of wind and water have eroded rock into bizarre shapes and stately colonnades.

As the canyon deepens, the rocks above it grow massive, even threatening. You have entered the Missouri Breaks, badlands, as rugged and inhospitable to a man on foot as any in the country; but from the safety of the river they are grandly picturesque.

There are numerous opportunities to follow trails up from the river to extraordinary rock formations that have inspired names like Hole in the Wall, Steamboat Rock, and the Citadel. Below Cow Creek, the badlands diminish. The cliffs draw back, leaving a wide river bottom.

Preparation for this trip should certainly include a reading of the Lewis and Clark journals, published in an abridged paperback edition by Houghton Mifflin.

For all its wild beauty along this stretch, the Missouri is not a river you can dip a bucket into for drinking water. Bring containers holding enough water for at least four days. You can replenish at Coal Banks and Hole in the Wall.

The fishing is good for catfish and sauger. During the height of the season, in July, you can expect a fair number of other boats on the river. And, yes, many will have motors. As the steamboats proved, all this stretch of the Missouri is navigable by power boats. The river is generally too slow for rafters, while kayakers will find it no challenge.

One of the best features of a trip on the Upper Missouri is the excellent topographical and historical map of the river entitled: *Historic Upper Missouri River*. You can get it by writing to Missouri River Cruises, P.O. Box 1212, Fort Benton, MT 59442. A free map and brochure are available from the Montana Fish and Game Department, Helena, MT 59601.

LITTLE WHITE RIVER

Time of year: May to October

Degree of difficulty: novice

Craft: canoe

Character: pastoral

Permit required: no

Rentals available: no

The Little White, in south-central South Dakota, is a peaceful and very popular stream of rare beauty. An enthusiast of it has written, "I will go a long way to find a place where I can paddle my canoe through wild country all day and camp alone wherever I decide to camp. The Little White River is such a place."

Swift and clear, it can be run for nearly one hundred miles, beginning at Ghost Hawk Park near Rosebud down to the dam at White River. There are rapids at the end, but nothing difficult. A canoe is the best craft. A fifteen-mile stretch below Highway 18 is choked with scrub growth and fallen trees, making too tight a squeeze for a raft.

The pleasure of the Little White is in its wilderness setting. The river passes through the Rosebud Sioux Reservation and the La Creek National Wildlife Refuge. This refuge, the whole river in fact, is a grand place for bird watching. Some 250 species are known to inhabit or pass through the refuge, including a giant race of Canadian geese and the once nearly extinct trumpeter swan, both of which breed there.

From the put-in at the Ghost Hawk Campground, the river meanders for about ten miles through Crazy Horse Canyon, three to ten miles wide, with walls rising abruptly three hundred feet. Above lies a treeless grassland, where herds of beef cattle graze. There are numerous gravel bars in the river, some large enough to camp on.

THE SOUTHWEST

IN spring the rapids on the rivers of the Southwest match those of any place on earth. Volcanic activity, shifting of lands, and rising mountains combined some forty million years ago to produce an awesome landscape. And what a place it is for river craft to float on calm, meadow streams through desert beauty and skinny passages as deep as any gorges in the United States! Rafts and kayaks are preferred, though there are many delightful canoe runs as well.

Most of the waters are supervised by either the National Park Service or the Bureau of Land Management. To run these rivers, registration is necessary with the appropriate agency and advance planning is essential, as the waiting list can be long. Of the watercourses in the Southwest, only the Upper Rio Grande in north-central New Mexico has been included for protection under the Wild and Scenic Rivers Act. But many others are as wild and scenic: the Yampa, the Green, the Chama, and sections of the Colorado, Dolores, and Gunnison.

River running in the area is generally on the Rio Grande, the Colorado and its tributaries, the Green, and the Chama. But smaller, short-season runs are well worth the trouble on such little-known rivers as the Gila and the Salt. In the Gila wilderness, a total of 750,000 acres of forest is maintained in its natural state. Mechanized equipment is forbidden in the area. Traveling by foot, horseback, or boat, one may sample mountain country as it was in the time of the pioneers, undeveloped and unsoiled. Only the mastodon and the camel are missing from the wildlife roster of days gone by.

At different times in history, stretches of these rivers were inhabited, but never for long. It is a land that attracts men not because they are able to bend it to their will, but because they cannot.

COLORADO RIVER

Time of year: *April to October*

Degree of difficulty: *various*

Craft: *canoe, kayak, raft*

Character: *wild*

Permit required: *yes*

Rentals available: *yes*

The mighty Colorado is complex, its flow unpredictable. Rising in the Wind River Range, in Wyoming, and the Never-Summer Mountains, northwest of Denver, it cuts a winding path for 1,440 miles southwestward across the Sonora Desert to the Gulf of California. In its delta, the highest temperatures in the world have been recorded.

And the river is unique. For more than two-thirds its length the Colorado has cut a deep gorge. Wherever a lateral tributary joins, a further gorge has been created, resulting in a labyrinth of deep trenches not to be found anywhere else on earth.

Star of the Colorado is, of course, the Grand Canyon, the world's most intricate and complex system of canyons, gorges, and ravines. Its creation was one of the grandest gestures in geological history. The canyon was carved as the river flowed and the land pushed upward against it. On the mile-high walls is revealed a stratified time scale in millions of years that reads like a textbook.

For centuries the Colorado, with its canyons, frustrated the explorations of conquistadores and remained on the map as a mysterious scrawl. Then in 1869 John Wesley Powell, a one-armed veteran of the Civil War, spent three months on the river, traveling nearly nine hundred miles through the "Great Unknown" of the Grand Canyon. The first recreational run through the canyon was made in 1909. However, by 1949, only one hundred persons had followed Powell's route. Then business began to pick up. Georgie White started a trend when she lashed three surplus bridge pontoons together, steered them with an outboard motor, and carried groups of fifty down the river. A successful uprun of the canyon in three Buehler jet boats made news in 1960. And finally the fight between dam builders and conservationists during the mid-sixties brought publicity and more tourists.

Today, to prevent crowding and overuse, aspirants must obtain permits to run the river. Issued on a first-come, first-served basis, these are in such demand that application must be made at least nine months in advance. For full details on the many requirements, contact the Inner Canyon Unit Office, Grand Canyon National Park, P.O. Box 129, Grand Canyon, AZ 86023. Trip leaders, for example, must be experienced, preferably on the canyon. Rafts must be at least sixteen feet long. And your lengthy list of required gear will indeed be checked by a ranger before you put in.

A trip through the canyon will generally take 14 to 21 days. From the put-in at Lee's Ferry, it is 225 miles to the Diamond Creek take-out or 280 miles to Pierce Ferry on Lake Mead. Most trips pull out of Diamond Creek to avoid 40 miles of still water on Lake Mead.

The best season on the Colorado is April through October. The desert climate will raise temperatures to over 100°F. during the day and keep them no lower than 65°F. at night. On beginning his trip through the

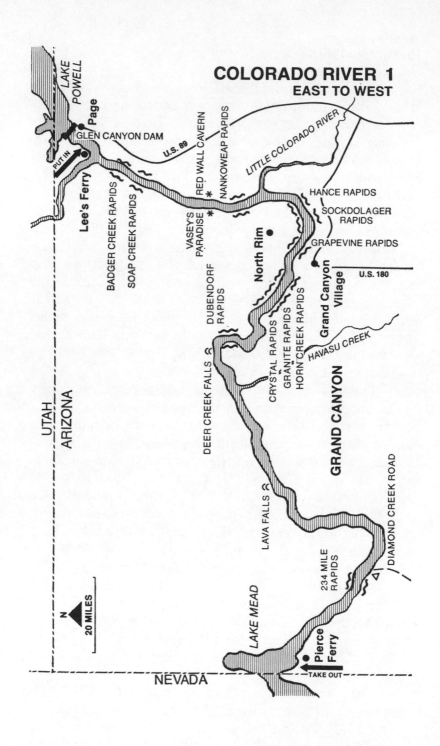

COLORADO RIVER 2

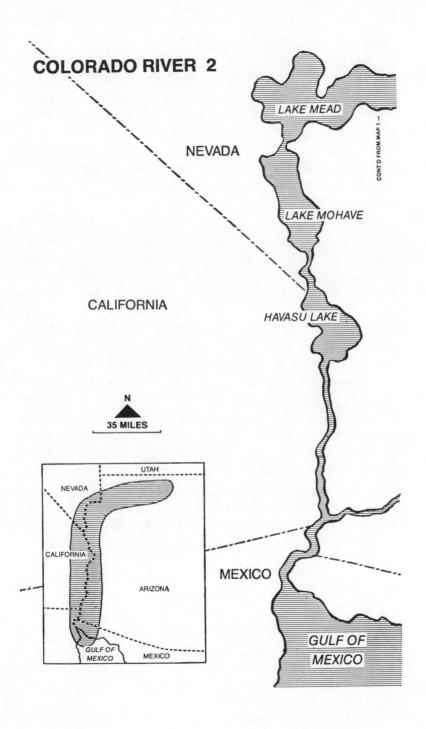

NEVADA

CALIFORNIA

LAKE MEAD

LAKE MOHAVE

HAVASU LAKE

CONT'D FROM MAP 1 →

N

35 MILES

MEXICO

GULF OF MEXICO

UTAH

NEVADA

CALIFORNIA

ARIZONA

GULF OF MEXICO

MEXICO

canyon, Powell wrote, "We are now ready to start on our way down the Great Unknown. . . . We are three quarters of a mile in the depths of the earth, and the great river sinks into insignificance as it dashes its angry waves against the walls and cliffs that rise to the world above; the waves are but puny ripples, and we but pigmies, running up and down the sands or lost among the boulders." The canyon, with numerous Class V rapids, is extremely hazardous but within the grasp of skilled boatmen.

Complicating the difficulty of the canyon run is Glen Canyon Dam, which controls water flow. As the dam responds to electricity demands from Phoenix, twelve-foot tides cause bizarre conditions in the canyon. Boats must be moored in deep pools at night so that they are not on dry ground in the morning. Some rapids become more difficult; others easier. A boater finding the water level at a rapids not to his liking can wait a few hours till it suits him, then proceed.

The most difficult rapids are probably Lava Falls, Crystal, and Hance. Hance looms up just after Papago Creek at Mile 76. Its huge holes, rocks, and twelve-foot waves are so jumbled that finding a passage through is a tricky maneuver. Crystal used to be a moderate and pleasant rapids, but in 1967 a torrent of rain caused flash floods to toss large boulders into the river. Now the river narrows at that point and gigantic back-curling waves hug the left-hand cliffs. Passage through means jumping a hole so big that a miss can mean a vanished boat.

At Lava Falls, Mile 179, Powell said, "What a conflict of water and fire there must have been here! Just imagine a river of molten rock running down into a river of melted snow. What a seething and boiling of the waters. . . ." And still today, the rapids remain steep and full of tremendous holes, overwhelming waves, and blinding foam. These rapids should definitely be scouted from both banks.

The canyon also boasts rapids that cannot be scouted at all, like Sockdolager and Grapevine. And then there is Mile 234 rapids whose hole blocks off the entire left side of the canyon.

The canyon is spectacular. Be sure to allow time for side trips and stops at Vasey's Paradise, where, as Powell described, "the river seems inclosed by a wall set by a million brilliant gems . . . fountains bursting from the rock high overhead and the rocks covered with mosses and ferns and beautiful flowering plants." And be sure to take moments to contemplate Red Wall Cavern, an overhang carved by the river on the outside of a bend. Some say this amphitheatre would hold fifty thousand people.

Off the river, watch out for scorpions. They like to spend the night in the folds of sleeping bags and the cozy insides of boots. Their sting is not fatal but a good precaution is to carefully shake out bags and boots each morning.

For further information on this trip, read the *Grand Canyon River Guide,* Canyonlands Press, Salt Lake City, UT 84101, and the *Grand Canyon National Park,* edited by Robert Scharff, David McKay Company. There is much good literature on this area, all of which will make your trip more enjoyable.

SALT RIVER

Time of year: March to June

Degree of difficulty: various

Craft: canoe (spring only), kayak, raft

Character: wild; semiwild

Permit required: no

Rentals available: yes

The Salt is for rafting, or at least that's the way some enthusiasts in the Phoenix area see the river each spring. Located in east-central Arizona, it runs east-west from near Phoenix to Seneca, where it merges with the Black River. The run is fifty-two miles, from Salt River Bridge at Route 60, to Route 288, at the upper reaches of Roosevelt Lake. Fed by the melting snows, the Salt cuts a path through a magical wilderness canyon, but there is sufficient water only in spring. By the end of June the level is already dropping, and by late summer the river is practically dry. When conditions are prime, depending on the snow cover of the previous winter, a number of tough rapids challenge the tubers and rafters. Scouting of several rapids, as well as a portage or two, may be necessary. The average gradient in the canyon is twenty-three feet per mile; with a forty-five-foot-per-mile gradient in one section. Apart from the rapids, the float is leisurely, giving time for relaxing afternoon trips from one campsite to the next.

There is an additional seventeen-mile section of the river in Tonto National Forest, from Granite Reef Forest Camp (close to Phoenix) to Saguaro Lake Guest Ranch. This run is a slow float, with established or undeveloped campsites located every two miles or so. The current averages about two miles per hour, and the run is predictable. Mesquite and large saguaro grace the riverbank. There are many access points and parking facilities, which make the section popular and suitable for trips of a couple of hours or a couple of days.

For information on running the Salt, contact Bert Coleman, Travel Information Section, 3303 N. Central Avenue, Phoenix, AZ 85012, and the Arizona Office of Tourism, 1700 W. Washington Street, Room 501, Phoenix, AZ 85007, or the Arizona Department of Economic Planning and Development, Travel Information Section, 1645 W. Jefferson, Phoenix, AZ 85007.

GILA RIVER

Time of year: late March to mid-April

Degree of difficulty: intermediate

Craft: canoe, kayak, raft

Character: wild; semiwild

Permit required: no

Rentals available: no

Compared to the Salt, the Gila River is undiscovered. Far from major highways and with a float season of only three weeks (usually the last week in March and the first two weeks of April), it has escaped notice by most river runners. And yet the state-protected Gila Wilderness, which surrounds the river, is scarcely changed from the days when Apaches camped there. In the conifer forests of the Mimbres and Pinos Altos ranges, bear, javelina, antelope, and elk make their way. The Gila Wilderness is a natural aviary, sheltering some 250 species of birds. And in the cliff dwellings of the prehistoric Pueblos, where paintings still adorn the interior walls, or in the City of Rocks, a natural formation, the past is palpable.

The land of the Gila was among the last in the lower forty-eight to be settled. Only a few decades ago it was still American frontier. Some forty miles of the river cut through this wilderness for a magnificent canoe, kayak, or raft run. As the season is so short, write the Albuquerque Whitewater Club, 804 Warm Sands Drive, S.E., Albuquerque, NM 87123 for up-to-date information on the time of the most dependable flow rates. An average of two to four feet in depth is recommended. Although the distance is short, allow a minimum of four to five days.

Make no mistake, this river can be dangerous during spring runoff. Expect a series of Class II and Class III rapids. Scouting is advised, not only to read the rapids but to check for logjams or occasional barbed wire fences crossing the river. Several short portages are necessary. Be prepared as well for violent changes of weather. Rain, hail, and snow, with winds up to sixty miles per hour, are not uncommon in spring. The Gila National Forest Office recommends that a trip itinerary be left with an on-land friend. Put in at the river crossing on Route 15 and take out at the Turkey Creek Landing Area or at Sapillo Creek, where there is an access road. Points not to miss are Skeleton Canyon, where a small waterfall drops through a chute and then is sprayed back up by a lip of rock, and the area just above Sapillo Creek, where the cliffs drop directly into the water. Below Sapillo Creek the river is mostly unrunnable because of the diversion of water for irrigation. For more information write the Chamber of Commerce, 925 Hudson Street, Silver City, NM 88061.

RIO GRANDE

Wild and Scenic River

Time of year: *May to mid-June*

Degree of difficulty: *various*

Craft: *canoe (spring only), kayak, raft*

Character: *wild; pastoral*

Permit required: *For information write Bureau of Land Management, P.O. Box 1449, Santa Fe, NM 87501.*

Rentals available: *no*

The Rio Grande is the second longest river in the United States, rising in the southern Colorado Rockies, vertically crossing the center of New Mexico, then veering eastward to form the natural border between Texas and Mexico before finally emptying in the Gulf of Mexico at Brownsville. Its nineteen hundred miles are only surpassed by the Missouri-Mississippi system. Western

THE UPPER RIO GRANDE

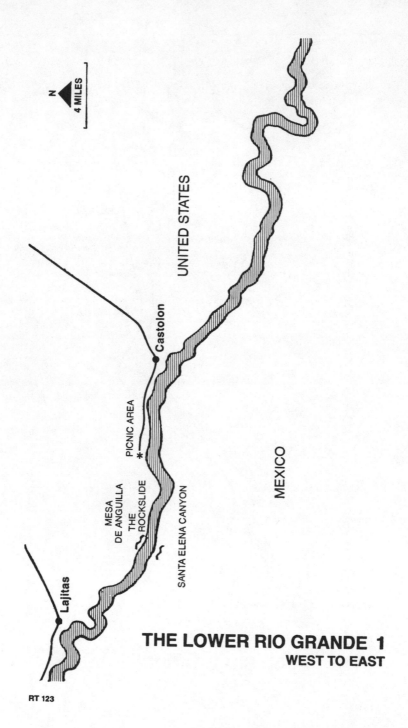

THE LOWER RIO GRANDE 1
WEST TO EAST

RT 123

THE LOWER RIO GRANDE 2

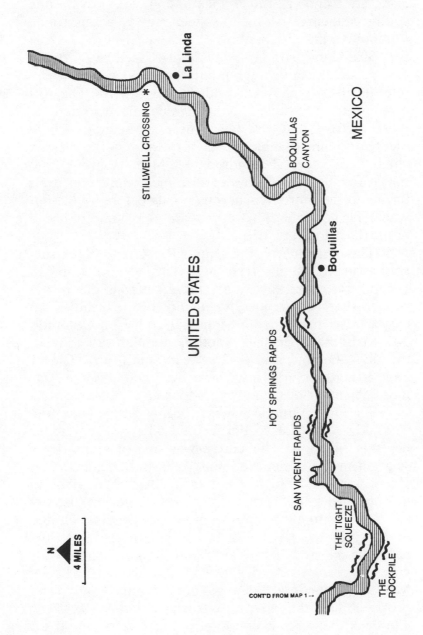

La Linda

STILLWELL CROSSING

MEXICO

BOQUILLAS CANYON

UNITED STATES

Boquillas

HOT SPRINGS RAPIDS

SAN VICENTE RAPIDS

THE TIGHT SQUEEZE

THE ROCKPILE

CONT'D FROM MAP 1 →

N

4 MILES

river runners give it top billing. Its headwaters, flowing clear, cold, and swift over rock and gravel, provide fine spring canoeing. Along the river valley, white frame farmhouses line the bank.

The Upper Rio Grande is a two-faced river. It can be a peaceful run through mountain meadows, or it can offer death-defying risk to white-water experts. The 150 miles north of Santa Fe, New Mexico, are wild and remote. Access roads are few. There are sections where the river is impassable in its fury, and portage trails climb banks several hundred feet high. A group that put in for more moderate class rapids could find itself having to run more treacherous points before a take-out would be possible. Therefore careful planning should be made before the trip.

The best time on the Upper Rio Grande is during spring runoff, usually from May through mid-June. In general, rafts and kayaks are more suitable, but in the calmer stretches, canoes would not be in trouble. An easy Class I trip is from Manassa Bridge on Colorado 142 to Lobatos Bridge. Another popular run is from the ghost mining camp at Creede to South Fork. Clever anglers can find large trout here. And annually the Alamosa Chamber of Commerce sponsors a raft race.

The Rio Grande Gorge begins just above the Colorado-New Mexico border and descends fifty miles to Taos Junction. The Gorge was one of eight rivers selected in the initial National Wild and Scenic Rivers system, and in 1970 it was the first American river to be thus dedicated. Trips down the gorge are usually run in one- to three-day segments, depending on the difficulty of the river. Put in at Lobatos Bridge. Surrounding the river here is sage and chamiso prairie with volcanos rising in the distance. As the river enters New Mexico, the landscape changes almost immediately. The broad sloping cliffs give way to sheer rock walls. Near Ute Peak the gorge is two hundred feet deep, but at La Junta Campground, where the Red River enters the Rio Grande, the walls rise vertically eight hundred feet. The side canyons become wilder and uninhabited. Bobcat, mule deer, coyote, and muskrat can be seen hunting in the tall grass lining the bank.

To end this twenty-four-mile section of intermediate Class II rapids, take out at Lee Trail. The climb from river to rim will be a rough 220 feet but far better to be fatigued from the climb than to face the next 12 miles of river. At this point, the river drops 650 feet creating thundering water that boating experts have ranked Class VI, one of the most difficult sections of water in America.

After Red River, the Rio Grande slows to a Class III rapids, only to pick up again between Dunn Bridge and Taos Junction in the wildest stretch of all. If you arrive in Taos right side up, you can take out. From this point, the river alternates between lazy floating and intermediate challenges. The most popular white-water run in New Mexico is a twenty-four-mile stretch through White Rock Canyon. Artesian springs are nearby to refill canteens. But not all springs on the river are potable. Fresh water should be carried and river water boiled before using.

The lower Rio Grande provides memorable white-water experience in the stretch between Lajitas and Langtry, Texas, on the Texas and Mexican border. At Ojinaga the river, bled nearly dry by irrigation, picks up new strength from the Rio Conchos and for some 250 miles to Langtry it snarls and strikes its way through deep, isolated gorges. Any number of different trips can be made through this water, taking four days to four weeks to wander about in the side canyons. To avoid the high summer temperatures, the best season for the lower river is October through February. As in the upper river, this section presents rapids such as Rockslide, near Santa Elena, that must always be scouted and often portaged in high water. But there is also a plentitude of less challenging water that will give the novice time to know his craft and increase his skill.

Some of the most isolated water in the United States is the 90 miles between Stillwell Crossing at the end of Boquillas Canyon to Langtry. Many river runners have drifted here for a week, some 130 miles, without seeing any other people. Companions instead were panthers, peccaries, road runners, and the tiny *brasita de fuego* bird flying at the willows. Even where civilization touches the river, the deep chasms and desert mountains maintain the strong sense of solitude. Access is through Great Bend National Park.

The ghosts of Cortez, Coronado, the other gold-hungry Spaniards who vainly sought the fabled Cities of Cibola haunt the Rio Grande. The cities were never found, but silver and gold were discovered. Most of the mines vanished with the explorers or hermits who happened upon them. So there are still treasures waiting along the Rio Grande—and there are spirits. In northern New Mexico, echoes of Indian shamans dancing atop their *kivas* as they ring out the pulse of the earth on their huge drums can still be heard on quiet nights, though some say it is the sound of the river.

For information on water conditions (and shamans) on the Upper Rio Grande, contact Rio Grande White Water Adventures, Inc., 3536 Arizona Avenue, Los Alamos, NM 87544, and Rio Grande National Forest, U.S. Forest Service, Monte Vista, CO 81144. For lower river details, contact Bob Burleson, President, Explorers Club, P.O. Box 844, Temple, TX 76501, or the Superintendent, Big Bend National Park, TX 79834.

THE WEST

THE rivers of the West flow out of the continent's mightiest mountains, young, muscular, still largely untamed, despite the imposition of dams that have drowned scores of wondrous gorges. This is the big league, the ultimate test, the supreme river experience.

It is true, there are times when a staid New England river in spring spate, dashing through a boulder-strewn rock garden like a football running back, will test the skill of the nimblest canoeist or kayaker; and there are incredible moments of stillness in the early morning on loops of the Buffalo River in the Ozarks, when the splash of a fish jumping resounds like a gunshot to ripple the image of dappled sycamores hanging over the banks. Should he find himself there, even an army engineer must feel it sinful to so much as sneeze. But on the Green, the Yampa, the Colorado, and the Tuolomne, the spell and the challenge begin at the beginning and play out to the end.

There is all manner of boating here, in pristine wilderness rich in natural and anthropological history, where the great canyons are cut sandstone towers, and sheer cliffs stand as testament to the geological events that shaped the land. The iron-stained Green River canyons of Labyrinth and Stillwater harbor the ancient stonework of the Anasazi dwellings and the huge rock paintings of manlike figures and animals—among the most impressive works of primitive man.

There is tumultuous white water, and there is quiet water that is ideal for swimming. Hiking back from the rivers, far from thrusting one back into civilization, puts one still farther into the wilderness, in touch with the country the way it was before the time of Columbus.

The water here belongs to two main systems: that collected by the mighty Colorado, flowing off the southeast flank of the Rockies into the Gulf of California, and the abrupt river-streams that pour down the western flank of the Sierras to the Pacific. There is no point in taking a trip on any of the rivers of the Colorado system if you have less than a week or two. Consider these more expeditions than river trips. If your time is short, plan instead a few days on one of the Sierra rivers—there are many besides the Tuolumne and the American.

Most western rivers worthy of attention flow through national or state parks. Because of the burgeoning demand and the admirable resolution to maintain the rivers in as wild a state as possible, most must be carefully regulated by one or another official agency, the Bureau of Land Management, the National Park Service, or the United States Forest Service. And the waiting list to get a permit may be a long one. Some rivers listed here do not need a permit as of this writing, but that is bound to change. Always check before you set out by writing to the agency responsible for the river you have chosen.

To run serious white water like the Grand Canyon, you will, in addition to getting into line, have to prove your ability and preparedness to the Park Service or to whatever agency is regulating the river you choose. You will have to have at least two boats in your party and experienced hands to man them, preferably people who have run that particular river before and can demonstarte the fact. If you are missing essential gear or if what you have is old and worn, you can expect to be turned back by the rangers.

For those who know what they are doing, regulation can be a pain in the neck. But it is a small price to pay to keep our rivers wild and for the right to run the finest water in the world.

YAMPA RIVER

Time of year: May to mid-July

Degree of difficulty: novice to intermediate

Craft: kayak, raft

Character: wild

Permit required: no

Rentals available: yes

The Yampa is the Colorado's last undammed tributary of any size. Called Bear River by early trappers, the Yampa flows westward through the deep sandstone canyons of the Colorado Rockies into Dinosaur National Monument, where it joins the Green at Echo Park. From here it continues into northeast Utah. Bone fishhooks and other objects excavated from Yampa canyon caves show Indians lived there as long as 3,500 years ago. A staple of the Ute Indians was the nourishing yampa root, dangerously similar in appearance to the poisonous water hemlock.

The scenery in Dinosaur National Monument makes a feast for geologists. The area was covered by seas more than twelve times, separated by intervals when the waters were pushed back by emerging highlands. The quarry in the monument contains one of the world's greatest concentrations of dinosaur remains. Allow plenty of time to explore the various side canyons and visit the fascinating archaeological remains, particularly the Indian storage cave near Mantel Ranch.

A seventy-two-mile trip down the Yampa from Deerlodge Park to Split Mountain Boat Ramp will take you through days of drifting, warm swimming, and a very fast ride on one of the West's most dangerous rapids. Warm Springs is a long stretch of furious water located forty-one miles below Deerlodge Park at the mouth of Warm Springs Draw. It features a series of holes on the left, jagged rocks on the right, and a huge hole dead center at the foot. The rapid is lethal and has claimed the lives of more than one professional boatman. Sensible river runners walk around Warm Springs. The other Yampa rapids are moderate, with the exception of Teepee Rapid and Big Joe.

The Yampa's route through the mountains is in a series of horseshoe bends. The canyon walls, almost continuous to Echo Park, have been eroded into beautiful distinct formations with such names as Haystack Rock, Cleopatra's Couch, Crow's Nest. Along the river there are fine campsites.

Allow a minimum of seven days for a trip on the Yampa. Raft size should be from twelve to thirty-three feet. Early May to mid-July is the best time to make the run, but it is possible for water level to be too low as early as July 1. An abundance of catfish, some trout, and Colorado whitefish will vary your river menus.

Permits are required. Write the Dinosaur National Monument and, for additional information, the Dinosaur National Historical Association, P.O. Box 127, Jensen, UT 84035.

AMERICAN RIVER

Time of year: May to September

Degree of difficulty: various

Craft: canoe, kayak, raft

Character: semiwild

Permit required: no

Rentals available: yes

From the rocky banks of the American River, at Coloma, John Marshall plucked the first gold nuggets in 1848 to herald the California gold rush. Today's travelers on the river may find not only some remaining gold but also a rich blend of relaxing calm and thrilling rapids. The American rises out of the Sierra Mountains, makes its way through the Mother Lode country, and near Sacramento branches into three main forks to flow into the Sacramento River.

The length along each fork is some one hundred miles, but dams and falls render much of the distance unfit for boating. A variety of trips, however, is still possible. The main branch is a big swift river, wide and deep, with quiet pools and some marshes. There is fast white water but plenty of maneuvering room, ideal for the intermediate canoeist. A twenty-four-mile run from Nimbus Dam to Discovery Park takes seven hours and can be made in a scenic overnight. The camping spots at Goethe Park, twelve miles downriver from the put-in, provide water and fire pits. Travel any month except April (too high), August, September, and October (too low).

The North Fork is also a Class II trip from Highway 49 and Folsom Lake. Take-out is at Rattlesnake Bar. The Middle Fork from Greenwood Bridge to Murderer's Bar can be more difficult, depending on water level. In one section the river makes an oxbow bend back to within fifty feet of its starting place. Old-time miners blasted a tunnel through this spot. Today some experts have boasted of negotiating this opening, but the chute is tumultuous and should be portaged by most.

The best boating is on the South Fork. May through September is the season for traveling from the Highway 193 bridge to the Salmon Bar Bridge on Folsom Lake. At normal summer flow, difficulty will be Class III, but several rapids are Class IV. This run has over fifty rapids. The first long rapid is Meatgrinder, so called because standing waves, called a haystack, hide a pointed rock that has slashed many raft bottoms. In the third section of the river, from Lotus to Folsom Lake, the riverbed is granite, the canyon walls jagged and fearsome when the river shoots into the American

Gorge. In the gorge, one rapid follows another for eight miles. Each rapid can be run, but it means hard work for the bailers to keep the raft from swamping. This twenty-mile trip will take from one to two days.

For more information contact the American River Touring Association, 1016 Jackson Street, Oakland, CA 94607, and the American River Canoe Trips, P.O. Box 5488, Sacramento, CA 95814.

KLAMATH RIVER

Time of year: June to October

Degree of difficulty: intermediate

Craft: canoe, kayak, raft

Character: semiwild

Permit required: no

Rentals available: yes

The Klamath is a long, large river rising above Upper Klamath Lake on the eastern side of the Oregon Cascades and making its way through northwestern California to the Pacific. Its upper reaches pass through rocky, arid canyons. In the central section near Happy Camp the canyon deepens and is abutted by many isolated gorges. In its final run to the Pacific, the Klamath is flanked by the gentler mountains of the Coast Range.

This rugged wilderness area is the land of Big Foot. It is said that the traveler along the Klamath will find that his food supplies have mysteriously run short. And very large boulders, again mysteriously, seem to shift around from year to year. If you miss Big Foot, you should at least glimpse great blue heron, osprey, bald eagle, killdeer, mink, otter, and bear. Be sure to take tackle for the Klamath's famous steelhead and salmon. Trout, sturgeon, and striped bass also live in these waters.

Because the Klamath is dam-controlled, its season is a long one—from June through October. During winter and spring the waters are too high and dangerous. A sixty-seven-mile trip from Horse Creek to Ti Bar takes about six days. If you have time for only a three-day trip, run the thirty-mile section from Happy Camp to Ti Bar. This stretch is the more exciting.

The rapids—Hamburg Falls, Rattlesnake Creek, Swillup Creek, and King Creek—are of moderate difficulty. Some scouting may be necessary. The stretch from Happy Camp to Salmon River is not for the casual boatman. Most of this run is through canyons, and there is little or no access in case of trouble. The most dangerous rapid of this run is Ishi Pishi Falls, an impassable series of hundred-yard-long sloping boulder fields, with several perpendicular five- and six-foot drops. Though you will not be running this rapids, you should try and time your trip so that you will be at the falls in early autumn, when the Klamath River Indians net fish in their ancient manner. There is also an annual Big Foot Celebration at Happy Camp. If possible, allow extra time to visit the Mount Shasta Caverns nearby.

For further information contact the Happy Camp Chamber of Commerce, Happy Camp, CA 96039.

DOLORES RIVER

Time of year: May to June

Degree of difficulty: intermediate

Craft: canoe, kayak, raft

Character: semiwild

Permit required: no

Rentals available: no

The Dolores drains the La Plata Mountains of southwestern Colorado, crossing into Utah to join the Colorado River some thirty miles north of Moab.

Winding through canyons and mesas, the river is fast, narrow, and scenic. Best of all, it has only recently been discovered by river runners. The season, however, is quite short. There is only enough water in the Dolores from May through early June.

An eight-day, hundred-mile trip can be made from Cahone to Bedrock. Or you can start at Slickrock for a forty-six-mile, three- to four-day trip. Put in at Slickrock or Gladel, as it is sometimes called, twenty-two miles north of Dove Creek on State Highway 141. Bedrock, your take-out, is on State Highway 90 southwest of Uravan. In season, this run is an easy one for rafters and kayakers. Canoeists must be very experienced. Though there are relatively few rapids and no obstructions, the hydraulics are tricky and the walk home is through extremely rough country.

Snaggletooth Rapids in Slickrock Canyon promises fast, exciting action. Farther on, in Gypsum Valley, before entering the sandstone walls of Bedrock Canyon, the river changes pace to meander in lazy loops. Camping is generally excellent, except in Big Gypsum Valley, which is fenced-off range land. Be sure and boil your water unless you have gathered it in a seep or spring. The clear welling of spring water in Bull Creek Canyon is pure.

Occasional farms and ranches are visible, and a road parallels the river. Numerous side streams rising out of canyons cry out to be explored on foot.

For further information contact the Uncompahgre National Forest, District Ranger, Delta, CO 81416. You will need the following United States Geologic Survey Quadrangle maps: Horse Range Mesa, Hamm Canyon, Anderson Mesa, Paradox, Davis Mesa, Red Canyon, Rock Creek, Juanita Arch, and Gateway.

GREEN RIVER

Time of year: May to October

Degree of difficulty: various

Craft: kayak, raft, dory

Character: wild

Permit required: yes

Rentals available: yes

The Green River headwaters lie in the Wyoming Wind River Mountains of the Bridger Wilderness. Tumbling from the Continental Divide, the Green flows south until it reaches the northwestern corner of Colorado. There it veers sharply eastward to merge with the Yampa and then continues down through Utah to arrive at its famous confluence with the Colorado near Moab. A great number of trips, some in true wilderness and others through carefully managed parkland, are possible.

The uppermost northern reaches are wild and free-flowing. The river is clear, swift, and shallow; the country remote. In a forty-mile stretch in western Wyoming, south of Grand Teton National Park, only two wooden bridges cross the stream. July through October is the season for this two-day trip. Put in at Whiskey Grove Campground off I-80 and take out at Warren Bridge Campground, where U.S. 187/189 cross the river.

Near Whiskey Grove, visit Warm Springs, with its indigenous Kendall dace, a fish found nowhere else in the world. Backtracking into the Bridger Wilderness and across the Continental Divide is almost irresistible. Here, early westward trails—the Overland, Pony Express, Mormon, and others—found their way through the Rockies. Though the country is wild, the river is not. Difficulty is only Class I and Class II. Rafts may be rented in the area; canoes must be car-topped in.

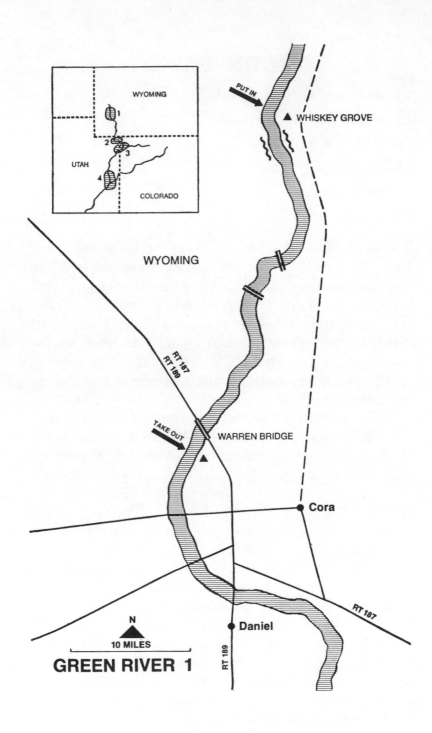

GREEN RIVER 1

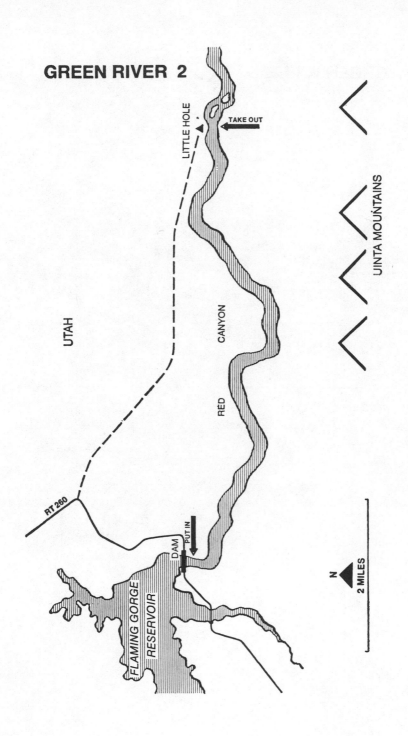

GREEN RIVER 2

LITTLE HOLE

TAKE OUT

UINTA MOUNTAINS

UTAH

CANYON

RED

RT 260

FLAMING GORGE RESERVOIR

DAM

PUT IN

N
2 MILES

GREEN RIVER 3

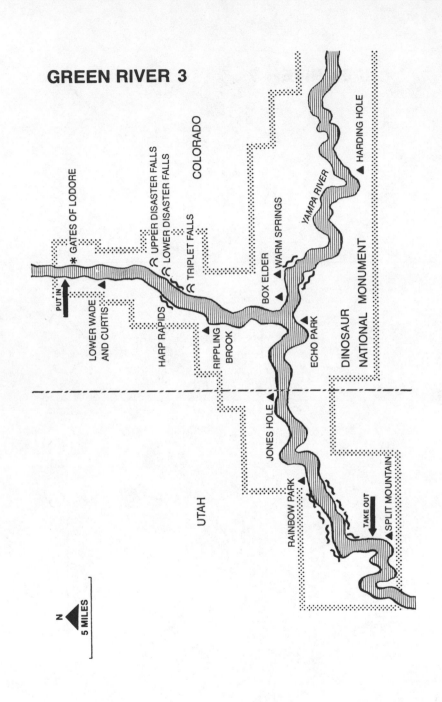

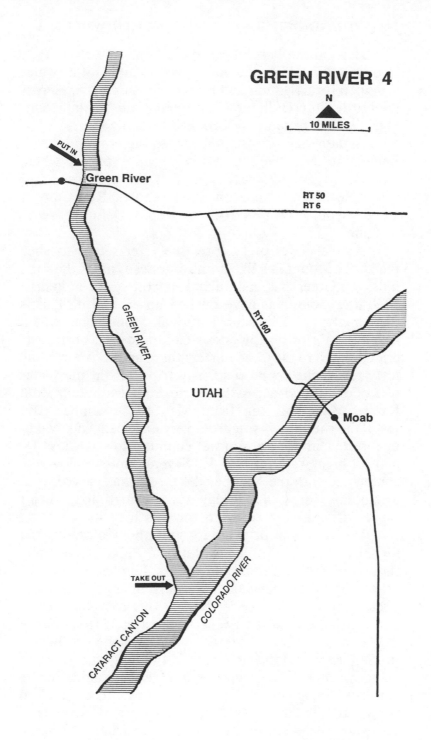

GREEN RIVER 4

N

10 MILES

PUT IN

Green River

RT 50
RT 6

RT 160

GREEN RIVER

UTAH

Moab

TAKE OUT

CATARACT CANYON

COLORADO RIVER

Beyond the base of the mountains, the river flows through a long, highland valley, where much of its water is tapped for irrigation and human consumption. Across the border into Utah the Green enters the Uinta Mountains through brilliant, red-rocked Flaming Gorge.

A dam was constructed across the gorge in 1962. Below the dam there is a twelve-mile run on which motors are not allowed. You can leave the river at Little Hole or continue on to the end of Red Canyon and test your skills at Red Creek Rapid. Definitely scout this one.

At the Gates of Lodore, the river seems to slice the Uinta Mountains like a knife. Indeed, older than the hills, the Green has maintained its course for millennia while the mountains have pushed up around it. This is the country of Dinosaur National Monument, which spans the tip of northwestern Colorado and northeastern Utah. Here the Green meets the Yampa. An exciting forty-four-mile, four- to six-day trip is from the Gates of Lodore (road access here) to Split Mountain Boat Ramp. Make this run from May to September. But make the run only if you are a very experienced kayaker or rafter. Difficulty at normal summer flow is Class IV and at high water, Class V. Several miles below the confluence with the Yampa, the Green has carved Split Mountain Gorge, a one-day run through four major rapids. Permits are required for this trip.

In Utah, on its way to join the Colorado, the Green crosses Canyonlands National Park, a geological fantasy of exposed color and shapes. Perched on shelves beneath overhanging cliffs, ancient stone dwellings argue irrefutably that man once lived in this rock-hard land.

The one hundred twenty-mile stretch from put-in at Green River State Park to take-out at the confluence of the Green and the Colorado is the longest section of smooth water on the river. There are no rapids in the canyons. Some four miles below the mouth of the San Rafael River, the Green enters Labyrinth Canyon and the walls rise sharply up to a thousand feet. At some point the water has undercut the rock faces so that they lean out overhead. Upheaval Canyon follows, and finally Stillwater Canyon with its abundance of prickly pear cactus and jimsonweed.

Wild burros, as well as bighorn sheep, live here. You will want to do much hiking in the narrow side canyons. Of special interest are the spectacular rock formations such as Turk's Head and Candlestick Tower in the final thirty miles. Good campsites can be found on sandbars in the sweeping bends where willows and tamarisks grow.

Take out at the confluence if you do not want to challenge white water. The next forty-seven miles, through Cataract Canyon, have been dubbed by early explorers "the graveyard of the Colorado." Be prepared for rapids that equal the Grand Canyon in power and difficulty. In the high water of May and June, they can become particularly fearsome.

Between the confluence and the take-out at Lake Powell, there are forty-two rapids. Mile Long rapids is actually six rapids in quick succession. Two miles farther is Bip Drop, where the gradient is so steep as to make the rapids seem to be a tilted waterfall. This rapid has been described as one of the toughest in America. It is runnable, but all caution is advised. The season for the run from Green River to Hite Marina on Lake Powell is May through October. Anyone making the run from the confluence must register and obtain a permit from the park authority. A permit is not required for the more gentle float on the Green River proper.

For further information, get in touch with the superintendents of the parks.

DESOLATION CANYON, GREEN RIVER

Time of year: June to October

Degree of difficulty: intermediate to expert

Craft: kayak, raft, dory

Character: wild

Permit required: no

Rentals available: yes

"The canyon is very tortuous, the river very rapid, and many lateral canyons enter on either side. Crags and tower-shaped peaks are seen everywhere, and above them long lines of broken cliffs: beyond the cliffs are pine forests of which we obtain occasional glimpses as we look up through a vista of rocks. We are minded to call this the Canyon of Desolation." So it appeared to John Wesley Powell in 1869. Modern-day travelers on the Green River's Desolation Canyon above its juncture with the Colorado are apt to see things differently. Viewing the colorful cliffs rising to skyline forests of pine and fir, riverside groves of giant cottonwoods, rare, delicate flowers in hidden rock gardens and ancient Indian petroglyphs, they are more likely to feel every emotion but desolation.

Yet from Powell's day, the canyon is little changed. Once a ferry at Sand Wash shuttled sheep across, but spring floods broke the cables in 1952 and they were never repaired. There was some early shale exploration in this area, and a few groups surveyed for dam possibilities, but fortunately the river has escaped the technological touch of man.

Both Desolation Canyon and the shorter Gray Canyon that follows it resemble the Grand Canyon in majesty and immensity. But this stretch of river is more a wilderness experience than the high white-water adventure to be had downstream in the Grand Canyon.

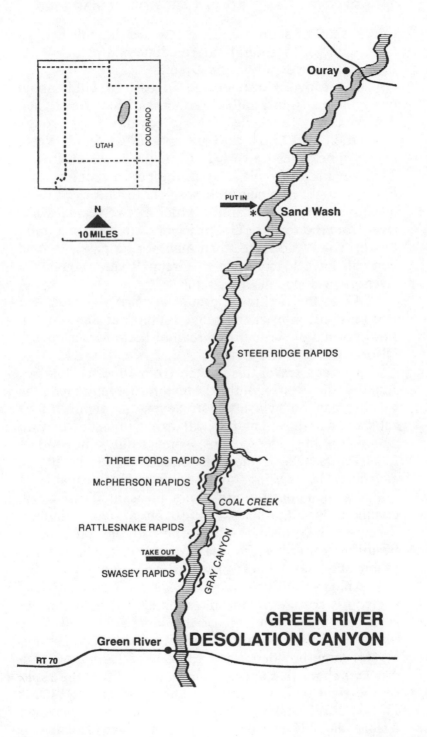

UTAH

COLORADO

N

10 MILES

Ouray

PUT IN →

* Sand Wash

STEER RIDGE RAPIDS

THREE FORDS RAPIDS

McPHERSON RAPIDS

COAL CREEK

RATTLESNAKE RAPIDS

TAKE OUT →

SWASEY RAPIDS

GRAY CANYON

Green River

RT 70

**GREEN RIVER
DESOLATION CANYON**

Of the sixty or more rapids, a few are difficult enough to be scouted. In general, intermediate boatmen will not be out of their depth on the Green.

The canyons are located in eastern Utah about one hundred twenty miles southeast of Salt Lake City. For an eighty-four-mile, five- to ten-day trip through Desolation and Gray canyons, put in at Sand Wash, twenty-nine miles downriver from the town of Ouray. The rough road from Ouray to the put-in requires daylight. At night it is nearly impossible to find the access. Take out at Swasey Rapids, which is twelve miles upriver from the town of Green River. After a heavy rain, the dirt road leading to town may not be passable, and you will have to continue to Green River, though the river is developed in this stretch.

As of this writing, permits are not required, but you must check in at the ranger station at Sand Wash. For information write the Bureau of Land Management, District Office, P.O. Drawer AB, Price, UT 84501.

You can travel this stretch from June to October. June is the best month. Later in the summer, the weather can be hellishly hot. Seven- to eighteen-foot rafts are suitable. Angling will bring in many catfish, and off in the side streams, some trout. The midget faded rattlesnake is the only dangerous reptile in the canyons. The two-foot snake is probably incapable of killing a man, but its bite is not pleasant. Poison ivy, common along the bank, is probably a greater danger. To offset this nuisance plant, the canyons offer more beautiful flora like the black sagebrush, shad scale, rabbit brush, and a host of wild flowering plants.

Among rapids to be scouted, Coal Creek in Gray Canyon is considered the most difficult. Run it on the right side but watch out for the large rock and wave on the extreme right at the head. Also, just downstream, several large boulders have caused the formation of a crooked channel. Land a quarter mile above the rapid on the right bank to scout it. The rapid is rated Class IV. At Rattlesnake Rapid, Class III, water piles up against the cliff, causing tricky angular waves. There is also a boulder in midstream near the foot. You should also be on the watch for Steer Ridge Rapid, which lies hidden around a bend ready to surprise the unsuspecting boatman; McPherson Rapid (Class III) and Three Fords Rapid, at the head of Gray Canyon, are also challenging.

The looming red walls dotted with piñon and juniper on the talus slopes that characterize Desolation Canyon in Utah give way to lower cliffs in muted browns, yellows, and tans. Plant life varies. One plant, however, should not be missed, the famous Green River melon.

For further information about the river, write the State Director at the Bureau of Land Management office listed above. And for guides, the Ute Indian Tribe provides service. Write Ute Trails and Rivers, Fort Duchesne, UT 84026.

TUOLUMNE RIVER

Time of year: May to September

Degree of difficulty: intermediate to expert

Craft: kayak, raft

Character: wild

Permit required: yes

Rentals available: yes

The Tuolumne boasts one of the last few stretches of wilderness white water left in the entire state of California. The Sierra Club, joined by others, has labored for the abandonment of O'Shaughnessy Dam and the old Lake Eleanor Dam and to block construction of any new dams on the river. In 1975 Congress named the river for consideration as part of the Wild and Scenic Rivers system. A study by National Park Service and various other government agencies is now taking place.

The one hundred fifty-eight-mile Tuolumne rises from under the Mt. Lyell Glacier in Yosemite National Park and flows down the western Sierra Nevada to join the San Joaquin River near Modesto, California. In that brief course the river has cut one of the world's most majestic canyons, irrigates some of the world's richest farmland, fills one of its largest reservoirs, and provides fresh water for the entire city of San Francisco.

With all that, it still remains a delight to river runners. Certainly, the eighteen-mile course from Lumsden Campground to Wards Ferry is among the most exhilarating continuous white-water runs in the country. The stretch is decidedly out of bounds for the canoeists, and only the most expert kayakers and rafters should attempt it.

The river begins in Yosemite National Park. The scenery is beautiful here. Above Early Intake, the Tuolumne canyon is U-shaped. Steep bare rock slopes, almost vertical at some points, drop into stream-side talus slopes and large alluvial flats. There are big pools and sandy beaches. Small footpaths and fishermen's trails give access to the area for hikers and campers. But the low water flows, dependent on O'Shaughnessy Dam, discourage any type of boating here.

The section from Early Intake to Lake Don Pedro is runnable. Access trails, however, dating from the early days of the Forest Service or those cut by miners and fishermen, are "hands and knees only." But the Tuolumne, more a giant creek than a river, is breathtaking, the water crystal clear, the canyon bedecked with greenery and wild flowers. In addition to life jackets and extra paddles, the many rock-choked passages demand crash helmets and wet suits. Rafts should be no longer than seventeen feet, and the man at the oars an expert, preferably with experience on the Tuolumne.

For an eighteen-mile, two- or three-day trip in this stretch, put in at Lumsden Campground, about fifteen miles west of the entrance to Yosemite National Park and two miles downstream from Lumsden Bridge. About a hundred yards upstream of the put-in, there is a public campground with toilets, picnic tables, and fire pits. Your take-out will be at the Wards Ferry Bridge. A dirt road there leads down to the water's edge.

You can run this stretch from May to September. Flow from the Hetch Hetchy Dam fluctuates, depending on the amount of electricity being generated. Bear in mind that the demand in San Francisco is greatest during the week and less on weekends. During late summer, volumes below six hundred cfs on weekends render this section unrunnable. Contact Hetch Hetchy Dam for up-to-date details, and remember that four thousand cfs is considered the upper limit of runnability on the river.

The gradient on this run is extremely steep, the rapids almost continuous. The drop from Lumsden Bridge to Clavey River is fifty feet to the mile. From Clavey River to Wards Ferry Bridge, it is thirty-five feet to the mile. Clavey Falls should definitely be scouted. At some water levels you can run it on the left, but at others you may have to run on the right or even line your boat or carry it. Below this rapids, there is more space between the falls, but the rapids continue to demand full attention. At extremely low water, the last rapid before Wards Ferry Bridge is the most challenging of all.

For information about permits, write the United States Forest Service, Groveland Ranger Station, Highway 120, Groveland, CA 95321.

A final section from La Grange Dam to Waterford is eighteen miles (six hours) of very gentle Class I river. The current is steady and strong, with mild riffles. Along the way you will see heron and snowy egret rookeries in the huge oak trees that line the south bank.

For more details write the American River Touring Association, 1016 Jackson Street, Oakland, CA 94607. Maps of the area are available from the United States Department of Agriculture, Forest Service, 630 Sansome Street, San Francisco, CA 94111.

THE NORTHWEST

THE Northwest (Washington, Oregon, and Idaho) is big country under big sky with big and wild rivers to match. They flow out of the Rocky Mountains and the Cascades and through the desert region of southern Idaho. Outside Alaska, this is the least tamed corner of the United States. It is possible to sample the richness of the Northwest with a raft trip of half a day or a full day on the Upper Snake River as it threads its way lazily across the flat bottom of Jackson Hole, Wyoming, under the peaks of the Grand Tetons. And each year some seventy thousand people do.

To do justice to the rivers of the Northwest requires, indeed demands, more than a day's time. Hell's Canyon on the Snake and the Salmon, the Bruneau, and the Owyhee are all rivers that deserve a week or more, whether you sign up with a commercial outfitter or take your own raft or kayak. There are plenty of sections in this part of the country that can be run in open canoes, but to do so is a little like using a Flexible Flyer sled on the ski runs at Vail. The appropriate craft are rafts, kayaks, and river dories, designed to handle big water. Kayakers will want to bring along a support raft to carry the camping gear.

Nearly all the rivers mentioned in this section—and in most of the others as well—are regulated by one government agency or another. If you are planning your own expedition, it cannot be emphasized too strongly that you must write for reservations well in advance— often as much as a year before you intend to go. If you have never been on really big water before, an advisable first step is to sign up for one of the many commercial float trips available in this part of the country. You can get a list of reputable outfitters from the Chamber of Commerce at a city in the vicinity of the river you have chosen or by writing to the headquarters of the nearest national park. The men who run these trips are usually excellent guides, more than willing to share their years of experience. Moreover, unless the weather happens to be foul during the entire trip, river running must be reckoned in terms of pleasure per dollar as one of the least expensive vacations one can imagine.

The weather in the Northwest can be a problem. Even in the dry desert regions of southern Idaho, storms brew up quickly to change a warm sunny day into one that is thunderous, drenching, and chill. So pack accordingly.

Other caveats include rattlesnakes and, to a lesser degree, poison ivy and an occasional too-inquisitive bear. A snake-bite kit should be included in any first-aid kit that does not already have one. Keep an eye out for poison ivy if you are allergic to it, and take the necessary precautions around camp to discourage bears (see Chapter 6). However dangerous a river may be, it is not ordinarily the rapids but the unexpected little mishaps that are most likely to tie knots in your trip.

Many of the rivers in the Northwest have longer seasons than you might expect. There is one advantage to dams and reservoirs—as, for instance, on the Snake. The flow can be spaced out and the river maintained at a runnable level earlier and later than on a truly wild river. Trips on unregulated rivers, therefore, should, where possible, be planned for the early part of the season. Trips late in the season often must be started at some point farther downstream. Always remember, too, that conditions vary enormously from year to year, depending on the amount of snow the previous winter and how much rain falls in the spring and summer. So if you are going on a free-flowing river, you will want to check with the local authorities immediately before departure—which you will have to do anyway, in most cases, to get your permit.

Alas, folks, the days of the independent mountain-man who took on the West as he found it are over; he has been replaced by the forest ranger and the power dam. But for those who like to pretend that it just ain't so, the Northwest is about the best setting you can find to re-create the way it was.

MIDDLE FORK, SALMON RIVER

Wild and Scenic River

Time of year: *July to September*

Degree of difficulty: *expert*

Craft: *kayak, raft, dory*

Character: *wild*

Permit required: *For information write Challis National Forest, Forest Service Building, Challis, ID 83226.*

Rentals available: *no; guided trips are available*

The Salmon River, with its three forks, drains central Idaho's 2.5-million-acre wilderness area, the largest remaining in the United States outside Alaska. The Salmon is unfettered by impoundments, rare for so vigorous a stream in this power-hungry age. The river rises naturally every spring, picking up driftwood and silt to run high, opaque, dangerous, for a few weeks. Runs at this time are rated "suicidal" by seasoned Salmon River hands.

When the snowmelt season is past, the Salmon clears and eases up, leaving behind what veteran river-man Verne Huser has called "the most beautiful camp-

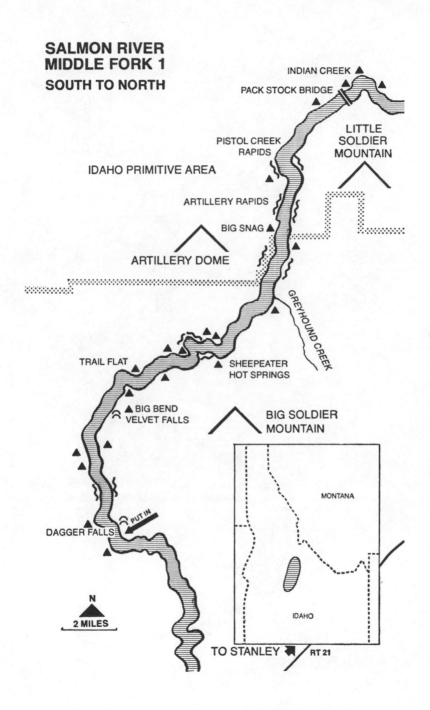

SALMON RIVER MIDDLE FORK 1

SOUTH TO NORTH

INDIAN CREEK ▲

PACK STOCK BRIDGE

PISTOL CREEK RAPIDS

IDAHO PRIMITIVE AREA

LITTLE SOLDIER MOUNTAIN

ARTILLERY RAPIDS

BIG SNAG ▲

ARTILLERY DOME

GREYHOUND CREEK

TRAIL FLAT

SHEEPEATER HOT SPRINGS

BIG SOLDIER MOUNTAIN

▲ BIG BEND
VELVET FALLS

PUT IN

MONTANA

DAGGER FALLS

IDAHO

N
2 MILES

TO STANLEY ← RT 21

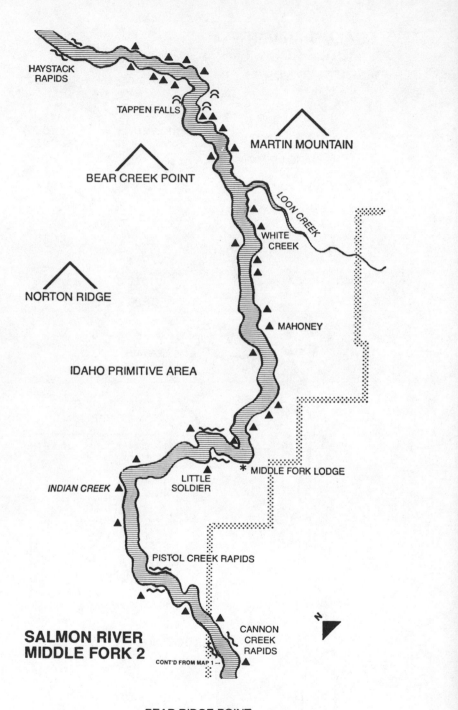

HAYSTACK
RAPIDS

TAPPEN FALLS

MARTIN MOUNTAIN

BEAR CREEK POINT

LOON CREEK

WHITE
CREEK

NORTON RIDGE

MAHONEY

IDAHO PRIMITIVE AREA

* MIDDLE FORK LODGE

INDIAN CREEK

LITTLE
SOLDIER

PISTOL CREEK RAPIDS

N

CANNON
CREEK
RAPIDS

**SALMON RIVER
MIDDLE FORK 2**

CONT'D FROM MAP 1 →

BEAR RIDGE POINT

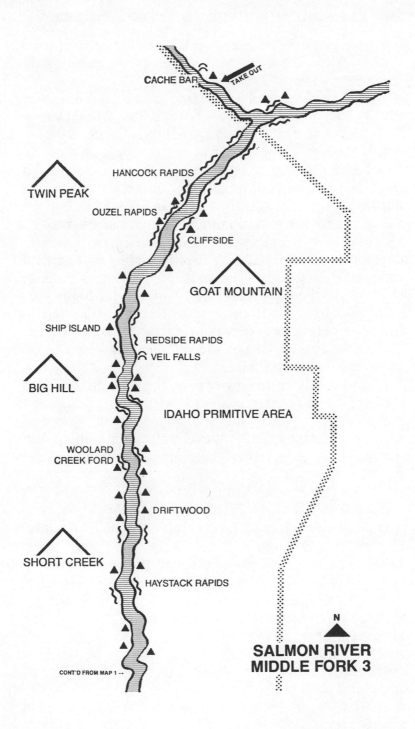

CACHE BAR

TAKE OUT

HANCOCK RAPIDS

TWIN PEAK

OUZEL RAPIDS

CLIFFSIDE

GOAT MOUNTAIN

SHIP ISLAND

REDSIDE RAPIDS

VEIL FALLS

BIG HILL

IDAHO PRIMITIVE AREA

WOOLARD
CREEK FORD

DRIFTWOOD

SHORT CREEK

HAYSTACK RAPIDS

N

CONT'D FROM MAP 1 →

SALMON RIVER
MIDDLE FORK 3

ing beaches I have ever known." The piles of driftwood thrown up on the bars and beaches make camping all the more pleasant.

The wildest, most interesting, and varied trip is on the Middle Fork, a ninety-six-mile run from Dagger Falls down to the confluence with the main Salmon, where there is a take-out ramp on the right side of the river. The trip may take anywhere from five to seven days, and a more rewarding week in the wilderness can hardly be imagined. At the beginning, the Middle Fork has the character of a mountain stream, narrow enough to heave a stone across, shallow, rocky, with nearly continuous Class III and IV rapids, ending in a vertical drop at Velvet Falls. The altitude at Dagger Falls is roughly six thousand feet. The banks are heavily forested with hardwoods and evergreens. Nights are crisp, the water clear and fresh—in fact, the water of the Salmon is considered potable all the way down to its confluence with the Snake.

Some sixty miles downstream the river grows. Here it enters desert country, with sagebrush, dry grasses, and barren rock replacing the high-mountain character of the upper stream. Finally, the Middle Fork plunges into a steep rocky gorge, which narrows as the mouth of the river is approached.

The free-flowing nature of the Salmon means that water levels can be expected to drop through the summer. The season is a short one, July through September. Earlier than that there is apt to be too much water; later, not enough. Halfway through the season the top twenty-eight miles of the river may be too low, and rafters will have their gear flown in to a little airstrip at Indian Creek. At any season the lower section of the river can be expected to be big and muscular, with heavy hydraulics. The rapids here need to be scouted. But experienced boaters should not find it necessary to make any portages.

The Middle Fork is a charter member of the Wild and Scenic Rivers system and is perhaps the best controlled river in the country, in the sense of recreational usage. It became so popular in the early 1970s that stringent regulations had to be instituted. In 1973 some four thousand five hundred people ran the Middle Fork, an increase from six hundred twenty-five in an entire decade. Before that, only Indians and miners and an occasional wilderness rancher bothered to enter this hard country. It is ironic that the heaviest usage our remaining wilderness areas are experiencing is from those who seek unspoiled solitude. Be that as it may, it has become necessary to limit the number of parties leaving Dagger Falls to six per day, which may seem like a lot until one learns how many more applications there are. On the plus side, the river is big enough and the land grand enough to swallow up that many river runners, so that once you are launched, it is quite possible to feel alone.

If you go with professional guides on an organized trip, registration is, of course, taken care of for you. Information on guided trips can be obtained from Western River Guides Association, 994 Denver Street, Salt Lake City, Utah 84111, or from Idaho Outfitters and Guides Association, Box 95, Boise, Idaho 83701.

To take your own raft or kayak—canoes, even closed canoes, are not seaworthy for this kind of water —you must write early. Reservations will be accepted beginning October 1 for the following season. Address your request to Middle Fork District Ranger, Challis National Forest, Challis, Idaho 83226. They will send you an application form and a list of the requirements you must meet in the way of experience and equipment. If all this sounds a bit much, the Salmon is worth it. Reservations have become a fact of life in the pursuit of wilderness. And it must be so if the character of the West's public lands is to be preserved.

Such heavy traffic has pushed back the wildlife along the river so that it is not so evident as it was a decade or two ago. The fishing, however, is excellent, though the steelhead trout, for which the Salmon is famous, have diminished in number lately.

The trip into this wilderness area is not as difficult

as might be imagined. Twenty miles west of Stanley, Idaho, on Highway 93, make a right turn on a road marked Dagger Falls. To get to the take-out, drive northeast of Stanley on Highway 93 to North Fork and follow the road along the river from there to the confluence.

All parts of the Salmon are well documented. The scroll map, *Middle Fork of the Salmon,* is a must if you are going to run that river; it is available from Leslie A. Jones, Star Route Box 13A, Heber City, Utah 84032.

ROGUE RIVER

Wild and Scenic River

Time of year: May to September

Degree of difficulty: intermediate

Craft: canoe, kayak, raft, dory

Character: wild

Permit required: For information write Bureau of Land Management, P.O. Box 2965, Portland, OR 97208.

Rentals available: yes

The Rogue is a wilderness highway tucked into the southwest corner of Oregon. Chinook salmon and steelhead trout go up to spawn, and river runners come down, and it is hard to say which bunch enjoys the trip more.

In the decade following the California gold rush, the Rogue and many western rivers like it were ravaged to a fare-thee-well. An army of unshaven prospectors tore up the riverbanks from Gold Beach on the Pacific right up to Crater Lake, some two hundred miles from the sea, where the Rogue rises in the heart of the Cascade Range. One hundred years have healed those scars, and long stretches of the Lower Rogue, protected now

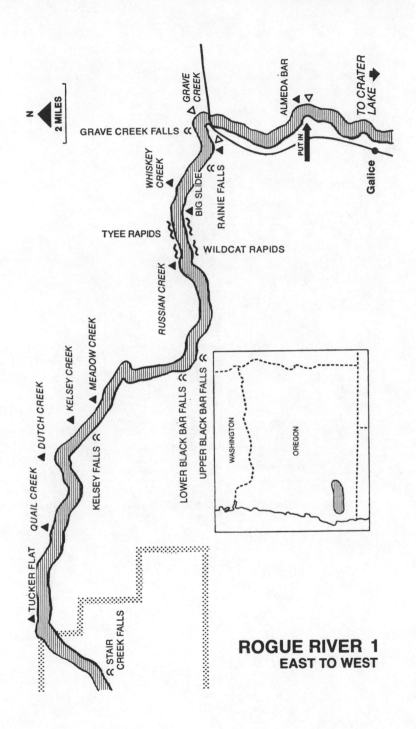

ROGUE RIVER 1
EAST TO WEST

N
2 MILES

TO CRATER LAKE

GRAVE CREEK

ALMEDA BAR

PUT IN

Galice

GRAVE CREEK FALLS

WHISKEY CREEK

BIG SLIDE

RAINIE FALLS

TYEE RAPIDS

WILDCAT RAPIDS

RUSSIAN CREEK

MEADOW CREEK

KELSEY CREEK

DUTCH CREEK

QUAIL CREEK

TUCKER FLAT

KELSEY FALLS

LOWER BLACK BAR FALLS

UPPER BLACK BAR FALLS

STAIR CREEK FALLS

WASHINGTON

OREGON

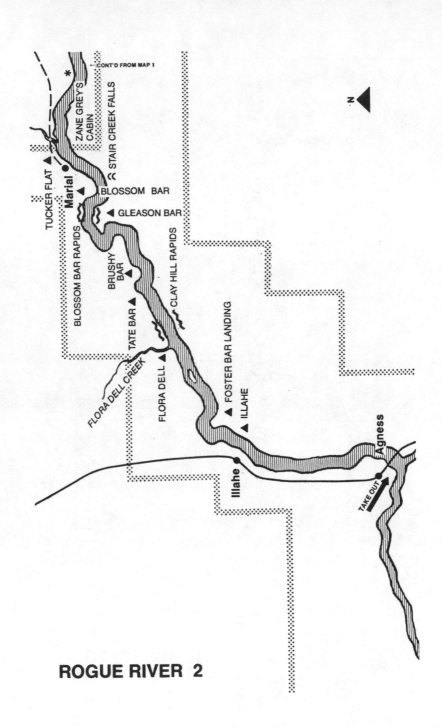

N

←CONT'D FROM MAP 1

ZANE GREY'S CABIN

STAIR CREEK FALLS

TUCKER FLAT

Marial

BLOSSOM BAR

BLOSSOM BAR RAPIDS

GLEASON BAR

BRUSHY BAR

CLAY HILL RAPIDS

TATE BAR

FLORA DELL CREEK

FLORA DELL

FOSTER BAR LANDING

ILLAHE

Agness

Illahe

TAKE OUT

ROGUE RIVER 2

as a charter member of the Wild and Scenic Rivers system, is looking once more like the first-class wilderness river it is.

A half century ago Zane Grey discovered the fabulous fishing the Rogue offered. The camp that was Grey's headquarters and where he wrote a number of his novels about the wild and woolly days of the West still stands at Winkle Bar.

The Rogue is a handsome mountain river, blessedly free along its lower section from the usual encroachments of civilization. Parts of the river are suitable to every sort of boating. The upper section calls for kayaks, rafts, or river dories. Stretches of placid water and deep green pools, great for swimming during the summer, alternate with challenging rapids. There is only one portage, at Rainie Falls, and that can be lined down a side chute maintained as a fish ladder. Below the little settlement of Agness, the trip can be made in an open canoe all the way to the sea. A road follows the river, but the major portion of the run is through national forest.

Though several commercial lodges are spaced along the river, the section from Grave Creek Bridge down to Illahe rates as prime wilderness, with only one access road at Marial. Here the Rogue has sliced down through the burgeoning mountains, laying bare awesome amounts of rock, a geologist's delight. The vegetation is ash and bigleaf maple in damp areas, madrone and white oak on dry ridges. Farther downriver western red cedar, yew, live oak, golden chinquapin, Douglas fir, and hemlock crowd the banks. Side streams, whose gin-clear water is the true glory of the Rogue, are lined with rhododendron, azalea, dogwood, grape, and a profusion of ferns. Otter, raccoon, mink, black-tailed deer, are often seen. Eagles, water oozle, woodpeckers, and osprey all work the river. The fishing is excellent, with spring the prime season, but there is a good run in the fall as well.

The recommended run is from Grave Creek Bridge

down to Agness. The distance is forty-five miles, and
the trip may take anywhere from two to five days,
depending on how much rambling up the side streams
one is inclined to. A hiking trail follows the river along
this stretch. If you intend to fish, get a license. This can
be done in any town in Oregon.

The Rogue rapids are generally rated Class II and
III, depending on the amount of water in the river. The
range is from about two thousand cfs to ten times that
figure. In low water it is the rocks you must look out for;
in high water, the hydraulics. It is possible to take an
inflated raft over Rainie Falls, but only the most expert
should try this, and even then they can expect a dunking. It is a straight ten-foot drop over boulders, and as
stated, the recommended route is to line your craft
down the fish ladder on the right bank.

There are many campsites along the way. As of
this writing it is not necessary to camp at maintained
sites. But if you intend to run the river, you will need
a permit. Write either to the Bureau of Land Management, Medford District Office, 310 W. 6th Street, Medford, OR 97501 or to the Forest Supervisor, Siskiyou
National Forest, P.O. Box 440, Grants Pass, OR 97526.
Either place will send you gratis a fine map of the river
covering both navigational and scenic points. Drinking
water is available at some locations. Otherwise boil the
water or use tablets. There is plenty of potable water
in the Rogue's many side streams. The river itself is less
savory at Grants Pass and above, because of commercial wastes that have been dumped into it. The swimming, however, is safe and fun.

The season to run the Rogue is May through September. In very wet years the river may be dangerously
high in spring. The Rogue is not dammed below Crater
Lake, a rare blessing these days. Traffic on the river
gets fairly heavy during July and August.

You can get on the river at any place from Galice,
twenty miles below Grants Pass down to Grave Creek,
where the river and road go their separate ways.

SNAKE RIVER

Wild and Scenic River

Time of year: *May to September*

Degree of difficulty: *intermediate to expert*

Craft: *kayak, raft, dory*

Character: *wild*

Permit required: *For information write Hell's Canyon National Recreational Area, P.O. Box 907, Baker, OR 97814.*

Rentals available: *no; guided trips are available*

The Snake is a monumental river with two entirely separate sections to interest boaters. It rises in Yellowstone National Park and draws strength from the melting snows and glaciers of the Grand Tetons before heading west across southern Idaho. Blocked by the coastal range, it turns north, forming the natural border between Idaho and Oregon, and finally west again into Washington to pour its water into the mighty, and mightily spoiled, Columbia.

The Yellowstone–Grand Teton section of the river is in Wyoming. Here, in Grand Teton National Park, commercial rafting is big business. Most outfitters run short trips of a day or half day, accounting for more than fifty thousand passengers per season. A favorite is the twelve-mile drift from Dead Man's Landing to Moose, costing about eight dollars per person. The scenery—snow-capped Tetons rising like white walls from the flat land of Jackson Hole—is as spectacular as any in the West, and the chatter from the guides is apt to be erudite, touching on everything from Pliocene gravel deposits to the eating habits of ravens.

A recommended solo day's run, for which you will need a permit (write to the Grand Teton National Park, Moose, WY 83012), begins at Buffalo Entrance Station

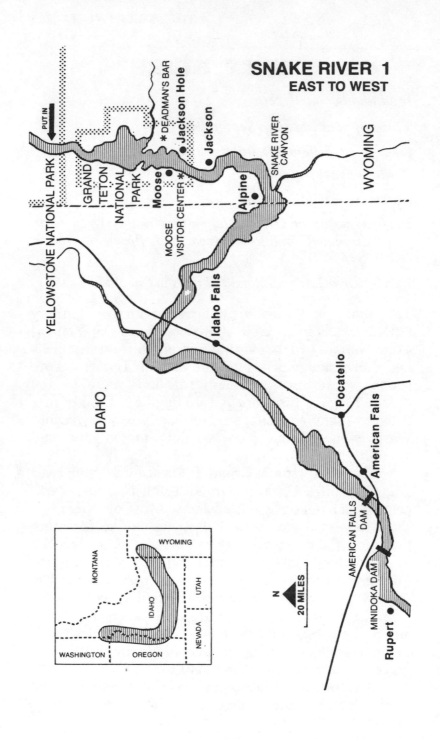

SNAKE RIVER 1
EAST TO WEST

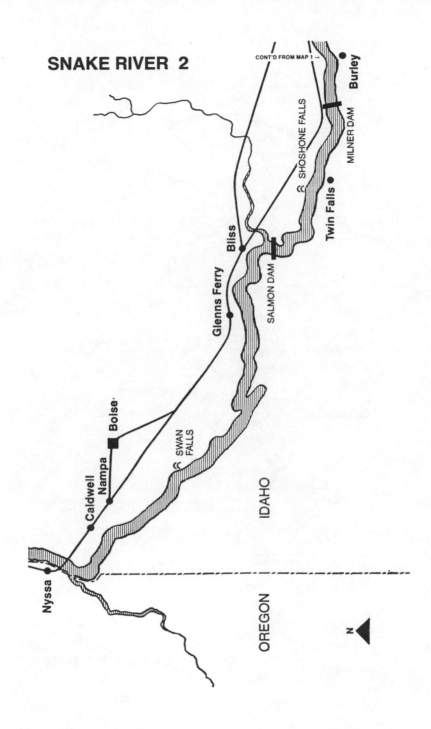

SNAKE RIVER 2

CONT'D FROM MAP 1 →

Burley

SHOSHONE FALLS

MILNER DAM

Twin Falls

Bliss

Glenns Ferry

SALMON DAM

Boise

Nampa

Caldwell

SWAN FALLS

IDAHO

Nyssa

OREGON

N

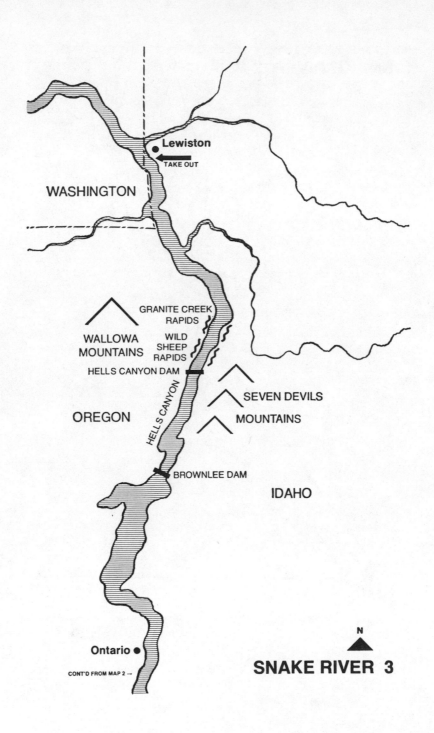

Lewiston
← TAKE OUT

WASHINGTON

GRANITE CREEK
RAPIDS

WALLOWA
MOUNTAINS

WILD
SHEEP
RAPIDS

HELLS CANYON DAM

HELLS CANYON

SEVEN DEVILS

OREGON

MOUNTAINS

BROWNLEE DAM

IDAHO

Ontario ●

CONT'D FROM MAP 2 →

N

SNAKE RIVER 3

and runs about twenty miles down to Moose Visitor's Center. There are no hazards or rapids above Class I, as the river meanders across the alluvial bottom land.

Below Jackson, where the river enters the Snake River Canyon, there is enough rough water to please river runners looking for more thrills. The wildest section of the Snake, however, lies several hundred miles downstream, where the river plunges through a magnificent defile called Hell's Canyon. Nearly half of this tremendous gorge that separates the Wallowa Mountains of Oregon from the Seven Devils of Idaho has been drowned by three major dams. But the Snake flows wild and free through the lower half of its grand canyon.

The put-in is just below Hell's Canyon Dam, from which point it is a hard four- or easy six-day trip to the mouth of the Grand Ronde, some eighty-five miles downriver, the first spot where one can conveniently get in with a conventional vehicle. Here the river passes between sloping mountainsides that rise seven thousand feet above the river. The water is usually clear and warm enough for delightful swimming, unlike the freezing Colorado River, its major rival for wild grandeur.

The two most challenging rapids come right at the beginning, Wild Sheep and Granite Creek, and either is equipped to capsize a dory or rubber raft. Both should be carefully scouted. Even the professional guides who take parties through Hell's Canyon week after week all summer and fall stop to look over these furious drops, because with each new change of water level the hydraulics change.

In between the drops and riffles the river runs gentle, deep, and easy. There are magnificent sand beaches to pull out and lunch and camp on—though campsites will be assigned when you get your permit (see below). Side streams provide excellent trout fishing (you will have to get licenses from Idaho and Oregon both if you wish to work both sides of the river).

Other interesting features of the lower Snake are the many abandoned mines. One shaft, several hundred yards long, pierces a Gibraltar-like headland of rock, all the way from the Snake through to the side of the tributary Imnaha River.

Hell's Canyon is strictly a kayak and raft course. Those taking kayaks through are advised to do so with a supporting raft to carry camping equipment, for there are no convenient take-out spots for nearly seventy miles below Hell's Canyon Dam. Rafting parties, of course, must include at least two craft and must secure permits. Write well in advance (this is a popular river) to Hornet District Ranger, Payette National Forest, Council, Idaho 83612, or Supervisor, Wallowa-Whitman National Forest, Federal Office Building, P.O. Box 907, Baker, OR 97814. Campsites will be assigned when you check in at the dam.

Camps include firepits and sanitary facilities and usually fresh water, though the river is considered potable. Despite the necessity for such accommodations for the growing traffic on the river, the upper stretches of the run must rate with the finest wilderness experiences in the country. A day or two downriver from the dam, however, one encounters jet boats coming up loaded with gapers from Lewiston, and the spell is broken.

The time to run Hell's Canyon is from May through September. July and August may see temperatures rising over the 100°F. mark—but there's always the river to cool off in. Even as late as October, the Snake is far warmer than the surrounding hills and can make quite a pleasant trip even while snow is falling in the Wallowa Mountains to the west. The Hell's Canyon section of the Snake is also well served by commercial outfitters. For a list, write the Lewiston, Idaho, Chamber of Commerce or the Western River Guides Association, 994 Denver Street, Salt Lake City, Utah 84111.

OWYHEE RIVER

Time of year: May to June

Degree of difficulty: various

Craft: kayak, raft, dory

Character: wild

Permit required: yes

Rentals available: yes

The Owyhee, in southeast Oregon, provides a vigorous and enormously picturesque six-day trip through high desert. The season, May and June, is limited. April is apt to be too cold to be pleasant, and after June the water may be too low. The Owyhee, a variation of the spelling of "Hawaii" (in memory of two Hudson Bay boatmen from the islands who were murdered on the river a century and a half ago), is not an overcrowded river, largely because of the limited season. The sense of remoteness and other worldliness is intensified by the canyon setting—sagebrush hills, lovely, welcoming sand beaches, weird clay badlands, rock gorges.

This is prime rattlesnake country, and the water needs either boiling or the addition of halazone tablets because of ranching upstream. But those are just about the only two negative points on the sixty-three-mile stretch of river between the recommended put-in at Rome Bridge and the take-out at Leslie Gulch. The camping along the way is excellent, though poor at both the put-in and the take-out. The section of the river below Rome can be run with rafts and kayaks by boaters with intermediate experience. The rapids are mostly Class II and III, with one Class IV, which can be portaged.

There is a thirty-five-mile section of the river above Rome, however, that is ranked among the greatest challenges to rafters and kayakers in the West. For those who can handle Class IV and Class V rapids with ease, and know enough to determine when to carry their boats, this little-run section of the Owyhee, through steep-sided gorges and breathtaking rock formations, makes a thrilling two- to four-day challenge. The put-in for the upper section is at Three Forks, Oregon, at the confluence of the North, Middle, and Main Owyhee rivers.

JOHN DAY RIVER

Time of year: March to June

Degree of difficulty: novice to intermediate

Craft: canoe, raft

Character: semiwild; pastoral

Permit required: no

Rentals available: no

The John Day, in north-central Oregon, is an accommodating stream when there is enough water in it— March through June in average years. Over one hundred miles of it is boatable in anything from rafts to open canoes. Its greatest challenge is a few Class II rapids. Most of the run is suitable for novices, though some stretches may require the inexperienced to portage during times of high water, above five thousand cfs.

The Day flows through high desert country, dotted with ponderosa pine, juniper, and sage. The upper section is free of roads, though there are some signs of ranching along the way. Put in at Service Creek on Highway 19. From here is is a two- to four-day trip down to Clarno, with the possibility of take-outs at ranches along the way.

From Clarno Bridge the Day can be run for another seventy miles down to Cottonwood Bridge, where Highway 206 crosses the river. The going can be a little rougher here than on the upper section, except for one very long rapid with a Class III drop in the middle. Anyone should scout the rapids just below Clarno, and novices will want to portage here and also, probably, Basalt Rapids some six miles farther downriver.

The water quality on the Day is not up to the rest of the remote feelings of the river. There is too much farming and running cattle along the way. Be prepared to boil water or bring a supply. The swimming, however, is excellent in June, the fishing, fair. No permits are needed. Much of the land along the way is private. When appropriate, ask permission to camp, put in, or take out.

SELWAY RIVER

Time of year: May to June

Degree of difficulty: intermediate

Craft: kayak, raft, dory

Character: wild

Permit required: yes

Rentals available: yes

The Selway is an Idaho river tailor-made for commercial outfitters. Many professionals rate the Selway as the king of white-water rivers in this part of the world, with waters flowing "swift and clear through primeval forests and panoramic mountains." That's the way it is in Idaho.

A typical five-day rafting expedition starts at White-cap and runs forty-nine miles down to Selway Falls, amid dense forests of pine and cedar, traversing the Bitterroot Wilderness Area. Sightings of elk, moose, bear, mountain goat, and bighorn sheep are practically guaranteed by outfitters' brochures, though, in truth, heavy usage has made the animals shy of the riverbank. No such reticence applies to the fish and birds.

Peak water flow is in the late spring and early summer. At other times the river is apt to be too rocky for enjoyable navigation. It is in the former mood that the Selway justifies its royal title among white-water streams. The camping and sense of solitude on this river are outstanding. But there is a price one pays. It is necessary to have a permit, and the request for reservations may be backed up as much as a year. Write to West Fork Ranger Station, Darby, MT 59829. They will also provide a list of reputable commercial outfitters, and this is not a bad way to approach the river for the first time.

A major challenge begins halfway through the run, at Moose Creek, a major tributary. Here one drops into a canyon for six miles without a campsite and with plenty of rip-roaring rapids, up to Class IV. Experts only, if you go alone.

BRUNEAU RIVER

Time of year: April to June

Degree of difficulty: intermediate to expert

Craft: kayak, raft

Character: wild

Permit required: yes

Rentals available: no

In the southwest corner of Idaho, reaching fingers southward across the Nevada border, lies the remote and until recently little-known Bruneau River system. It veins a desert canyonland that, except for a spate of nineteenth-century mining fever, offered little to attract development. The maze of gorges that beckon like open doors in a bordello are an explorer's dream. The main stream during the spring and early summer offers some of the wildest white water in the West. The Bruneau has a fierce temper when aroused and should be attempted only by expert kayakers and rafters.

All-weather roads cross a number of headwater streams near the Idaho-Nevada border, but access to the river proper is limited. A bridge at Blackrock Crossing, another at Indian Hot Springs, are two access points. Beyond, there runs some fifty miles of boatable canyon through dry country, gorges down to Hot Springs, a few miles south of the town of Bruneau near the confluence of the Bruneau and the Snake.

In 1973, when a study was made of the river for inclusion in the growing list of Wild and Scenic Rivers, data showed that there had been only about ten to twenty parties a year on the Bruneau. Use is increasing, but it remains a relatively unspoiled river. For more information write to the Idaho Department of Commerce, Room 108, Statehouse, Boise, ID 83707, or Idaho Outfitters and Guides Association, Box 95, Boise, ID 83701.

Give this one at least five days, and twice that if you have a mind to explore.

SKAGIT RIVER

Time of year: May to July

Degree of difficulty: intermediate

Craft: canoe

Character: semiwild

Permit required: no

Rentals available: no

The Skagit rises in British Columbia and gathers muscle in some of the wildest and most spectacular country in the Cascade Range. The boatable part of the river in Washington State is not, strictly, a wilderness stream. A road runs beside it from the Newhalem power house all the way to the sea. Farms, homes, and bridges do not exactly crowd its shores, nor are they conspicuous by their absence. For all that, the Skagit and its tributaries, Cascade and Sauk rivers, make good sport for a day or a week, in almost any craft one chooses. The scenery is ruggedly spectacular, the country accommodating and fit for camping. The abundance of forest helps screen some of the signs of civilization.

The Skagit reaches salt water near the mouth of Puget Sound, and even today, despite heavy pressure from sportsmen, it remains a superb salmon- and steelhead-trout-spawning ground and fishery.

On the twenty-mile section above Rockport on Route 20, the Skagit plays the part of a bumptious mountain stream. It is canoeable in spring and summer, though the rapids may match Class IV in times of high water. Below Rockport, where the Skagit meets the Sauk, the river gentles some and broadens. Civilization is more evident, but the view of the glacier-clad North Cascades, Sauk Mountain, and the Eldorados more than makes up for man's intrusion.

Hamilton, some thirty miles below Rockport, makes a good take-out spot. Below Hamilton the river spreads out into multiple channels and loses it appeal save for those determined to run from the mountains to the sea.

Fishing, of course, is excellent all the way. And the presence of the road makes it possible to launch and take out almost anywhere one wants.

CANADA

CANADA, second in size among nations only to the Union of Soviet Socialist Republics, contains over half the world's supply of fresh water. Bogs, ponds, lakes, brooks, and rivers lace the country coast to coast and around its ragged Arctic fringe. Since prehistory, Canada's vast-reaching waterways have dictated the settlement and commerce of this remote northland. A quick glance at a map is enough to understand why it was here that the canoe, and in the far north the kayak, reached a peak of refinement in the hands of the natives.

In Canada the canoe became what the horse was to the Mongols in Eurasia and, later, in a brief flowering of the Great Plains, to Indians of the American West. When Europeans reached Canada, they naturally adopted this proven mode of travel. And until recently, when iron rails and ribbons of cement were laid across the continent, it remained the *sine qua non* of exploration, commerce, and exploitation.

Now fashioned of modern materials but very little changed in shape, the canoe, once again, is reclaiming Canada in the name of sport and recreation. Canoe trails range from strings of ponds to wild stretches of white water. Commonly, so many lakes and rivers are joined together that it is possible to take loop trips in which you end up back at the point of embarkation. So vast is its intricate network of waterways that a canoeist may easily travel from ice-out to freeze-up with only an occasional portage and never retrace his route.

Cruises range from much-used trails in the more readily accessible parks to the lonesome lakes and rivers of the north country. There are still waters where only the Indian's canoe has passed, and there are waters that no man has paddled. A canoe trip in Canada can mean not only the experience of challenging water and a test of survival and endurance but a real likelihood of discovering entirely new and uncharted paths.

The preeminence of canoe country in the central part of the continent is due to the gentle upward curving great bowl of the Canadian Shield. As the ice sheet retreated, the glacier scoured mountain shapes and etched the wild rivers and tranquil lakes. The shield, exposing the most ancient rock on earth, covers much of Quebec, Ontario, and the Northwest Territories.

Canada's wealth of woods and waters defies the imagination. It is possible to cross Canada by canoe and see country much as it was in 1613 when Samuel de Champlain dared the wilderness in search of the gateway to the Orient. In fact, one could paddle from practically any Canadian city to the Atlantic, Pacific, or Arctic oceans, or, indeed, to the Gulf of Mexico.

The Hudson's Bay Company, with posts scattered throughout the dominion, offers a U-Paddle Canoe Rental Service. Canoes can be picked up at one company post, paddled to a distant post, and dropped off without backtracking. Canoe posts are now at Yellowknife, Waterways, Ile à la Crosse, La Ronge, and Norway House, with many more to be added soon.

Many of Quebec's rivers have been sheltered in parks such as La Verendrye and Laurentides, site of the sixty-mile run on the Metabetchouan. Along the north shore of the St. Lawrence are a number of south-flowing rivers like the Moisie and the Romaine. In the great drainage basin of James Bay, other paradises of canoe camping like the Megiscane can be found.

Ontario, with its 250,000 lakes and connecting streams and rivers, provides still other such Edens. You might try paddling in the Algoma section, northeast of Lake Superior, or in the Algonquin Provincial Park. This latter area, a vast 3,000-square-mile arc of wilderness of sparkling water and virgin forests, was set aside exclusively for canoe camping. In the Superior National Forest and the Quetico Provincial Park, there are an estimated 2,500 miles of canoe routes. Or you can enjoy shorter and delightful wilderness trips on the Flint and Wanapitei rivers.

The Canadian Shield also supports various mighty river systems that flow generally east and north: the Albany, the Assiniboine, and Red, the Saskatchewan with its two large branches rising in the Rockies, and above all, the Churchill. These rivers, with their immense drainage basins, formed the main highway that led from Montreal west and north by way of the Great Lakes and the border-lakes region. They connected in turn across two divides with the headwaters of the Columbia River and the awesome Fraser, which flow to the Pacific. Or they joined with the Peace and Athabasca rivers in Alberta, draining through a series of huge lakes into the Mackenzie River and into the Arctic Ocean.

The resplendence of the northwest wilderness is nowhere more evident than in British Columbia along the Fraser, Thompson, Bowron, and Canoe rivers. Railroads and highways are infrequent but sufficient to provide access.

The rivers and lake systems of Canada offer hard work for rafters unless small motors (forbidden on some rivers) are used, but too much tame water for kayakers. Thus the canoe reigns supreme on the dominion's waterways.

Canoeists planning voyages throughout northern Canada should be expert paddlers, experienced at river camping and woodcraft. A knowledge of navigation with map and compass is essential. Rations must be carefully planned and arrangements made for resupply. Travelers in deep wilderness must notify the Royal Canadian Mounted Police of their route and estimated time of arrival. Familiar as they are with the area, the police may deny permission if they believe a trip is beyond one's level of skill and experience.

To travel more frequented waterways of Canada, you may write the Ministry of Natural Resources or the Department of Tourism, Fish and Game in the various provinces for initial information on the area you have selected.

BOWRON RIVER

Time of year: June to October

Degree of difficulty: intermediate

Craft: canoe

Character: wild

Permit required: yes

Rentals available: yes

The Bowron River winds through the forest of British Columbia. Within the Bowron Lake Provincial Park, over a quarter million acres of protected wilderness, sprawl six major lakes and connecting waterways. A circuit of seventy-five miles—through lakes Bowron, Indianpoint, Isaac, Lanezi, Sandy, and Spectacle, with connections made by the Bowron and Cariboo rivers—makes one of the great canoe trips of western Canada. Framed by the rugged Cariboo mountains, seven thousand feet high, the area is studiously undeveloped.

The Parks Administration (established in 1961) has seen fit to tack up signs indicating portages, routes, shelters, and campgrounds, but that is it. The campgrounds are primitive; latrines must be dug, and what shelters there are are for emergencies only. It is not uncommon for travelers to be stormbound for days on end. You are not forgotten, however. All travelers of the circuit must register in the park's information center before departing and must check in on returning.

Be prepared to meet a few bears, and take the usual precautions around camp. Be wary also of moose.

BOWRON RIVER

N

10 MILES

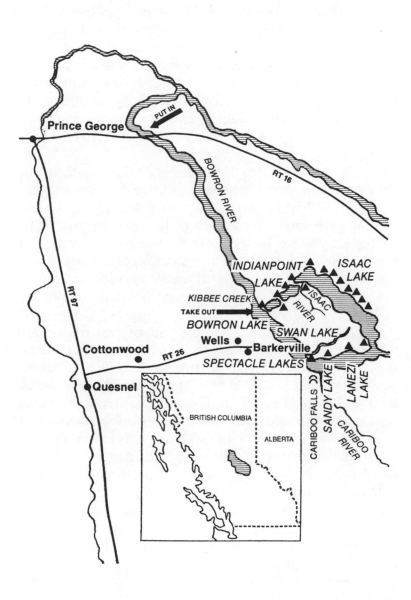

Prince George

PUT IN

BOWRON RIVER

RT 16

INDIANPOINT
LAKE

ISAAC
LAKE

KIBBEE CREEK

ISAAC
RIVER

TAKE OUT

BOWRON LAKE

SWAN LAKE

RT 97

Wells

Cottonwood   RT 26   Barkerville

SPECTACLE LAKES

Quesnel

BRITISH COLUMBIA

ALBERTA

CARIBOO FALLS

SANDY LAKE

LANEZI
LAKE

CARIBOO
RIVER

Generally, your silent canoe or kayak will not disturb them. But moose have been known to attack when crowded or with young. Caribou and mountain goat also inhabit the park, along with waterfowl and beaver in the marshes. Beaver dams, in fact, may necessitate several portages. No hunting is allowed, and only on Bowron Lake are motorboats permitted.

Fishing is best on Indianpoint and Isaac lakes. But in all the waters, you may find kamloops trout, dolly varden, lake trout, and Rocky Mountain whitefish. Fishing licenses are required, and in dry seasons campfire permits may be necessary. Check at park headquarters.

The park, located about ninety miles southeast of Prince George, has remained a primeval wilderness because it has had so few visitors over the years. Today, travelers are encouraged to keep their parties small. The nearest towns are Wells, population eight hundred, and Barkerville. Barkerville, a historic gold rush town, named after a Royal Navy deserter who found gold in the 1860s, is now a ghost town that should not be missed.

The lake and river circuit can be run from June to the end of October. In June high water may inundate many of the beaches, and in July flies can be a nuisance. Many travelers prefer September, when the deciduous trees add their blaze of fall color to the steady presence of the white spruce and alpine fir. You should allow at least one week but preferably ten days for your trip.

There are seven portages. The first, a two-mile carry from Bowron Lake Campground to the beaver dam on Kibbee Creek, is the hardest. All trails are in fair condition, but in wet weather—and there is plenty of that—they may be muddy and slippery. Experienced canoeists should have no trouble, but some of the best have capsized in the fast waters of the Isaac and Cariboo rivers. On the big lakes, stay close to shore and watch for squalls. In your equipment, you might include a pair of hip waders useful on Three Mile Creek where the canoe must be lined and pulled over many beaver dams. And remember that the nights are cool and even cold during the summer.

In the fast-moving Cariboo River, a major hazard is tree trunks extending out from the bank across the current. In Lanezi Lake shallows and deadheads in the narrows demand careful reading. A narrow entrance at Unna Lake will bring you to the not-to-be-missed eighty-foot-high Cariboo Falls. From Spectacle Lake on, your paddling will be downhill to your take-out at Kibbee Creek.

The Bowron River drains the west and north sides of the circuit and flows north to enter the Fraser River near Prince George. A separate run, taking a minimum of three days, can be made on the river. If you are in Swan Lake, keep close to the west side and you will find the outlet stream. The current is slack there, giving you time to enjoy a magnificent marsh where moose and waterfowl often visit. If you are not already in the circuit, then put in from the secondary road, Route 26, east of Quesnel. The run on the Bowron is generally leisurely, with a few small canyons constricting the stream to add spice (difficulty nowhere greater than Class III).

The season for running the Bowron is in late June or early July. Water level is critical. If too low, rocks and shoals will make for very tough going. And if too high, water will be very rough in the canyons. Falls of ten feet have been reported on occasion. Once through the short canyon, you will be in the calm water and free to look upon the windowless ghost cabins that dot the bank. Midway down to the Fraser River, the river is squeezed by five short and beautiful canyons. The third provides the most challenging white water of the run. There are tricky boils of fast water, heightened by eight- to ten-foot waves at the base. The portage, if necessary, is not difficult. The final canyon is steep with magnificent rock formations. The water runs smoothly.

Take out at Highway 16 bridge, opposite the coal

mine, or paddle a few more miles to the Fraser and end at the car ferry. For more details write the Parks Branch, Department of Recreation and Conservation; the Department of Travel Industry; or the Director of the Survey and Mapping Branch, Geographic Division, Department of Lands, Forest and Water Resources. All three are located in the Parliament Building, Victoria, British Columbia.

CHURCHILL RIVER

Time of year: June to September

Degree of difficulty: intermediate

Craft: canoe

Character: wild

Permit required: no

Rentals available: yes

The Churchill has always been a water highway. Traveling up the river to its source, the voyageurs crossed the northern divide (over the backbreaking twelve-mile Methys Portage) into waters that carried them ultimately to the Arctic and across the mountains to the Pacific coast and Alaska. Today the Churchill is still one of the grandest waterways on the continent, a thousand-mile string of great and lovely wilderness lakes narrowing occasionaly to a wide, fast river thick with rapids.

The Saskatchewan portion of the river rises in the sedimentary lowlands of northwest Saskatchewan, flows in a generally eastern direction skirting the southern edge of the Precambrian Shield into Manitoba and then drains into Hudson Bay. Along its course there are rapids, falls, narrow chutes, broad expanses of lakes dotted with islands, and long placid stretches of smooth water. Traveling this route, a modern-day voyageur may well feel the memory of the early fur trade rivalry between the Hudson's Bay Company and the North West

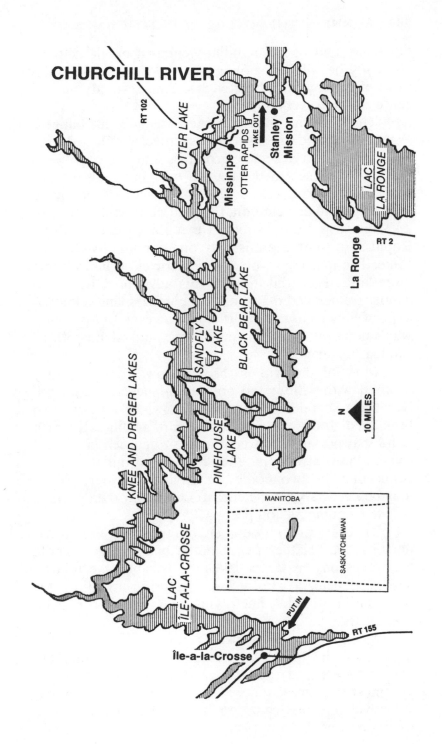

CHURCHILL RIVER

RT 102

OTTER LAKE

Missinipe

OTTER RAPIDS

TAKE OUT

Stanley Mission

LAC LA RONGE

La Ronge

RT 2

BLACK BEAR LAKE

SANDFLY LAKE

KNEE AND DREGER LAKES

PINEHOUSE LAKE

N

10 MILES

MANITOBA

SASKATCHEWAN

LAC ÎLE-A-LA-CROSSE

PUT IN

RT 155

Île-a-la-Crosse

Company and of Cree Indians camped on the shores. Certainly he will see snow geese and the large populations of pelicans and bald eagles. And certainly he will sense solitude everywhere.

The Churchill has remained virtually unchanged. Water has erased the signs of past travelers. Only deeply worn portage trails, campgrounds, and an occasional cabin bear witnes to the legions who have passed this way. For the experienced wilderness canoeist, equipped with maps and due caution, the Churchill offers a superb 240-mile trip from historic Ile à La Crosse to Otter Rapids. En route there is only one community—Snake Lake. The journey involves much travel on lakes, some quite large. Essential tools of this adventure, besides a canoe, are detailed maps, a good compass, and a knowledge of how to use them. It is all too easy to lose one's way among the many channels, bays, and islands of this sodden northland.

Most of the trip is through low, rocky country forested with willow and poplar, birches and conifers. Because a shoreline may be overgrown or a portage so little used, trails are sometimes hard to find. Keep in mind that portages between lakes or between lakes and rivers almost always parallel the natural outlet or inlet connecting the two bodies of navigable water. But it may be necessary, in the end, to chart your own portage course by compass and pacing.

The varied conditions encountered requires a canoe of at least sixteen feet. Smaller boats cannot handle the waves on the larger lakes. If you become injured and need help, a smoky fire will bring attention. Or paddling in a circle and waving may attract a passing aircraft.

Mosquitoes and blackflies can drive strong men mad. Early in the season (before June) and late (in September) this particular hazard is minimal. Otherwise you must take precautions. Insect repellent is essential. Wherever possible, camp on an island or on large bare rock outcrops and sand spits.

To cut down on grub weight, carry fishing tackle. The Churchill offers excellent northern pike, walleye, whitefish, and lake trout. And don't overlook the huckleberries, blueberries, raspberries, and strawberries you will find in season.

Before starting, fill out a permit at one of the registration river points. The program is voluntary, but it is a sensible precaution for all canoeists in the northland. Allow at least fourteen to eighteen days to reach Otter Rapids, where Route 102 crosses the river. Beyond Otter Rapids the Churchill continues for several hundred miles to the Hudson Bay at the town of Churchill.

You can put in at either of the two Saskatchewan Department of Natural Resources "camp kitchens" on the west side of South Bay at Ile à la Crosse, or from the community of Ile à la Crosse. All accesses are by gravel road. Take-out will be at the bridge across Otter Rapids or at the Missinipe town site on Walker Bay at Otter Lake. Here car or air transportation to La Ronge and points south can be arranged.

Prevailing winds are from the northwest. Ice on the lakes or the river does not usually disappear until the middle of May. The first rapids you will encounter are Shagwenaw Rapids, linking the north end of Lac Ile à la Crosse with Shagwenaw Lake. The rapids are little more than fast water at normal water levels. Drum Rapids, which is separated into four parts, and Leaf Rapids may be run, but often a safer course is to portage. The trail at Leaf is eight hundred and seventy yards long and in fair condition. It starts as a break in the willows on the right shore. In all there are from fifteen to twenty white-water stretches on the route which may be run, lined, or portaged, according to your skill and inclination. White-water chances that one might take on a river in more settled country are folly in the vastness of the North Country.

Some consider Sandfly Lake the most beautiful along the route. Shallow in spots, it has rocky islands that provide virtually an unlimited number of camp-

sites. Black Bear Lake is filled with islands, and navigation becomes tricky. On the exposed rocks and cliffs
Indian paintings, which once may have acted as sign-
posts, can still be seen. In the fall, great flocks of geese
and ducks congregate on the marshy section between
Knee and Drager lakes. Cree Indians still hunt, trap,
and fish the Churchill, using outboards these days instead of canoes. At campsites you are likely to find
Indian traps, snowshoes, and dog harnesses hanging
in bushes and trees. Obviously these should not be disturbed. Nor should you burn any cut poles, which are
used to dry fish and nets. Cree handicrafts are available
in the villages near Ile à la Crosse.

For further information write the Department of
Tourism and Renewable Resources, P.O. Box 7105,
Regina, Saskatchewan, S4P 3N2, or the Department
of Northern Saskatchewan, Provincial Buildings, La
Ronge, Saskatchewan.

METABETCHOUAN
RIVER

Time of year: June to September

Degree of difficulty: intermediate

Craft: canoe

Character: semiwild

Permit required: yes

Rentals available: yes

The Metabetchouan River area in south-central Quebec
reeks with history. Indians of the lake region and from
other neighboring groups always held their assemblies
adjacent to the river. In 1671 a Jesuit father counted
more than twenty nations camped along its banks. The
first European to visit the area was the Jesuit Father
Jean De Quen, in 1647. A score of years later he estab-

lished a mission there and the site became one of the King's Posts with store, chapel, and hostel for fur traders and missionaries. A farm was established to provide food. The navigable segment of the river, heavily traveled by trappers and missionaries, came to be known as the Jesuit Trail.

In 1821 the Hudson's Bay Company acquired the site and made it a principal post. Settlers arrived in 1861, built a sawmill, ironworks, and a dairy industry along the river. In 1876 the mission and trading post were transfered to the Indian reserve of Pointe Bleue. When you visit the town of Metabetchouan, note the remarkable Gothic church made of pink granite.

The river rises in Laurentides Park and flows north for eighty-five miles to Lake St. John. For a considerable distance its course marks the western boundary of the park, which lies just north of Quebec City, a day's scenic drive from Montreal. With an area of four thousand sixty squares miles, Laurentides Park provides semiwilderness canoeing with hundreds of miles of marked canoe trails and many more miles of unmapped waters in lakes and streams. The fish in these waters range from pike, whitefish, smelt, and turbot to yellow perch, speckled trout, and Arctic char. A license is required. Write the Direction Générale du Tourisme, 150 East Boulevard Saint Cyrille, Quebec, G1 R4 Y3.

The Metabetchouan river trip is newly established. It is a sixty-mile run that will take about four days. But you should allow extra time for side trips, hikes, and just stopping to enjoy the stunning scenery. A chain of lakes and streams lead southward into the river. Although a forest road parallels part of the route and there are established campsites, the region still smacks of genuine wilderness. Canoes can be rented from the Parks Service. If you bring your own, the put-in point is at Lac Montagnais, seventeen miles west of Lac Kiskisink at the end of a gravel road. Take-out will be at the bridge, back at the Kiskisink–Camp Montagnais road.

The route, going south then northerly, will include some fourteen short portages, mostly around rapids, although the longest (taking about twenty minutes) is between lakes. If desired, your trip can involve only Class II rapids, with portage trails marked around those of greater difficulty. For more experienced canoeists, there are Class III and Class IV rapids on the run. The route describes a rough V shape.

To make this run, registration at Camp Montagnais is required. Write the Department of Tourism, Fish and Game, Parliament Buildings, Quebec City, Quebec. And also make contact with the Direction des Parcs, Parc Laurentides, Quebec.

FLINT RIVER

Time of year: June to September

Degree of difficulty: intermediate

Craft: canoe, kayak

Character: semiwild

Permit required: no

Rentals available: no

Wilderness boating in Ontario can be enjoyed in ventures of expedition proportion. Or the cross-country road traveler, with a canoe or kayak lashed to his car, can find numerous two- and three-day excursions. The thirty-mile, three-day trip down the Flint is such a run. The Flint flows northeast in the Sudbury District to the Kenogami River.

Put in at Klotz Lake Provincial Park on Highway 11 out of Longlac. Longlac, thirty miles west of the lake, is the nearest outlet for groceries. As canoes and camping equipment are difficult to rent locally, they should be brought with you. During the summer months the river can become quite shallow. A downstream trip only to the Canadian National Railroad tracks may be as far as you can go when water level is low. The Ministry of Natural Resources recommends that before you start you get in touch with the railroad ticket agent in Nakina for information on the approximate time that the train will be traveling between Pagwa and Nakina. Arrangements can then be made for the train crew to watch out for you and be prepared to stop and pick you up if necessary.

At the put-in on Klotz Lake, there is a provincial park that provides a good base camp and starting point. The fishing in Klotz Lake and Flint Lake for northern pike and walleye is excellent. The first portage of the run is seventy-five yards long on the right side of Hoiles Creek just at the outlet of Klotz Lake. From Klotz Lake you pass into Flint Lake, with fine campsites on the northern end. From the outlet of Flint to the railway tracks is about nineteen miles.

About eleven miles downstream from Flint, the water picks up speed. Look for brook trout. A dense network of windfalls on the left side of the river requires a one hundred-yard portage. A third easy portage lies around the next bend on the right side of the river.

Downstream you will come to a number of small falls or rapids—"lift-overs," or if water level is high enough, they can be run. All subsequent portages are well marked.

The take-out will be at the railway's north line tracks off the Flint River. If by this time you have indeed fallen in love with this country, and if water level permits, you can continue down into the Kenogami and the Albany River to Fort Albany. This run is not to be taken idly, however. There are no serious difficulties, but the distance is some two hundred and fifty miles.

For further information write the Ministry of Natural Resources, P.O. Box 640, Geraldton, Ontario P0T IM0. Topographic maps (you will need the Kenogami and the Taradale section maps) are available from the ministry office. Canoes and camping equipment are difficult to rent locally, and you should bring them with you.

WANAPITEI RIVER

Time of year: June to September

Degree of difficulty: intermediate

Craft: canoe, kayak

Character: semiwild

Permit required: no

Rentals available: no

The Wanapitei, in Ontario, flows south through Wanapitei Lake into Georgian Bay. The Huron Indians called the forested north shore of Georgian Bay *Ouendake,* or "one land apart." The area of hill country, with thousands of lakes and waterways, is very much a land apart. A great deal of it has been designated as Recreational Reserve by the Canadian government. The combinations and permutations of routes are many and varied.

A good and pleasant week can be spent coming down from the lake, which lies some twenty-five miles northeast of Sudbury, and can be reached by gravel road off the Trans-Canadian Highway. Expect rapids, wilderness enough, and a number of portages, depending on the water level. Summer is the time of year. For further details write the Department of Tourism and Information, Province of Ontario, Parliament Buildings, Toronto, Ontario.

MOISIE RIVER

Time of year: July to August

Degree of difficulty: intermediate

Craft: canoe

Character: wild

Permit required: no

Rentals available: yes

Along the north shore of the St. Lawrence estuary in Quebec, there are rivers still little touched by man. They begin high in the rugged Laurentian Highlands, and as they course southward, have cut deep valleys. The most challenging is the Moisie, that runs from southwest of Opocopa Lake, three hundred and fifty-two kilometers to Sept Iles, on the Gulf of St. Lawrence. Along its course, majestic cliffs and steep valley walls create a magnificent backdrop for a canoe trip.

White and black spruce, balsam fir, white birch, and trembling aspen fill the forests. Because of the river's swift current, waterfowl are few. But the Moisie is one of the best salmon rivers in eastern North America. And as you fish, moose and caribou may come down to drink.

The best time to make this three hundred four-kilometer, two-week run is at the end of July and into August. Water levels after the spring ice breakup in May will have returned to medium to low level, exposing cobbles, gravel, and sand bars that provide relatively bug-free campsites. Rapids are also more runnable in midsummer, and lining and portaging are less of a chore. The Parks Canada office recommends aluminum canoes for this trip as well as an emergency survival kit that when well packed can be worn on the belt.

Access to the headwaters of the Moisie is by float plane from Sept Iles or Labrador City. The planes are chartered at Sept Iles. Put in on the lower Pekans River, about ten kilometers upstream of the river mouth in order to avoid the Moisie's shallow and rapid headwaters. Take-out will be at Moisie settlement at the river's mouth. A road from Moisie will bring you twenty kilometers to Sept Iles, where road, air, and coastal ferry services are available.

In the first ten kilometers of the run, the forest changes character dramatically. Taiga gives way to black spruce, and white birch finally predominates. The birch marks the beginning of difficult water with strong currents, ledges, and two gorges. The rapids are very long, cover the entire width of the river, and are difficult to scout and line. The Moisie is only for very skilled and experienced canoeists.

At the mouth of the Taoti River, the Moisie valley narrows to canyon proportions, producing three major rapids. At the entry of the Caopacho River, it widens once more and islands appear. This alternating of canyon, then wider river, continues throughout the trip, making the scenery diverse and the run always interesting. Just below the Nipisso River confluence, high clay terraces appear. One must climb to the top of them to find flat ground for camping.

Itineraries and expected time of arrival should be checked out with a responsible agency—the Quebec Police Force or the Ministère du Tourisme, de la Chasse et de la Pêche (Minister of Tourism, Hunting, and Fishing) in Sept Iles. Permits for fires and fishing may be required. The above offices can provide maps and further details. National topographic maps can be obtained from Canada Map Distribution Office, Department of Energy, Mines, and Resources, 615 Booth Street, Ottowa, Ontario K 1A OE9.

BRAZEAU RIVER

Time of year: June to September

Degree of difficulty: intermediate

Craft: canoe

Character: wild

Permit required: yes

Rentals available: yes

In Alberta are many wild rivers with thrilling rapids and glorious mountain scenery. Long portages are rarely necessary, and most of the upper reaches of the rivers are accessible by road. Supplies and assistance are never far away. But the area appears isolated and trips can be long and rewarding.

The Brazeau River begins near Nigel Pass on the east slope of the Rockies and extends to just below its confluence with the Cardinal River, ending in the Brazeau Reservoir. To get there the Brazeau passes through the high ranges of the Rockies into a piedmont valley and finally through flat, forested lands at the edge of the prairies. The trip from Nigel Pass to the reservoir, a distance of one hundred thirty-seven miles, should take canoeists from a week to two weeks.

During high water, in June and early July, the river runs fast and powerful. Logjams make hazards at sharp bends. The climate in this season is generally dry, broken only by an occasional quick thunderstorm. Continuous bad weather is rare, but one must allow extra time for contrary winds and driving rain. Trip registration should be made either with the Royal Canadian Mounted Police or with the Alberta Ministry of Lands and Forests, Legislative Buildings, Edmonton, Alberta. Permits for fires and fishing may be required.

The put-in is at a roadless area in Jasper National Park. Access is limited to a pack trail over Nigel Pass. The trail is good, however, the scenery beautiful, and the ascent a mere one thousand feet.

The next portage is around a rock garden where the river enters a shallow but steep-banked canyon. Once out of the canyon, you will soon be in a banging and scraping stretch of moderate white water where a strong, high-bowed, aluminum canoe will be appreciated. Then the river slows as it passes through lush meadows of wild flowers on the open valley floor. Pine and spruce forests cover the flanks of mountains rising steeply beyond.

After Four Point Creek, the rapids begin again. Some require scouting. The more difficult are characterized by large boulders, strong currents, and standing waves up to four feet. At points the river narrows to only seventy-five feet. A particularly tricky spot is where the Brazeau accelerates over a shallow bedrock reef in a canyon and hurls itself against the left wall as the canyon veers to the right. At the reservoir, just before the dam, you will find the access road that leads to Drayton Valley and Rocky Mountain House.

National topographic maps are available from Canadian Map Distribution Office, Department of Energy, Mines, and Resources, 615 Booth Street, Ottawa, Ontario K 1A OE9.

CANOE RIVER

Time of year: June to September

Degree of difficulty: intermediate

Craft: canoe, kayak

Character: wild

Permit required: yes

Rentals available: yes

The aptly named Canoe River in British Columbia is navigable for some eighty to ninety miles from Valemount on the Canadian National Railroad, west of Jasper, to the river's confluence with the Columbia River at Boat Encampment.

The river headwaters are in an ice field high on Mount Sir Wilfrid Laurier. In many spots the drop is almost vertical, falling some eight thousand feet in twenty miles. Beyond this point, the river gushes out of a narrow chasm into the Canoe River valley, two or three miles wide and one hundred miles long, inhabited by grizzlies, moose, mountain goat, and beavers. Deep in woods, the river country gives an awesome feeling of unchanged time and nature. The valley has been little frequented by man. Deer and other wildlife bask fearlessly on sun-washed gravel banks as you slide by.

To bring your boat to this beautiful, isolated country you can ship it by railroad to Valemount on the Canadian National Railroad or haul it up by car.

Put in at the railroad bridge in Valemont. Intermingled with the giant ferns at the water's edge are tangles of raspberry bushes. But, of course, where there are berries, there are bear. If you are not visited by any, you will surely see tracks on the sandy banks along with the tracks of mink, wolverine, marten, and raccoon.

The first rapids will be theYellowjacket, tame but with an approach so smooth that you can be in them before you have time to get ready. Shallow rocks will require deft maneuvering. Creeks the size of small rivers enter at many points from the mountains, and below each junction expect mild rapids. At Bulldog Creek a rock wall one hundred fifty feet high forms the west bank of the river. The river here drops forty feet and narrows to create confused water with high standing waves.

Near Beaverpelt Lake you can find magnificent rainbow and dolly varden trout. And off a side trail near Bulldog Creek you can enjoy a wonderful hot springs bath in the utter stillness of a ravine.

The take-out at the confluence with the Columbia is reached by a mountain road, Highway 23, which leads back to civilization. The trip will take four to five days. The current is leisurely, but hazardous logjams may be encountered. None of the rapids is dangerous. In case of trouble, however, a dirt road used by loggers parallels the river for part of the trip.

For more information write to the British Columbia Travel Bureau, Department of Recreation and Conservation, Victoria, British Columbia.